Agency and Knowledge in Northeast India

The Nagas of Northeast India give great importance to dreams as sources of divine knowledge, especially knowledge about the future. Although British colonialism, Christian missions, and political conflict have resulted in sweeping cultural and political transformations in the Indo-Myanmar borderlands, dream sharing and interpretation remain important avenues for negotiating everyday uncertainty and unpredictability.

This book explores the relationship between dreams and agency through ethnographic fieldwork among the Angami Nagas. It tackles questions such as: What is dreaming? What does it mean to say 'I had a dream'? And how do night-time dreams relate to political and social actions in waking moments? Michael Heneise shows how the Angami glean knowledge from signs, gain insight from ancestors, and potentially obtain divine blessing. Advancing the notion that dreams and dreaming can be studied as indices of relational, devotional and political subjectivities, the author demonstrates that their examination can illuminate the ways in which, as forms of authoritative knowledge, they influence daily life, and also how they figure in the negotiation of day-to-day domestic and public interactions. Moreover, dream narration itself can involve techniques of 'interference' in which the dreamer seeks to limit or encourage the powerful influence of social 'others' encountered in dreams, such as ancestors, spirits, or the divine.

Based on extensive ethnographic research, this book advances research on dreams by conceptualising how the 'social' encompasses the broader, coextensive set of relations and experiences – especially with spirit entities – reflected in the ethnography of dreams. It will be of interest to those studying Northeast India, indigenous religion and culture, indigenous cosmopolitics in tribal India more generally, and the anthropology of dreams and dreaming.

Michael Heneise is an American anthropologist exploring indigenous religion, ecological knowledge, and medical pluralism in the Asian highlands. He is editor of the *South Asianist Journal* and co-editor of the *Highlander Journal*, both published by Edinburgh University. In 2017, he launched *Highlander Books*, an open access academic press that works in tandem with the journal. He edited *Passing Things On: Ancestors and Genealogies in Northeast India* (2014) and co-edited *Nagas in the 21st Century* (2017). In 2016, he earned a PhD in South Asian Studies from Edinburgh University and is the founding director of the Kohima Institute for Advanced Studies, Nagaland, India.

Routledge/Edinburgh South Asian Studies Series
Series Editor
Crispin Bates and the Editorial Committee of the Centre for South Asian Studies, Edinburgh University, UK.

The *Routledge/Edinburgh South Asian Studies Series* is published in association with the Centre for South Asian Studies, Edinburgh University – one of the leading centres for South Asian Studies in the UK with a strong interdisciplinary focus. This series presents research monographs and high-quality edited volumes as well as textbooks on topics concerning the Indian subcontinent from the modern period to contemporary times. It aims to advance understanding of the key issues in the study of South Asia, and contributions include works by experts in the social sciences and the humanities. In accordance with the academic traditions of Edinburgh, we particularly welcome submissions which emphasise the social in South Asian history, politics, sociology and anthropology, based upon thick description of empirical reality, generalised to provide original and broadly applicable conclusions.

The series welcomes new submissions from young researchers as well as established scholars working on South Asia, from any disciplinary perspective.

Neoliberalism and the Transforming Left in India
A Contradictory Manifesto
Ritanjan Das

Urban Marginalisation in South Asia
Waste Pickers in Calcutta
Nandini Sen

Agency and Knowledge in Northeast India
The Life and Landscapes of Dreams
Michael Heneise

Provincial Globalization in India
Transregional Mobilities and Development Politics
Edited by Carol Upadhya, Mario Rutten and Leah Koskimaki

Global Health Governance and Commercialisation in India
Actors, Institutions and the Dialectics of Global and Local
Edited by Anuj Kapilashrami and Rama Baru

For a full list of titles, please see: www.routledge.com/asianstudies/series/RESAS

Agency and Knowledge in Northeast India

The Life and Landscapes of Dreams

Michael Heneise

Routledge
Taylor & Francis Group

LONDON AND NEW YORK

First published 2019
by Routledge
2 Park Square, Milton Park, Abingdon, Oxon OX14 4RN

and by Routledge
52 Vanderbilt Avenue, New York, NY 10017

First issued in paperback 2020

Routledge is an imprint of the Taylor & Francis Group, an informa business

British Library Cataloguing-in-Publication Data
A catalogue record for this book is available from the British Library

Library of Congress Cataloging-in-Publication Data
A catalog record has been requested for this book

ISBN 13: 978-0-36-758789-5 (pbk)
ISBN 13: 978-1-138-47964-7 (hbk)

Typeset in Times New Roman
by Apex CoVantage, LLC

Contents

vi　*Contents*

Figures

Acknowledgements

Npezie we to the people of Kohima, with whom I shared dreams, mugs of *zu* and philosophies of life over the course of two years, living in the life-conferring sentient landscapes of the Naga Hills. The dream-world that you opened my eyes to has profoundly changed me, and for that I am forever grateful. My hope is that you will accept this book, an imperfect but sincere study, as one among many possible approaches to understanding the richness of Angami culture, knowledge and dreams.

Before reaching Kohima to begin fieldwork, the idea for an ethnography of dreams was already gestating for some years. The initial inspiration came in 2001 when I met Nelson and Sandra Hayashida, veteran missionaries who had spent several decades in sub-Saharan Africa and were relocating to the United States. I volunteered to help them unload a shipping container of books, and in the process discovered a manuscript that left me gobsmacked: 'Dreams in the African Church: The Significance of Dreams and Visions Among Zambian Baptists' – a doctoral thesis that Nelson completed at the University of Edinburgh under the mentorship of Andrew Walls. At around the same time, I received an invitation to visit Assam to lead a workshop on ethnomusicology. When I returned for short visits the following three years – to Mokokchung and Kohima in Nagaland, to Imphal in Manipur, and to Diphu in Karbi Anglong – I was struck by the fact that dreams seemed to be on everyone's lips in everyday conversation. These early impressions, the life-long relationships I developed and the magnetism of the landscape cemented my affection and commitment to the region – and it became the obvious choice when the time came for me to take up doctoral studies in anthropology.

The context, the research topic, the methodology and, indeed, the very institution where I would find funding and intellectual support were all there in front of me in these early years. That hot summer afternoon in Pennsylvania, as we rested surrounded by Nelson's books, I remember Sandra recounting their time in Edinburgh with great fondness – warm pubs on rainy days and myriad alleyways and courtyards offering clever shortcuts from New College to George Square. It was frankly not until my own nose throbbed in the cold wet Scottish air that I realised I was in some sense back to a familiar starting-point.

This book is based, with few alterations, on the doctoral project I took up at Edinburgh University in 2011, and defended in 2016. It is a project that would have been impossible without the generous financial support of Edinburgh's Graduate School of Social and Political Sciences, the Centre for South Asian Studies and the Tweedie Exploration Fund. I also wish to thank friends in Edinburgh, Glasgow and Manchester who opened their homes as we traversed the many in-between places awaiting special clearances, permits and visas for fieldwork. I am especially thankful to Anne Lowe, Lindsay Graham and Arkotong Longkumer, Gordon Graham, Yulia and Tima Cheprasov, Javiera Sepulveda and Pablo Briceño. I also wish to thank Edinburgh's Department of Religious Studies at New College for inviting me on multiple occasions to present my research and to interact with some remarkable minds. Equally remarkable were those with whom I shared time, space and ideas in the Department of Social Anthropology. I am particularly grateful to Jacob Copeman, Ian Harper, Janet Carsten and Magnus Course for adopting me into their family and providing multiple platforms, doctoral seminars, teaching opportunities and all-expenses-paid retreats in the Scottish Highlands where I met and interacted with many of the greats of contemporary anthropology. Above all, however, I wish to thank Crispin Bates for inviting me to Edinburgh, for supporting my research and publication projects, and for inviting me to participate fully in the life of the Centre for South Asian Studies.

Many of the ideas I shared and refined in the company of the Scottish anthropological community are thoughtfully incorporated into this book. I have also presented portions of my argument at the University of Oxford, the University of Wales, Lampeter, the University of Leiden, the University of Tezpur, and the Asiatic Society in Calcutta. An earlier version of chapter 1 appears in the *South Asianist* and in the book *Nagas in the 21st Century* published by Highlander. There is also an earlier version of chapter 4 published in the book *Democracy in Nagaland*, also with Highlander.

Arriving in Nagaland, technically a conflict zone, and bringing a family with small children was not an easy decision to make. A lot of planning went into it, and I am particularly thankful to Ketuselie and Vizolazeu Kuotsu for the arrangements they made for our stay. I am also thankful to Luochalie, Rovithono and Kekhrieluo-tuo Yhome for their incredible hospitality, as always. Going to the field, one invariably leaves an intellectual community behind, but it would be a mistake to suggest that such communities are not to be found in the 'field'. In Kohima, I happened upon intellectual giants, and I thank especially Richard Belho, Visakhonü Hibo, Niketu Iralu, Theyiesinuo Keditsu, Easterine Kire, Neikolie Kuotsu, Kevilhounyü Linyü, Keviyiekelie Linyü, Abraham Lotha, Vizovol Mekro, Achan Mungleng, Viketoulie Pienyü, Kekhriehoulie Yhome, and Thepfulhouvi Solo for welcoming me into their midst and challenging me as a scholar, but most of all for being true friends.

I was also tremendously fortunate to have been mentored at Edinburgh by Jacob Copeman in the Department of Social Anthropology, and Arkotong Longkumer in the Department of Religious Studies. Their insightful comments, constructive critiques and depth of knowledge inspired me to stretch my thinking beyond conventional categories and to embrace creatively the multidisciplinary nature of my anthropology. Moreover, they went above and beyond what would be expected of a supervisory team, meeting separately to discuss my progress, visiting my field site and engaging in the kind of pastoral accompaniment that can only be equated with old world mentorship.

My gratitude also goes to a few friends that over the years have inspired me in my academic pursuits. In addition to Nelson Hayashida, I wish to thank Dale Olsen, a pillar in ethnomusicology who introduced me to ethnography through Andean indigenous music, Obed Arango Hisijara for infecting me with the passion for anthropology that drives me still, the late Wesley Brown, who taught me how to write, and Antonio Albert for teaching me to persist always in matters close to the heart. I also wish to thank Xavier Andrade, Iliyana Angelova, Catriona Child, Mark Elliott, Jon Froehlich, Vibha Joshi, Daniel Kortsch, Peter Matthews, Edward Moon-Little, Roland Platz, Akshaya Tankha, Dharamsing Teron, John Thomas, Zhoto Tunyi, and Jelle J. P. Wouters for their constant encouragement and support through the years. Finally, I am indebted to Samantha Hurn, Penny Dransart, and especially Piers Locke, who mentored me when I first embarked on an exploration into Himalayan dreaming at the University of Wales and offered invaluable insights on my final chapter.

But it is to the Athens of the North that I direct my highest appreciation. I wish to thank Heid Jerstad who took time away from her own fieldwork in North India to visit me in Nagaland, and Grit Wesser who carried a five-kilo package of coffee on her trip to Bangladesh to post it to her deprived colleague in Kohima – unforgettable! I also thank my good friend Pablo Briceño for our evening talks about Latin America, inspiring me to remain a believer in the kind of society that I experienced as a youth in Nicaragua, and for which I hold the deepest longing. I also thank Don Duprez, Hannah Lesshhaft, Diego Malara, Stephen McConnachie, and Katka Ockova for trudging through the bloody trenches of my unwieldy writing, emerging unscathed and smiling with brilliant critiques. Also, I thank Leila Bright, Merily Em, Sandalia Genus, Luke Heslop, Hanna Mantila, Agathe Mora, Gilda Neri, Jon Schubert, and Javiera Sepulveda, all of whom effortlessly mix brilliance with laughter and occasionally bare their teeth in spirited discussion. Similarly, within the Centre for South Asian Studies, my sincerest gratitude is reserved for Tsvety Bandakova, Supurna Banerjee, Aurora Bardoneschi, Feyza Bhatti, Shruti Chaudhry, Bashabi Fraser, Hugo Gorringe, Aya Ikegame, Patricia Jeffery, Roger Jeffery, Deborah Menezes, Ada Munns, Shahid Perwez, Saad Quasem, Piyush Roy, Kanchana Ruwanpura, Jeevan Sharma, Thomas Solinski, and Wilfried Swenden, whom together with Crispin Bates were my Edinburgh family, and in many ways remain so.

A few people engaged with the text in its entirety. In addition to Jacob Copeman and Arkotong Longkumer, I am grateful to Yulia Egorova and Ian Harper for their thorough, constructive reviews, and especially to Lindsay Graham for her critical insights and meticulous editing from the title page to the footnotes. I also wish to thank the anonymous reviewers, and Crispin Bates and the Editorial Committee of the Centre for South Asian Studies for admitting this project into the *Routledge/Edinburgh South Asian Studies Series*. Finally, I wish to thank Dorothea Schafter and Lily Brown at Routledge for believing in this project to the extent of securing the simultaneous release of a South Asia edition. I cannot thank them enough for this vote of confidence in my work. The South Asia edition features a unique cover by Guwahati-based designer Arpit Agwarwal, featuring the artwork of renowned Naga artist Temsuyanger Longkumer.

My family in the United States, of course, has been my rock throughout my academic career, and as my mother decided to begin her doctorate at around the same time as I, we have enjoyed talking 'shop' together. Reflecting back to the 1980s, when she enrolled me in a rural public school in Nicaragua, it is hard to believe I would end up in India via Scotland. It has been a long, rich journey, and this book is for my parents Stephen and Sheila Heneise, my big brother Andy, and my little sister Becky – pues. . . 'porque fuistes rebeldes, luchando noche y dia contra la injusticia de la humanidad!'

The dedication of this book, however, goes to my sons Tristan and Salvador, but especially to Asanuo, my wife. Your patience and companionship made things like power outages and bucket showers seem somehow meaningful. Your fluency in three of the languages spoken in my field site was humbling. Fortunate for me, I could also express my frustrations in a colourful language only you understood – Spanish! I thus never quite took the beating – the 'rite de passage' – that marks an anthropologist's first, truly committed journey into the unfamiliar, and I give you all the credit. *A nkhrie, Asanuo.*

A note on vocabulary, naming and currency[1]

Tenyidie words, employing the Kohima dialect which is largely accepted as the 'official' Angami language (e.g. *ruopfü, mhotékezhamia, tekhumiavi*) are italicised and translated at the first mention, in parenthesis (see also the glossary). Words or sentences in square brackets are comments when further clarification is required.

I have also italicised common terms carried over from the British colonial period and still in use, though borrowed from other languages. For example, *khel* (Pashto for 'clans', drawn from the Pashtun or Afghan tribes in Afghanistan and Pakistan); Gaonbura [Gaon Bura] (Assamese for 'village elder' or village head); and *Bara Basti* (Urdu for 'great settlement', the vernacular term used to refer to the historic *Kewhimia* village settlement).

Place names, such as the Peace Camp, the Local Ground or High School Junction, are capitalised but not italicised. The same goes for names of institutions, such as Angami Youth Organisation, the National Socialist Council of Nagalim – Isaak-Muivah (NSCN-IM), Baptist Revival Church, etc.

The correct spelling of *Tenyidie* proper names, such as Neisazonuo, is complicated by the general use of typically shorter, pet or nick-names that often bear little resemblance to the full name, such as Asanuo derived from Neisazonuo or Fifi derived from Rovithono. Generally, the names of persons in this book follow the Angami naming tradition: normally, people have one given name, which is usually a short phrase, such as Neisazonuo (to be joyful) or Kevizakie (to bring forth goodness), followed by the father's clan name, such as *Meya*. Upon marriage, a bride will usually take the husband's clan name. In cases of divorce, the bride always reverts to her father's clan name. Typically, younger generations will refer to most women and men in their parents' generation as auntie, or *anie*, or uncle, *anie-u*; while those in their grandparent's generation are grandmother, or *atsa*, or grandfather, *apfutsa*. In this book, I have used these latter two terms to describe only one specific elderly couple and refer to others of their generation by their anonymised proper names.

I have given aliases to most of my informants, though public personas are identified with their real names. Aliases are denoted by an asterisk at the first mention in the text. Acronyms are in common usage, in conversation, in the local dailies and in most publications, and though I spell out the full name of the organisation at first mention, I only use the acronym thereafter, regardless of the chapter.

Finally, translation work from *Tenyidie* and *Nagamese* was done by myself in consultation with a local native speaker, but direct, word-for-word translations are not included in the book unless specific words pointing to important Angami ideas or concepts, such as *mho* (dream) or *tekhumiavi* (man in the shape of a tiger) are employed, in which case they are drawn into the text.

Though money was an important aspect of fieldwork, it is not central to the ethnography, appearing only intermittently in the text. Nevertheless, I will employ the term 'rupees', instead of the international standard abbreviation INR or currency symbols like Rs. At the time of my arrival, in November 2012, the exchange rate was 87 rupees per 1 pound, and when I returned to the UK in June 2015, the exchange rate was 101 rupees per 1 pound.

Sample prices at the time of research:

1 small cup of tea at a local shop: 10 rupees
1kg of tomatoes: 100 rupees
1 taxi ride from the village to the town: 80 rupees
Primary school teacher (private) base wage: 5,000 rupees/month
1 full day of labour for a mason or carpenter: 400 rupees/day

Note

1 This section draws on a schema developed by Jon Schubert for his 2014 University of Edinburgh doctoral thesis "Working the System: Affect, Amnesia and the Aesthetics of Power in the 'New Angola'", which I have found helpful and adapted for this book.

Glossary and acronyms

ACAUT	Action Committee Against Unabated Taxation
Akhuni	a traditional dish of fermented soya
Angami	A Naga people numbering 130,000, mostly settled in Kohima district, Nagaland state, India. The word 'Angami' is the British pronunciation of *Gnamei*, used by the Meitei of Manipur in the 19th century to refer to the northernmost *Tenyimia* communities settled along the Barail Range.
Chekrü	male member of the clan who can be trusted not to break taboos
Kemovo (Thevo)	head village man/founder of the village
Kepenuopfü	Angami supreme creator or God. *Kepenuo* – lit. 'birth' + *pfü* – lit. 'mother'. Christian *Ukepenuopfü* 'Our God'
Lidepfü	an elderly widow selected as the first reaper.
Lhisemia khel	*Lhi-se-mia* – lit. 'together-three-peoples', a clan family of nineteen clans (*chienuo*) created in 1958, bringing together three historic and related Kohima clan families (*thinuo*), namely *Huruotsumia* (7 clans), *Rhiepfumia* (7 clans), and *Tsieramia* (5 clans)
LYO	Lhisemia Youth Organisation
Meya clan	Anonymised name of one of the nineteen *Lhisemia* clans of Kohima village within which (and with whom) much of the research for this project was conducted and consulted.
Mho	Dream in *tenyidie*
Mhorüvemia	Dream traveller (a person who can consciously navigate their dreams, and sometimes engage in out of body 'remote viewing')
Mhoté	Short for *mhotekezhamia*, but less severe, suggesting instead 'lucky dreamer'
Mhotékezhamia	Prophetic dreamer; lit. 'true dreams foretelling person'
Morung	traditional men's dormitory
NNC	Naga National Council. The NNC is the oldest Naga nationalist organisation
NSCN-IM	Naga Socialist Council of Nagalim – Isak Muivah. The NSCN-IM is the largest Naga nationalist organisation, and the

	main partner in dialogue with the Indian Government regarding Naga nationalist demands.
Pitsu	ritual practitioner
Ramei	Angami ornamental headdress
Ruopfü	Spirit. The Angami use *ruopfü* for human 'spirit', 'soul' (reflective of Christian uses), and spirit beings generally, usually with modifiers to distinguish 'my spirit' (*a ruopfü*), 'your spirit' (*puo ruopfü*) and 'river spirit' (*dzü ruopfü*) from recently deceased human spirit or ghost (*kesiamia ruopfü*) and ancestral spirit (*upfutsa ruopfü*, lit. 'grandfather spirit' or 'elder spirit'). Angel is *terhuomia* and evil spirit is *terhuomia* all the same (lit. invisible man or 'person'), though the context of its use may suggest 'messenger' or divine intermediary. Whether *terhuomia* and *ruopfü* are ontologically different is entirely unspecified. Fairies, dwarf spirits, different theriomorphic spirits are generally *terhuomia* – and there are seemingly countless. Animal spirits fit very much into the polymorphism that underwrites much of the folklore, and the various stages of the Angami afterlife. So some *terhuomia* may be ontologically undifferentiated from some *ruopfü*, and some may be different. In this book, I follow the common usage of *ruopfü* as 'soul' and 'spirit', and capitalise the 'R' of *Ruopfü* to denote 'supernature' (following Hamayon 1996, p. 76 and footnote) – the transcendent spirit of nature endowing all of nature with life from which the Christian 'Holy Spirit' or *'Kemesa Ruopfü'* (capitalised in the Bible, thus lit. 'Clean Spirit') is drawn. *Ruopfü* as 'supernature' resembles in many ways the Native American concept of 'Great Spirit'.
Tehuba	elevated, circular space where elders meet for clan meetings
Tekhumiavi	Tiger-man – lit. 'man in the shape of a tiger', a person who, while asleep, can project his or her soul into a non-human animal, either a leopard or a tiger.
Terhuomia	Non-human, non-physical beings or minor deities, often characterised as ambivalent if not generally unfriendly toward humans.
Themumia	Angami traditional healer aided by spirits, or 'shaman'.
Urra uvie!	Our land is our own
Whinuo	Warrior and legendary founder of Kohima village, roughly 500 years ago (based on the oral history and genealogy of the Tsieramia, Whinuo's clan.
Zhevo	Highly respected, and typically oldest male member of a clan, clan ward, or small settlement, in charge of announcing and administering important community rituals.

1   Introduction

This book explores the relationship between dreams and agency among the Angami Naga and is based on two years of fieldwork (2012–2015) in Kohima, the combined village and administrative capital of India's Nagaland state (Figure 1.1). It reflects on the fact that, despite the many changes the Nagas have undergone as a result of British colonialism, widespread conversion to Christianity, political conflict and global capitalism, dreams and dreaming remain important avenues for negotiating uncertainty and dealing with the future. Through dreams and dreaming, one may glean knowledge from signs, gain insight from ancestors and potentially obtain divine blessing. As such, dreams and dreaming continue to assert themselves in the ordinary and extraordinary lives of people, and thus merit closer anthropological examination.

The Angami are one among as many as 88 distinct cultural-linguistic ethnic groups that self-identify as Naga settled in the mountainous Indo-Myanmar borderlands.[1] Nagaland, which in 1963 became India's 16th state, is home to roughly half of this larger transnational Naga community and had a population of 1,978,502 in the 2011 India census.[2] The Angami are roughly 130,000 in number, are settled largely in Kohima district and are considered one of the '16 major tribes' of Nagaland state.[3] Angami villages are generally identified as 'Western Angami', 'Northern Angami', 'Southern Angami' and 'Chakhro Angami' (in the lower hills and plains near Dimapur), loose divisions based primarily on their distinct *Tenyidie* dialects. Kohima is considered 'Northern' Angami and is home to the 'official' *Tenyidie* dialect used in educational curriculums and publications.[4]

The state capital Kohima's diverse population was 114,773 in the last census (including 15,734 in Kohima village)[5] and is the centre of Angami intellectual and political life. The Angami generally live in and own the majority of the land encompassing 25 main villages in Kohima district in southwest Nagaland state. Within each village there are typically three or four *khels* (clan families), and my fieldwork, which forms the basis of this book, was primarily conducted among members of the *Meya** clan within the large *Lhisemia khel*. The *Lhisemia khel* (hereafter *L-khel*) brings together three clan families instead of one, *Lhi-se-mia* – meaning 'three peoples' in *Tenyidie* – joining nineteen exogamous clans. One among four large *khels* in Kohima village, *L-khel* is located in its northwest quadrant of the hilltop settlement (Figure 1.2).

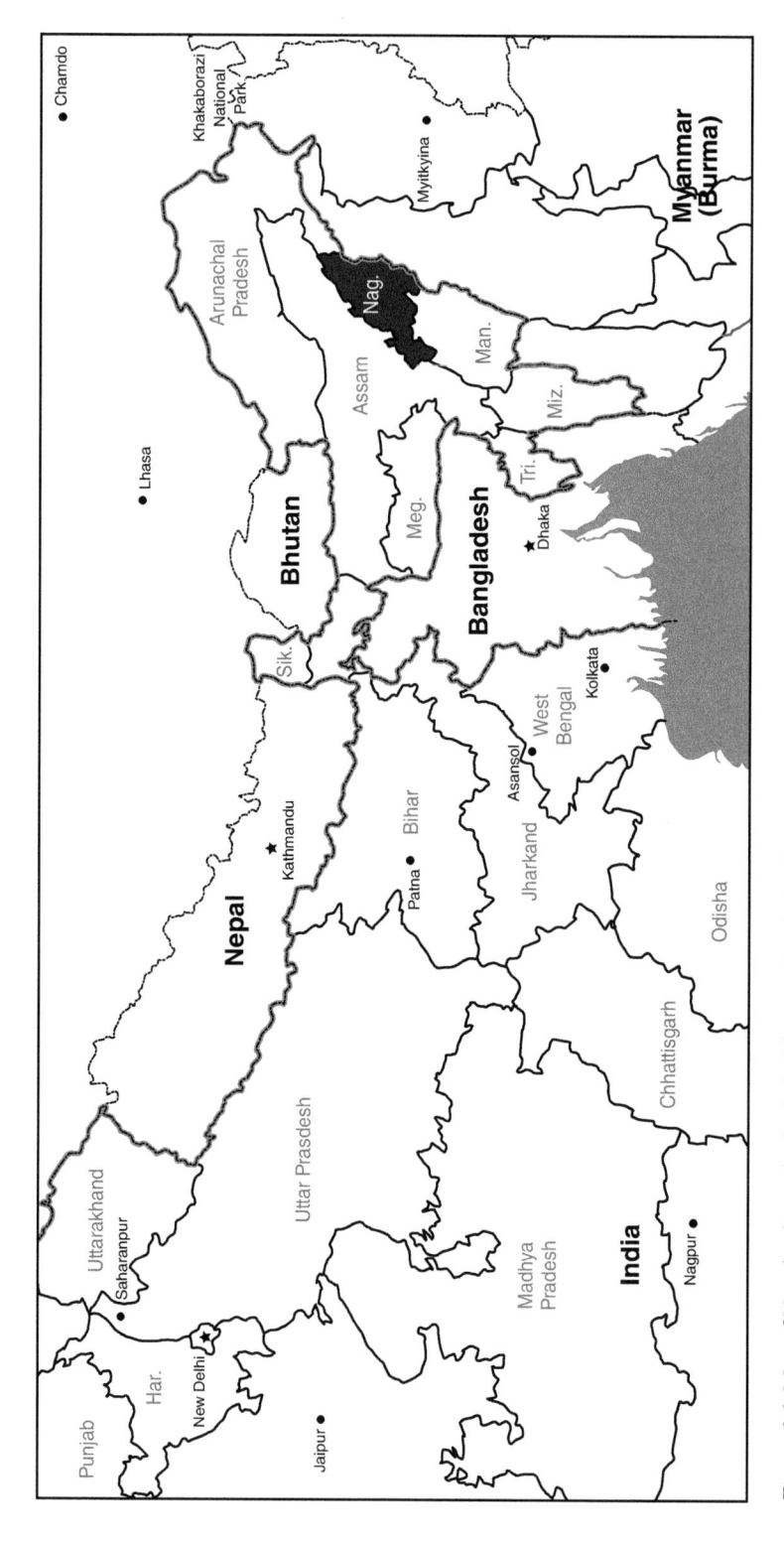

Figure 1.1 Map of Nagaland state in the Indo-Myanmar borderlands

Source: Author's drawing

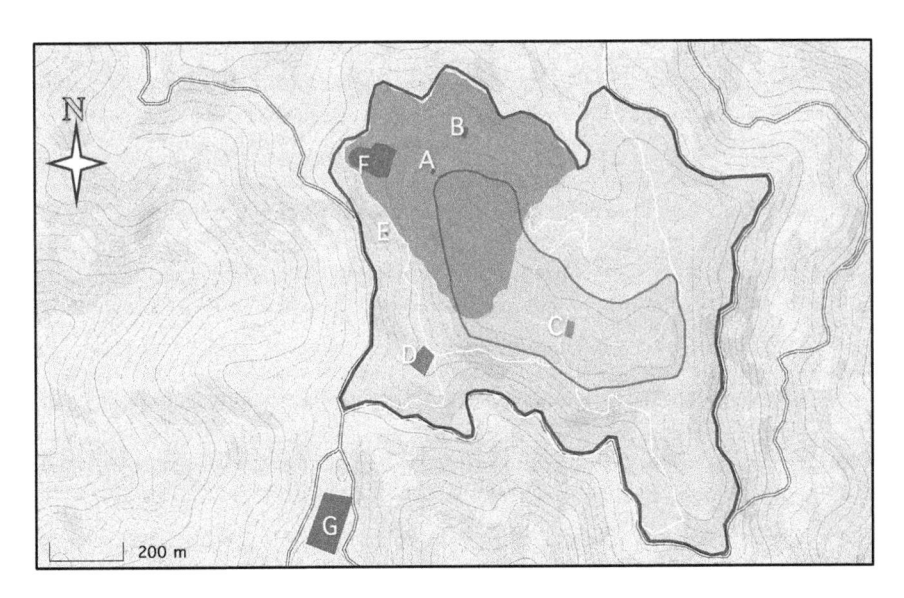

Figure 1.2 Map of Kohima, showing the Lhisemia khel (dark grey area), old village
boundary (thin outline in village centre), new village boundary (dark outer
outline), main village road network (thin white line), and key structures:
A. fieldwork residence; B. Baptist Revival Church; C. Traditional Baptist
church; D. Mission Compound; E. Atsa's house; F. NNC Peace Camp; and
G. Kohima local ground

Source: Author's drawing

The areas comprising the various western and northwestern districts in Nagaland were part of the 'administered area' under British control until India's independence in 1947. Leading up to this point the Nagas had called for assurances,
both from the outgoing British administration and incoming postcolonial government, that the Naga areas would not be included in independent India. However, a
combination of crossed communication and mal-intent led to India including the
Naga areas within the new Indian union, and a fraught relationship with India has
overshadowed the Naga groups ever since. I discuss these developments in greater
detail below; however, this is the general social and political context in which the
Angami find themselves presently, and in which we must understand their culti-
vated practices of appeal to ancestral knowledge, including in their dreams.

In this introduction, I first advance the notion that dreams and dreaming can be
studied as indices of important relational, devotional and political subjectivities.
By examining their practical and symbolic dimensions, they can elucidate the
ways in which, as forms of authoritative knowledge, they influence daily life and
figure in the negotiation of day-to-day domestic and public contingency. Dreams
are also a mode of experience. Here I advance an ethnographic theory of 'reversibility' which will be explained in detail in chapter 3. Simply stated, reversibility
describes the continuity of consciousness between dreaming and waking states,

a concept I borrow from Maurice Merleau-Ponty (1968). However, my use of reversibility relates to the way Angamis understand the relationship between personhood and the moral order of the spirit realm perceived in dreams, and in particular their articulations of *ruopfü* – the *tenyidie* word for soul, spirit or life-being (see glossary) – which closely resemble Merleau-Ponty's concept of 'flesh'. By understanding the ways dreaming and waking experiences fold into and out of each other, we can gain insights into the ways people negotiate this coextensive communicative system involving knowledge received from the spirits of deceased relatives or from the divine. Moreover, by examining the particular settings, audiences and narrative devices employed in interpreting such messages, and making sense of this broader human and non-human 'sociality', we can observe how 'vernacular' divinational practices form counter-narratives to dominant 'institutional' forms of knowledge, especially the passed-down genealogical knowledge that underwrites clan patriarchy.

Having briefly summarised some of the key ideas that I will be using in the book, I now turn to the structure of this chapter. In the first section of this introduction, I briefly touch on the main themes of the book that will show how dreams can take an authoritative role in shaping people's daily lives because they can offer glimpses of the future and are thus capable of altering a family's fortunes. For some, dreams offer more than a glimpse, allowing entry and sometimes communication with ancestral spirits, animal spirits and other kinds of beings. In the second section I introduce Angami community life and social structure and situate the discussion within a historical trajectory intersected by colonialism, Christian missions, postcolonial Indian state-making and global consumerism. I then discuss my entrance as an ethnographer, including the day-to-day issues, struggles and small victories that made fieldwork on dreams both a challenge and an exciting research exercise. Finally, I briefly address some of the limitations of this research and outline the plan of the book.

The social life of dreams

Dreams (*mho*) are routinely shared in close family gatherings, around kitchen hearths in the morning hours or among close neighbours while engaged in household chores in the clan neighbourhood. They are generally interpreted as experiences of the 'self', a term closely associated with the person's soul or spirit, namely *ruopfü*. Thus, dreaming and waking states are equally understood as modes of experiencing the world, and thus are experiences of the *ruopfü*, thereby problematising the assumed suspension of perception or experience of the world in sleep. These diverse understandings can help us navigate the world of Angami dreaming that is interpreted by the people according to the context of the dream experience. First, dreaming is closely associated with ancestral and spirit-mediated knowledge. Properly interpreted, dreams offer glimpses into a privileged form of knowledge where eventualities, often concealed in signs, are both perceivable and negotiable through various devices of daytime 'interference', such as sharing the dream publically, getting a dream blessed by an elder or seeking intercessory prayer at a local church or prayer centre. Second, dreams reveal specific information about a particular situation, but in oblique ways, and there are individuals in the community, who are particularly gifted at deciphering oblique messages. Unlike the 'external' influences from ancestors and spirits, these individuals use long accumulated wisdom in interpreting their own dreams and the dreams of others, enabling the community to understand how the images and signs within the dream can become a part of daily life. Such gifted dreamers tend to be called *mhotékezhamia* or simply *mhoté* ('one whose dreams come true') and within each clan there are individuals, generally elders, that people point out as being especially *mhoté*. Thirdly, there are individuals whom I simply call *mhorüvemia* – 'dream travellers' – that can engage in lucid dreaming, namely their dream 'self' or *ruopfü* is fully conscious and has agency. This ability to consciously navigate outside the body can be experienced both within dreams and outside dreams, in this case entailing a form of 'remote viewing'. Finally, there are individuals with shamanic-like abilities known as *themumia* (lit. 'person who speaks to spirits'). Resembling the variously abled shamanic practitioners and healers found throughout the wider highland Asian region, the *themumia* generally work with spirit agents, and thus have the ability to communicate with ancestral spirits and other spirit agents in waketime and sleeptime all the same. Like the *mhorüvemia*, the *themumia* can lucidly navigate their dreams and return to their bodies to wake up at will. However, unlike the *mhorüvemia*, they are bound to the spirits that aid them in their work and thus must inhabit both spaces simultaneously. In present-day Nagaland, there is disapproval of such practices by many Christians so their work as healers is relatively concealed, though they are regularly consulted by Christians and non-Christians alike, often to discern troubling dreams and perceived omens (cf. Joshi 2012).

Although dreams, of course, begin as intimate experiences of the individual, there are many occasions when many of the Angami share these experiences. If, for example, the dreams contain vivid signs or imagery, they are most often shared in the first instance with close kin, typically a mother or elder. In many instances dreaming and dream interpretation have a particular pattern or structure. The process unfolds in this manner. (i) Within the close kin, one typically seeks out someone who can offer a positive interpretation or who may be predisposed to interpret a dream as a blessing. However, sharing a dream at all is understood to enhance, usually in a positive way, the dream's forecasted outcome in waking reality. (ii) Then the dream narratives may be shared within the community or neighbours, and through this they enter an arena in which other signs and omens, and their possible meanings, are being deliberated. (iii) These interpretations then are understood to be at play or active in an unfolding process of materialisation, possibly resulting in an event, thereby impacting on social reality. Indeed, the search for significance in dreams is, as one scholar put it, 'a profoundly social act'.[6] The inspiration or source of the pattern of dreams is believed to originate from ancestors, spirits or *Kepenuopfü* – the Angami supreme creator – with the intention of informing or warning their human kin of what lies ahead. Dream narratives connected to significant family events are remembered and passed down through several generations, sometimes achieving mythical status within the clan. Such narratives, in turn, become important elements in shaping group identity, give a sense of divine purpose to clan members and influence such practices as the naming of children. Names, which are often phrases, are intended to forecast the outcome of a person's life, and in a sense pre-empt his or her fate. Two examples are: *Ruokuoneinuo* 'to be very lucky' or *Pelerovi* 'to be trustworthy'.

As I have already suggested, dreams are not constructed in the moment but are related to other signs and omens that once they emerge remain in the memory of the interpretive community. How these are remembered and the role memory plays are crucial to the link between memory and dreams. This process by which supernaturally-imparted messages in dreams are transformed into passed-down clan narratives may be traced in orated family histories during special clan meetings or in less formal settings in which clan members recollect the way clan fortunes (and misfortunes) link back to particular signs culled from dreams or daytime omens (discussed in chapter 2). These clan narratives, in turn, inform the categories and indices of interpretation taken up by successive generations of dreamers, as they carry on seeking to interpret and glean meaning from their dreams in light of their clan history and new contingencies.

But communication with spirits animating the landscape beyond the village boundary – generally believed to be *terhuomia* (see glossary) – was once a central concern in Angami community life. For example, Prior to widespread conversion to Christianity among the Eastern Angami (now Chakhesang) the office of the *Kemovo* – the village head and representative of the original founder's kin – was still more or less active into the 1930s (Fürer-Haimendorf and Mills 1936). While the *Kemovo's* youngest son inherits his father's house and clan plot (which remains a custom today amongst most Angami clan families and is a pattern found in many other Naga groups), the eldest sons were expected to expand the clan territory by settling in new areas and becoming village heads or *Kemovos* themselves. When a new village site was identified, he would go ahead, build a fire with wood from his father's hearth, and lay down and dream. In his dream he would seek out the *terhuomia* or spirit masters of the land and negotiate for a new human settlement, use of the land and permission to hunt wild game. In exchange, the new village, which would be settled by usually at least two other exogamous clans, would agree to an annual village-wide public ritual. Therefore, in order to safely cultivate, hunt and engage in such things as drawing water from local water sources, there had to be an agreement of exchange already in place or the *terhuomia* would cause the settlers considerable harm. Thus the balance in the exchange had to be closely and continuously negotiated by the *Kemovo* (ibid., *see also* Pascal Bouchery 2007, pp. 111–112).

The spirit guardianship of land is a recurring theme in this ethnography, and in several accounts I discuss the ways in which these terrains of power are often revealed in dreams. In chapter 6, I discuss the ways in which an informant negotiated safe passage. In a separate case, the same informant unwittingly enters a sacred forest, falls immediately ill and requires significant intervention from a Christian charismatic dream prophetess and the spirit of his deceased mother. His spirit was then 'smuggled' across military checkpoints, thus also revealing the ways in which the militarised terrains of Indian state-making in the Northeast, can overlap with the terrains controlled by powerful spirits.

The *Kemovo* was in many ways charged with understanding the delimitations of these terrains and thus mitigated these kinds of risks to villagers, and in chapter 4 I touch briefly on some of the relationship dynamics between the early *Kemovo* and his local community as observed by Fürer-Haimendorf and Mills (1936). Nevertheless, territorial expansion has its limits, and Pascal Bouchery (2007, p. 112) notes that the *Kemovo's* elder sons eventually began to stay home, thus setting up a power struggle among siblings, which lead to a breaking down of the once lofty position of the *Kemovo* as representative of the original village founder's kin.

As noted earlier, the conditions set by the *terhuomia* for settling their land entailed the establishment of annual village-wide rituals. And in many respects, we see how the political and religious offices of the *Kemovo* were not distinguished by the Angami. As ritual practitioner, as well as the repository of clan knowledge as representative of the village founder's kin, the *Kemovo* was concerned for both genealogical orthodoxy and ritual orthodoxy, and thus ensured and enforced their strict observance. However, as the *Kemovo's* siblings came to challenge his authority, and indeed sought to influence clan councils – through sheer personal charisma, power in accumulated wealth or as respected warriors – the relationship between the *Kemovo* and the village-wide ritual practices became blurred (Bouchery 2007, p. 114). Indeed, religious practitioners were chosen by clan councils, and the details of the original exchange prior to the village founding were soon lost.

The institutionalisation of public rituals translated into annual rituals that principally followed the cultivation and harvest cycles. But, more and more, ritual practices associated with appeasing or keeping peace with the *terhuomia* – in cases of child birth, in terms of securing a good cultivation for the family, and the like – became a domestic concern. Large public ceremonies were largely dominated by men and consisted of village-wide work and hunting freezes, fastidious attention to food abstentions and the reading of omens. Indeed, the 'humbling' of the *Kemovo* meant that there was no definitive mediator for all, checking always to see where there may be imbalances in need of pre-emptive attention (Fürer-Haimendorf and Mills 1936; *see also* Hamayon 1996, pp. 80–82). It is in this vacuum that attentiveness to ritual orthodoxy became increasingly a domestic concern, and the insights that may be gleaned in waketime and sleeptime omens became a significant preoccupation at the family level.[7]

With the arrival of Christian missionaries in the 1870s, the more visible public ritual practices were targeted while those practices found in the domestic sphere, and in many ways concealed from public scrutiny, remained active. As a result, and similar to other practices within the ambit of the domestic sphere, such as field cultivation practices and food preparation, Angami dream culture represents an uninterrupted stream of continuity with the potential to elucidate a great deal about Angami social and religious life in the midst of significant change. These practices and continuities also have political ramifications, especially since the Nagas have been engaged in a nationalistic struggle with the Indian state for over 60 years, and the introduction and spread of Christianity has brought with it a certain moral ambiguity in terms of how to negotiate traditional culture with the modern teachings of Christianity.

The ethnography draws primarily on three co-habitating generations of the *Meya* clan and identifies two general cultural spaces characteristic of Angami patrilineal clan life, and thus is attentive to the ways in which dreams and dreaming culture may be perceived and interpreted within a given community setting. Patrilocal life tends to distinguish between those born into the clan and those who have kinship relations outside the clan lineage – typically married women. The history behind these segmentations can be traced to the exclusionary clan policies that entail limited participation in public discourse and decision making for non-lineage members. Here, clan authority is routinely justified through an invocation of clan histories and genealogies. The notion of clan 'perpetuity' within kinship structures is illuminated in the work of Meyer Fortes, who identifies some important linkages between African Tallensi social processes and the lineage system, which resemble those found among the Angami:

> If we visualise the social structure as a sum of processes in time, then the lineage system, which embodies the patrilineal principle, emerges as the source of the enduring pattern, the relatively fixed form of . . . social organisation . . . The lineage system unites the ancestors, the living, and the yet unborn in a uniform integrated sequence actualised at a given time in determinate corporate groups.
>
> (1949, p. 342)

This 'enduring pattern', in which at least some conceive of the whole as composed not of individuals but of descent groups into which individuals are accorded membership through birth or recruitment (Hershman 1981), is a spatio-temporal order – a spatially constituted and inter-generationally transmitted collective imaginary. The 'enduring pattern' and the laws that secure this spatio-temporal domain of group lineage-in-perpetuity, is an important modality of group consciousness. Other forms of knowledge such as that communicated by ancestors, spirits and sometimes *Kepenuopfü*, through dreams, visions and prophecy, form important resources for community members that do not participate in the elaboration of clan genealogical knowledge.

Though this research was conducted primarily in Kohima, it incorporates insights drawn from neighbouring Angami villages, and on occasion beyond Angami areas throughout contiguous Tenyimia Naga cultural-linguistic region. This includes communities in southern Nagaland, eastern Assam and northern Manipur. This larger area was explored in relation to important clan ties, inter-village friendships and cultural parallels with Naga communities that share ancestry with the Angami. More generally, however, I found it helpful to venture further afield in terms of the ethnographic sites I spent time in, because dream narratives

Figure 1.3 Morning sharing in Khonoma village
Source: Author's photo

often describe landscapes/dreamscapes that extend far beyond the perceivable horizon of village life in Kohima (Figure 1.3).

I unpack these ideas further in the following sections, but first I contextualise the discussion by tracing some of the key practices and viewpoints that underpin Angami social and political life. Of particular importance are the early observations by British colonial officer and anthropologist J.H. Hutton while he was stationed in the Naga Hills between 1912 and 1915. Hutton was the first to reflect on the social significance of dreams among the Angami and penned the first ethnographic monograph on the Naga, *The Angami Nagas* (1921a) on the region. I now summarise a few of his key observations as they relate to this study, before turning to the recent political history of the region.

The Angami Nagas

As briefly touched on earlier, the Naga-inhabited mountains and plains areas that presently form the western half of Nagaland state were part of a series of British annexations of hill areas in eastern Assam that began in 1866 in response to Angami raids on the expanding tea plantations. In 1874 these annexations formed the 'Naga Hills District', a 'Scheduled' district under the newly formed Assam province (Gundevia 1975, p. 47). At the same time, a line of control was instituted (Bengal Eastern Frontier Regulation of 1873) to restrict unofficial movement and trade with the 'plains'.[8] This 'Inner Line' restriction remains in effect up until today for Indian nationals. Foreigners, on the other hand, were required to obtain a special two-week 'Restricted Area Permit' to enter Nagaland, though this has been suspended at present to attract tourism for the annual Hornbill Festival, which happens every December.

Kohima was ultimately occupied in 1878 as the last major advance into the Naga areas – what Hutton described as 'the insidious ravages of the "Pax Britannica"' (1921a, p. 44) – and the headquarters for British administration of the Naga Hills was established on 'Garrison Hill' adjacent to Kohima village. They were thus able to monitor Angami antagonism better and gradually established control over settlements concentrated along the north-south Barail mountain ridge. A new road along this range connected, for the first time, British India with the Manipuri Kingdom and ultimately British controlled Burma (Hodson 1911). This and a new network of offshoot roads connected villages that until then had operated as independent political entities (Hutton 1921a, p. 44).

American Baptist missionaries, having developed a strong rapport with the British in the establishment of educational and medical institutions in Assam from as early as the 1830s, were allowed to cross the Inner Line and expand their efforts among the Naga in the 1870s (Downs 1986). Administration of the hundreds of Naga villages now under British protection was characteristically pragmatic, recognising the authority of village headmen and the efficacy of local customary laws. British officials, thus, directly adjudicated only in severe cases such as in the case of significant inter-village disputes (Hutton 1921a). The abolition of martial practices related to inter-village feuds and head-taking eventually lessened the power of village councils to wage war. This also affected many ceremonial and ritual practices related to war. And new forms of trade and the increasing use of a single currency introduced by the British began to gradually transform local village economies. Hereditary village heads such as the Angami *Kemovo* were identified by the British as *de-facto* village chiefs and given red shawls. These they wore as uniforms while engaging in their new duties of collecting taxes, based on the number of hearths in each village clan. They were called *Gaonburas* (ritual headmen), and this village-level office was instituted by the British throughout the administered Naga areas. The British also hired *Dobashis* (translators; the word meaning 'two languages' in Assamese) from each Naga linguistic group. *Dobashis* did not generally work in their own villages, and thus were spared the stigma that sometimes accompanied the *Gaonburas*, who would collect taxes in their own villages. *Dobashis* were very often relatives of the *Gaonbura*, but lived and travelled with the British officers as they toured extensively throughout the Naga-inhabited areas. These administrative decisions would greatly influence the dynamics of authority both at the village level and with regards to the shape of the new social elite. This idea of authority, a discussion developed further in chapter 6, is closely linked to the politico-religious tradition implied in notions of 'ownership' of Angami land. While these changes were occurring all over the Naga hills and amongst the Angami, it is interesting to note that some traditional practices persist. In the case of land, for example, which I will discuss in chapter 6, the relationship between land and ownership is influenced by human and non-human claimants. While modern practices such as the monetary value put on land have become widespread, in certain cases dreams still index this exchange.

Though the American Baptists arrived in Kohima in the wake of the British administrators, it was not until the 1930s that their evangelism, through literacy and education programmes, made any significant inroads. A veteran Angami pastor wrote, for example, that Angami opposition to the new religion was,

> because they [Angami] were rich; because they possessed a very close-knit, democratic social organisation; because of the unwillingness to give up zu [rice beer]; because of a higher intensity of anti-foreign attitudes; and because the Angamis possessed a very high degree of self-respect which included a pride in those customs and traditional institutions that the missionaries were condemning as 'pagan'.
>
> (cited in Van Den Brul 1980, p. 112)

But the advantages that schools and medical services brought to the region soon became evident and tipped the scales in favour of the missionaries. A newly educated elite was inculcated with Western forms and institutions for governing and organising society, and new committees were established in churches and in civic life – women's committees, deacon's committees and finance committees – as ways of educating lay-persons about building efficiency, planning events and developing strategies that continued to fuel evangelistic efforts. As the world wars drained Western mission coffers, the Nagas became the ones evangelising, and the last missionaries to work among the Angamis left in 1948. By 1955 all Western missionaries in Northeast India were forced out by the new Indian administration (Van den Brul 1980). In the 1941 census 34,000 Nagas are listed as baptised Christians, and by 1951, in the aftermath of the Japanese invasion, the number grew to 98,068, roughly 45% of the Naga population in the administered areas (ibid., p. 114; *see also* Eaton 1984). While Angami Christians were initially more reserved about their newfound faith than other Naga groups, by the 1950s, with their increased leadership role in Christian institution-building, there was a marked shift towards asserting distinction from their non-Christian neighbours. This assertiveness of difference – particularly with their employment of distinct Western dress – spread from the now increasingly urbanised centres of Baptist evangelist activity, and would constitute an initial public display in the development of a self-conscious pan-Naga Christian identity. Van Den Brul suggests that many new believers sought to mimic the behaviours and lifestyle of the American missionaries:

> The early Christians imitated the missionaries as far as possible, responding to the exhortation, often proclaimed from the pulpit, that they must 'put aside the old man, put on the new'. Dress and appearance were the most conspicuous aspects of the change, often resulting in an unconscious parody of western fashion. For Christians, frock coats and long dresses were a symbol of

modernization and of adherence to the new religion; they indicated changing values and standards of achievement motivation.

(1980, p. 117)

I touch on the importance of the early Christian movement in greater depth in chapter 5 and the development of a new ritually mediated social bond that can be closely linked to a pan-Naga identity. Two significant charismatic religious outpourings – the Christian 'revivals' of the 1950s and 1970s – were linked in many ways to the intensification of the Indo-Naga conflict, but unlike the early mission movement, it saw the spontaneous incorporation of older pre-Christian religious practices in their gatherings. The 'revivals' were widespread and would challenge the hegemony enjoyed for some time by traditional Baptists. This divide continues today, and in many respects mirrors the divide I will discuss throughout the book between the 'enduring pattern' of clan patriarchy and the 'hearthen economy' linking domestic productivity and relationality with non-clan members. I now turn to a few observations regarding traditional Angami dream culture and some key observations by early British administrator ethnographers.

J.H. Hutton is the first to point out the significance of dreams in Angami culture. He notes, for example, that apart from the everyday community dream narration and interpretation a variety of specialist practitioners employ dreams as a primary medium of divination. Professional 'dream-women', for example, used dreams to divine the outcome of hunting expeditions, business ventures or other concerns proposed by a client (Hutton 1921a, p. 245), whereas a *themumia* might be consulted for more serious matters such as in cases of drought or a serious illness – dreams being also a primary source in his or her endeavours. 'Their powers', Hutton writes, 'vary from merely dreaming dreams to the practice of genuine black magic' (ibid., p. 242). Other practitioners include *terhuope* (lit. 'bridge of spirits', or person believed to be inhabited by multiple spirits), who would answer questions while in a dream-like trance; and *tekhumiavi* (lit. 'man in the shape of a tiger') who would lie in a dream-like state in their darkened homes, while their animal spirits roamed the forest outside (ibid., pp. 244–247).

An Angami myth of origin, shared by other tribes such as Sumi, Rengma, Chakhesang and Lotha Nagas, details how the people came to be and their connections with the spirit and animal world. *Kepenuopfü* – lit. 'birth spirit' (the *pfü* suffix denotes female gender) – is the creator of all living beings, as well as ancestor of humans and is the term used for God and Creator in the *tenyidie* Bible. The origin myth holds that *themia* (man), *tekhu* (tiger) and *ruopfü* (spirit) were the sons of the same mother. Upon her death, the three brothers became estranged, and *Kepenuopfü* is generally held to be in spirit form living in the sky.[9]

Ruopfü is, as one of my informants explained, 'one with nature', and a central concept in this book. It is articulated in two general forms. *Ruopfü* (capital 'R') is the life-giving force animating animals, forests, rivers and all of the natural world. Here, I draw on Hamayon's (1996, p. 76 and footnote) term 'supernature' in an effort to avoid the binarisms entailed in the phrases 'supernatural world' or 'supernatural realm'. But *Ruopfü* as 'supernature' is not to be mistaken with the

Angami term for soul and spirit, namely *ruopfü* (with a small 'r'). Hutton seems to conflate both, thus leading to a somewhat broad conceptualisation, namely:

> a mysterious spiritual force which seems to combine the attributes of guardian angel, familiar spirit, Destiny, and in some cases it would seem even of a man's own soul. The description is vague enough, but the danger to be avoided in transcribing any Angami ideas upon the supernatural is, above all, the danger of distinguishing what is vague, of giving form to what is void, of defining what is not finite.
>
> (1921a, p. 183)

Animals, all except tigers, were brought by the *terhuomia*, who are believed to be lower deities. Chief among the lower deities is *Rutzeh*, who is evil and on whom such things as sudden death are blamed. There is also the mischievous *Telepfü* who is held responsible when men, women and children go missing. It is believed that *Telepfü* steals the senses of her captives so they are unable to scream or run, but does not kill them. Benevolent *terhuomia*, on the other hand, include *Miewenuo* who is known to visit farmers and blesses people with good crops or livestock; *Ayepi*, a sort of fairy who lives with humans in their homes and brings prosperity; *Tsükho and Dzürawü*, male and female spirits represented as dwarfs, are believed to live in the forests and are guardians of the wild animals; and *Metsimo*, who, as Hutton writes, 'guards the approach to paradise, a sort of Angami St. Peter', possessing attributes (according to the Memi Tenyimia tradition) that could qualify him as *Kepenuopfü's* husband (1921a, p. 182 and footnote).

Tekhu-rho, the god and guardian of tigers and leopards, is considered a very powerful deity, and believed to be responsible for the disappearance of humans (primarily hunters) in the jungle. At the moment of a disappearance, village elders in pre-Christian times would declare a *genna* or 'prohibition' (in this case entailing a community-wide freeze on field labour) in an effort to appease the angry deity. Search parties would then enter the forest. *Terhuomia* are numerous, and every village will have a variety of *terhuomia* that a neighbouring village may not have heard of. But what is important for this book is that *terhuomia* represent spiritual forces that are not 'kin'. Negotiation with *terhuomia* is done by specialists, and in this regard is unlike negotiation with the spirits of deceased relatives or 'ancestors' that communicate in dreams. The hundreds of myths, legends, folktales and songs that are still shared around kitchen hearths are firmly contextualised within this hidden world where *terhuomia* inhabit stones, trees, forests, rivers and mountains. According to one of my informants, even today 'the spirits demand respect and enact harsh punishments on those who are careless and don't follow the ancestral laws'.[10]

Though specialists such as the Angami shaman, or *themumia*, that inhabit human and non-human worlds openly practised well up into the 1930s and were integral to clan life and culture, their present-day contemporaries, possibly just as numerous and similarly gifted, operate largely in concealment due to the strong disapproval of such practices by the traditional Baptist church. For traditional healers, whose services remain in great demand, acceptance is achieved by a balancing act of respectability through holding an ordinary job of sorts, and perhaps maintaining membership in a local church, while visiting clients after hours, and only accepting tips (cf. Joshi 2012).

Hutton's observations of Naga cosmology, and the Angami 'science of dreaming' specifically, are punctuated with a set of first-hand experiences which he himself describes as personally perplexing. These accounts confirm many local accounts of the ways dreams foretell future events, how they can often be linked to specific locations and how they may be a channel for supernatural volition. The following is a series of brief examples drawn from archival materials, including personal notes and letters sent to colleagues in Britain while stationed in Kohima.[11]

In a 1923 letter to C.G. Seligman, Hutton describes his experience in a bungalow, used by the British inspectors, which he built in 1915 along a new road about 140 kilometres northeast of Kohima. Local villagers had warned him not to use the proposed site as it was believed to be haunted. The Baimho villagers, they informed him, had used the site to perform sacrifices to the spirit of a man who had drowned in the Tizu river. However, he ignored the warnings, argued that it was conveniently situated and had a good water supply.

> A few months after the bungalow was finished I went and stayed in it for some local business. I occupied the west bedroom and my night was spoilt by a horrifying nightmare in the course of which I saw a creature like a human child with a monstrous big head creeping across the floor; the principal feature of the dream was the quite unreasonable fear which I experienced and which caused me to perspire so freely (the weather was quite cool) that my pyjamas and sheets had to be dried in the sun the next day. I thought it was a bad, a very bad dream and put it down to having eaten the roe of some fish they had brought me from the river, and thought no more about it.
>
> A little later Mr Mills had occasion to come to Kohima, some 70 miles, to consult me about some matter, and in the course of his stay he asked me if I had ever had an unpleasant experience in any of the Mokokchung inspection bungalows. I mentioned a scorpion in the bathroom at Nankam, but he explained that he referred to psychic experiences. I said I thought not. He asked me 'not at Baimho?' To which I replied then that I had experienced the worst nightmare I remembered since my childhood there, but that was all. When I started to recount it he stopped me and went on. The only difference in our accounts seemed to be that whereas the creature with the big head that I had seen had unkempt hair, he had seen it bald – or it may have been the other way round. We agreed that we would tell no-one of this experience but would find excuses to send people to Baimho and find out later if they had such dreams.[12]

Their first 'victim' of their experiment was a man by the name of Meikeljohn of the Assam Forestry Department who transferred to the Garo Hills and had stayed in the Baimho bungalow prior to leaving. Hutton asked if he had experienced anything unusual there, and he said he had not. Sometime later a second person, Dr N.L. Bor, also in the Forestry Department, left the Naga Hills to fill in for Meikeljohn in the Garo Hills – though Hutton and Mills had forgotten to ask him about Baimho. When Bor and Meikeljohn met, however,

> Meiklejohn asked him whether he had been to 'the haunted bungalow' while in the Naga Hills. He replied that he supposed Baimho was meant. He had gone to sleep in a chair on the veranda after he had arrived, having walked some ten miles from his last halting place, but was so frightened by a dream that instead of sleeping at Baimho as planned he had packed up his kit again and walked on another twelve miles to the next bungalow the same afternoon.[13]

In the same letter to Seligman (1923) Hutton shares a second personal account that was included in his monograph (1921a, p. 144), dealing with a foretelling dream that appeared to the dreamer in symbolic form. Hutton likely understood that Seligman, keen to test Freud's theory of 'dream types' (discussed further in chapter 2), would be interested in Angami dream symbols and their meanings. He thus begins with a brief set of examples, namely

> to dream of being bitten by a tic, which cannot be pulled out is an omen of approaching death, while to dream of a man dressed entirely in new clothes is a sure premonition of the death of the man thus seen. A curious instance of this came within the writer's own experience. He left Kohima for a tour in the Kezama villages on September 8th 1913. At the moment of leaving, his own interpreter, Zelucha of Jotsoma, came up to say that he was not feeling very well and would prefer to join later after two or three days, so another interpreter, Vise of Viswema, was taken in his place. Mao was reached on the 10th, Kezakenoma on the 11th, Razama on the 13th. At Razama, Zelucha was expected to arrive, but another interpreter, Solhu of Kezakenoma, came instead, saying that Zelucha was going to die. When asked how he could possibly say this, as Zelucha had been quite well a few days before and had not been really ill when Vise saw him, Vise said that he had dreamt of him on the night of the sleeping at Mao, and had seen him dressed entirely in new clothes. This, he said, left no doubt. The news of Zelucha's death reached camp at Tekhubama on September 16th.[14]

Hutton does not dedicate much time to dreams, but the two accounts he does provide are significantly detailed (and not included in full here), and reflective of his attempts to verify, however possible, the absence of chance or coincidence. Indeed, he leaves little doubt regarding his own bewilderment, though he does not attempt any kind of theory or explanation of what he implicitly suggests is a kind of dream-mediated spirit volition active in dreaming and dream interpretation. More importantly, his accounts are consistent with the two general forms of contemporary dream experience documented in this research, namely 'iconic dreams' and 'indexical' dreams (discussed in more depth in chapters 2 and 3). Put simply, Hutton's dream experience (and generally shared by his colleagues) in the Baimho bungalow, constitutes an 'iconic' dream, because there was a direct correspondence between his dream-self and the approaching demon, recounted in hindsight in a logical narrative sequence. 'Indexical' dreams do not have this kind of direct correspondence. The image of a well-dressed man is a sign or symbol translated as portending the man's death and based on the interpreter's memory of past correlations between 'well-dressed' and 'death'.

Generally speaking, as observed by Hutton and confirmed by my fieldwork, dreams among the Angami continue to figure prominently in day-to-day community life, in ritual practices and in the retelling of clan histories. Although these dream practitioners no longer operate as openly as in the past, charismatic Christian groups such as the Baptist Revival Church have found ways of incorporating inspirational religious experiences, in many cases dreams, into their worship (see chapter 5). This project has also confirmed some of Hutton's insights in observing the underlying logic of dreaming, namely that dreams are understood as experiences of the soul or spirit. There is a general understanding that dreams communicate knowledge from spirits, sometimes from ancestors and often from the divine, or *Kepenuopfü*. Dreams are shared, whether in the morning hours by the kitchen hearth or with a counsellor at a prayer meeting in the local church, and they may also prefigure future events. The quotidian practice of sharing and interpreting the highly symbolic knowledge of dreams reveals the continuous concern with the way the imaginary and real are interwoven. An examination of these processes elucidates the linkages between the dream and the real, the intimate and the public, the subjective and the political. And although Hutton never explored the issue of Angami dreams beyond his two descriptions, and did not venture a theory that might explain the two very different kinds of dreams he detailed, his descriptions are nevertheless useful in building a case for important continuities in Angami dream experience over the course of a century.

An overview of Nagaland and Kohima

Upon closer examination, the visitor discovers that Kohima is in fact two bodies existing side-by-side: Kohima village ('Bara Basti' or 'Great Village' is how it is commonly referred to in the town) is a more or less traditional settlement of clan families; whereas Kohima town, which hosts and services Nagaland's government and development apparatus, is culturally diverse and reflects the kind of 'busy-ness' found in commercial centres throughout the Northeast. Technically separate from the village, the town in reality subsumes it in one continuous sprawl. The juxtaposition of these two bodies provides a stimulating environment for studying the shifting relationships that local inhabitants have with the ongoing cultural and material processes of social change. In addition, it provides a unique vantage point from which to observe the interplay between two very contrasting understandings of time. Kohima village, for instance, continues to follow traditional forms of cyclical time marked throughout the calendar year with carefully programmed re-enactments of important Angami festivals such as the weeklong *Sekrenyi* festival of purity after the New Moon in February. Other festive events coincide with cultivation and harvest seasons (cf. Hutton 1921a; Joshi and Arya 2004; and Joshi 2012). Kohima town, on the other hand, will host Christmas and Diwali alike, and generally accommodates festive events that appeal to its diverse population. The town is also host to the offices of the state government, a massive Assam Rifles headquarters and camp in the centre of the city, World War II cemetery and trendy boutique shops and is a hub for transport across Nagaland. The activities and orientation of Kohima Town suggest more linear understandings of time consonant with Indian development discourse, and the trajectories associated with local-national-global markets. In this book I am seeking neither to underplay nor overstate this binary relationship, in this case between village and town, and between Kohima and Delhi. But these are discursive positionings that are conjured daily in casual speech, and thus demonstrate a symbolic relationship that informs understandings concerning what is perceived to be 'backward' and what is 'modern'.

Beyond its historical and political importance in relation to World War II, the Battle of Kohima and its memorial serve as a semiotic text for Kohima's unique place as a locus of friction and convergence between differing political visions (i.e. Empire, nation-state and autonomous village republics); the various origins of influence (e.g. Japan, Southeast Asia, India and the West); contrasting understandings of time (i.e. cyclical, ritually re-enacted time and linear time spurred by innovation); and different visions of change (e.g. social conservatism, Christian apocalyptic, nationalist-populist and modernity). Moreover, the discursive binary between Asia's highland corridor and its powerful neighbours China and India – with their ambitious modernising designs and political technologies that underwrite these processes – can be viewed as a macrocosm of a more subtle interplay and tension between urban and rural, village and city; a binary that is daily at play in casual conversation, in comments about someone's sense of fashion, village accent or choice of private school for the children (Bach 2010).

The manicured lawns of the World War II cemetery in Kohima town also serve as a reminder of early British preoccupations with administrating the boundaries of British India. Part and parcel of surveying, taxing and arbitrating disputes between the dozens of distinct Naga groups was the task of recording, the 'fading histories' of the Nagas (Peal 1894). Hutton, the administrator ethnographer, was Deputy Commissioner of the Naga Hills from 1905 to 1935 and for most of this time resided in Kohima. Given his dual responsibility as an anthropologist as well as the highest ranking British official in the region, Hutton had the power and influence to summon his informants to his hilltop bungalow (on Garrison Hill just behind the cemetery), where he would meet with village elders to discuss their daily affairs, customary laws, religious beliefs and practices, folklore and language (Hutton 1921a). There is little evidence to suggest that Hutton's relationship with his subjects was anything but amicable, and many Naga scholars have engaged with Hutton's anthropological work, due to his powerful position as administrator. However, the problematisation of this very relationship – between the Western social scientist and his object of study – is inextricably a part of the research design for this book, and my own ethnography, and will need to be continually scrutinised, adjusted and scrutinised again.

Yet the difficulties inherent in studying such complex processes should not distract us from attempting to understand the ways in which marginal groups 'construct different identities in order to create a constituency' to move their own ideas and interests in opposition to political, economic and cultural hegemony (Goh 2002, p. 28). As state-sponsored modernisation processes in India and Nagaland attempt to formulate new identities and ideas of how people perceive themselves, individuals and families interpret, construct and are impacted by these processes of contemporary change. These changes are critical threads of inquiry that can shed new light on the dark corners of the 'political' situation that characterises much of highland areas in this part of Asia. Finally, the shifting relationship between individuals and the state becomes the arena for understanding more internal, even subconscious forms of knowledge construction, conversion and translation. Anthropologists studying dreams, local dream theories and the ways in which dreams are communicated have provided invaluable tools for engaging in this kind of work.

Having briefly contextualised the Angami Nagas within the broader colonial and postcolonial history, Christian missions and contemporary conflict, I turn now to an account of how this project was carried out in Kohima and in the Angami context more generally.

Fieldwork successes and challenges

When Hammersley writes that 'the aim [of ethnography] is to "get inside" the way each group of people sees the world' (1985, p. 152), what he describes should, in many respects, be the 'crowning achievement' following a lifetime of committed and focused observational participation. But how is the unobservable to be documented? How can dreams, which cannot be directly observed by anyone except a single dreaming subject, be a viable object of investigation? The only way to 'participate' in this, as an ethnographer, was to work to establish a great deal of trust, to establish knowledge of family histories, of dream signs and local meanings, and to recognise that dreams accompanied daily routines generally hidden in intimate familial spaces. Secondly, 'getting inside' in the real sense of seeking to experience something of what informants experienced entailed, in many ways, relinquishing one's preconceptions and exposing oneself to new experiences and understandings. Over more than two years of fieldwork, I learned about participating in an attentive, communicative and interpretive culture, and my knowledge on the subject also translated into my being asked to listen to and interpret the dreams of others.

In general, I was always mindful of the criticism aimed at Western anthropologists and the discipline (Goh 2002; *see also* Clifford and Marcus 1986; Marcus and Fischer 1986; Fox 1991; and Comaroff and Comaroff 1992) of the desire to create a consistent 'system' out of observed social processes. Beng Lan Goh articulates this aptly:

> The traditional anthropological goal of achieving an understanding of other non-Western cultures as coherent, meaningful, discreet, and integral systems has been criticized for reifying and Orientalizing other cultures and as implicated in the constitution and maintenance of anthropology's authority.
>
> (2002, p. 30)

Responses to this scrutiny have varied in the last two or three decades, and anthropologists have retooled to incorporate new levels of auto-critique, primarily through ethnographic experimentations which are more cognitive, experiential or, in some cases, self-ethnographic. These place the ethnographer's own impressions, thoughts and perspectives at the centre of the research, alone or along with other subjects. Such approaches aim for a kind of coeval epistemological scrutiny (Reed-Danahay 1997).

My own approach draws somewhat from this thinking in that my presence during moments of dream narration and interpretation evolved into my direct participation in the practices. Though I had begun to pay closer attention to my own dreams, I realised relatively early in my fieldwork that I was also welcome to share my dreams. As a result, I grew more attentive to, and began to recall, longer dream episodes and describe them in greater detail. As these accompanied others' dream narratives, I found my own dream signs and fragments joined the signs and narrative fragments of other dreams being shared. Together, like pieces of a puzzle, they sometimes might begin to form a picture. Often there seemed to be little in the way of a clear picture, and indeed they were quickly forgotten. Once in a while, however, the collective narrative pointed to some important eventuality, and everyone in the group sharing the dreams would be attentive through the morning hours and the day to news coming from relatives, or perhaps neighbours, of some event. In these moments of dream sharing, I began to memorise, and record, much of what is undoubtedly a very extensive lexicon of dream signs and their possible meanings.

One main challenge in dream research has been the problem of how to document the unobservable private dream-events of others. Anthropologists studying dreams have circumvented this problem by focusing not on the events themselves, but on the performance of dream narrations, and in some instances what are termed 're-enactments' (e.g. Graham 1995). Indeed, the attention has remained on aspects of dream culture that *can* be readily observed. Here, analysis has followed their contexts of communication and, necessarily, in dialogue with the interpretive community that decides their value and their social meaning (Tedlock 1991). This approach also corresponds with a general move away from some of the central concerns of psychoanalysis which privileges dream symbolic meaning over the communicative context. Anthropologists for much of the 20th century were concerned with dream signs similar to the way scientific specimens might be collected, for the purpose of comparative analysis irrespective of local dream theories and communicative practices (e.g. Lincoln 1935; Schneider and Sharp 1969, cited in Tedlock 1991). Hutton himself was asked by the ethnologist, C. G. Seligman, for his work on dreams for Seligman's own work on cross-cultural dream typologies.

The turn towards ethnographies encompassing practices and situations that are 'naturally occurring' has also opened avenues for increasingly nuanced research (Bourdieu 1978; Tedlock 1979). Barbara Tedlock, for instance, suggests that analysis should centre on daily routines – 'practice, interaction, dialogue, experience and performance, together with the individual agents, actors, persons, selves and subjects of all this activity' (2003, p. 105). This requires a longer time commitment and closer participation in routines, as well as careful consideration of meanings associated with communication outside the highly ritualised events that typically dominate anthropological monographs. The highly subjective spaces that conceal intentionality, motivation, anxiety and aspirations are spaces that one enters based on high levels of trust.

This notion of trust – let's say in the crudest way, between ethnographer and informant – has been of central importance to my method of research, and I attribute my ability to explore Angami dream culture to my longstanding association with, and family connection through marriage, to one of the large clans of Kohima village. My entry into the field in November 2012 was a return to spaces I was familiar with, shaped by familial routines I felt comfortable participating in, having developed trusting relationships there in previous years.

My first visits to the region were between 2001 and 2004, when I stayed with a host family. In the early morning hours, I would sit and listen to Ruokuoneinuo, a mother of five, as she shared and interpreted her dreams. Based on the insights she gained in interpreting signs in her sleep, she offered suggestions about the day's activities. For example, dreaming of handling fish or, oddly enough, human faeces she interpreted as positive signs. They indicated safe passage, or opened up the possibility of financial gain. Positive signs were blessings, and they seemed to express a sense of gladness in the broader cosmos. She was also attentive to messages perceivable during the day. A dog howling or a window breaking in the wind, for example, were bad omens: 'Oh, how unfortunate; I wonder who is going to die', she might say. Ruokuoneinuo's attentiveness to dreams and omens was shared by her neighbours, whom she would meet while tending her garden or visiting the local shop. When they shared their observations, they sometimes believed they caught glimpses of a single impending event. This community of perception seemed constantly on guard, navigating and managing a field of forces that I could not perceive except through the intensity of their expressions. However, I grew to respect the practice, and when Ruokuoneinuo had bad dreams, I was increasingly inclined to listen. During one of my stays, her message was to stay in. I had grown accustomed to traversing the epicentre of Asia's longest running conflict, for instance, to check my email. However, that day I listened to Ruokuoneinuo's advice and settled with a book on the roof. Within a few hours, a message reached us of a clash between two underground insurgent groups roughly a block away from the cybercafé I frequented.

I thought: What did all this mean? Here is a culture that believes dreams hold truths about the future. One's life is entangled with broader society and social relations, and the daily practice of interpreting the oblique fragments of knowledge one receives through dreams is a way of forecasting and managing one's life possibilities within this reality. My initial interest in exploring Naga dreams and dreaming was ignited by its link to the problem of political violence present in the community. The concept of fear held promise as a category for a discussion of both unpredictability and agency. Recent anthropological work by Carolyn Humphrey (2013), for example, suggests that the study of fear is one way of exploring agency in relation to cultural practices that involve the reading of omens. I have argued elsewhere (Heneise 2017) that in urban centres such as Kohima new spatial configurations associated with late modernity amplified both the imagined distance and temporality between city and village practices, indeed creating an urban-rural binary. This effectively accelerated the process by which 'old' village practices became caricatured and regarded as popular mythology, though this was increasingly invoked in Naga nationalist discourse. My investigation revealed that the once widely practised and documented 'tiger-man' phenomenon – the practice of men and women with special capacities to project their souls into large feline predators and control their movements – though almost entirely subdued by Christianity – remained a contemporary practice found in much of the region. The mechanics of human-animal transformation revealed a connection with sleep and dreaming. More importantly, I discovered a few possible entryways for approaching the subject of non-human agency empirically; of attending ethnographically to beliefs about spiritual forces actively engaged in human affairs. By situating my research among individuals such as traditional healers who appeared to breach the divide between sleeping and wake states, as well as between humans and non-humans, I could 'observe' someone inhabiting two distinct realities. The approach I assumed at the beginning of this research was to investigate and formulate a 'communicative theory' (following Tedlock 1992) of Naga dreams as a kind of heuristic for studying social processes. By studying the 'interpretive community' that I identified, particularly among village women, I was attending to a given set of social dynamics articulated through language and the uses of space and time in the crucible of kinship relations.[15] This methodological shift was prompted by the work of Sylvie Poirier. She suggests, for instance, that

> To the extent that dreams are capable of informing us about local notions of the person, local theories of human and non-human action, the cultural construction of experience, and the status of the imaginary – in short, about the specific modes of being-in-the-world, dreams are of interest to anthropology.
> (2003, p. 108)

It was clear to me that dreams were but one – albeit very critical – aspect of a bigger sphere of activity described by my informants, and this, it seemed to me, merited a different approach from analysing situated dream narratives and the various analysable communicative registers. 'How', I often asked myself during fieldwork, 'can I learn to feel, to perceive, to gain awareness of this pre-conceptual field of unobservable phenomena that elicits verbal and nonverbal reactions; phenomena of which dreams and signs appear to be but glimpses, without immediately sieving them intellectually?'

The accounts of many of my informants spelled out something along the lines of a moral universe in which humans and non-humans are engaged, in one form or another, in day-to-day knowledge exchange. Human social processes were but a subset of a larger coextensive web of agency. Therefore, among the Nagas, questions of a political nature extend, as Eduardo Kohn suggests, 'beyond the human' (2013, p. 14). Indeed, they are a kind of 'alter-politics' (Hage 2012, cited in Kohn 2013), a politics emerging 'not from opposition to or critique of our current systems but one that grows from attention to another way of being, one here that involves other kinds of living beings' (ibid., p. 14). This broader engagement in the field, Kohn later suggests, is an ethical responsibility for the researcher, since 'the political problems we face today in the Anthropocene can no longer be understood only in human terms. This ontological fact demands another kind of ethical practice'.[16] This book seeks to describe 'what happened' (Humphrey 2008, p. 358) in the field according to my informants, remaining mindful of the broader 'field' of activity that remains often only in faint traces in their descriptions. Dream sharing, in particular, enters an interpretive community that does not necessarily require all the details. Much of what is shared about a dream is implied, indicated, pointed to in a kind of gesture-like use of language. Indeed, dream sequences are sometimes shared in a kind of abridged form, not because the dreamer has trouble recalling details, but because his or her audience, the listener/interpreters can 'fill in' much of the plot based on a lifetime of similar sessions. Indeed, dream sequences can be said to be 'composed' upon hearing. For the researcher, this simply requires time and patience, and I often requested my informants to 'fill me in' on details that were taken for granted when first shared upon waking.

Finally, and to conclude this methodological discussion, it must be stated that this ethnography is but one among many possible approaches to the study of Angami culture and personhood, and indeed anthropological research in the region generally. Whereas the few anthropologists that have studied Angami culture have, for instance, approached notions of personhood in relation to social and legal processes of recognition (e.g. Joshi 2012; Das 1992; and Hutton 1921a), this study employs the term differently, seeking to elucidate Angami notions of 'self', of 'being' and of 'knowledge'. Inspired a great deal by Kohn's advocacy for an anthropology 'beyond the human' (ibid., p. 14.), the approach in this book is to conceptualise the 'social' as encompassing the broader, coextensive set of relations and experiences – especially with spirit entities – reflected in the ethnography, and particularly in dream accounts. Moreover, my use of the term 'personhood', as distinct from 'subjectivity', relates specifically to my interest in the concept's integrative quality. Drawing from phenomenology (which informs the theory in this book), my use of 'personhood' points to the unity of multiple 'subjectivities' within the person (developed in chapters 2 and 3). Whether one speaks of passive, active, unconscious or conscious perception, and indeed the 'self' or 'subject' of dreams, which are of critical importance in the anthropology of dreaming, these, it is generally agreed among my informants, are constitutive of the person and come together in unfolding social process.

The outline of this book

I have divided this book in two parts: the first three chapters together encompass the 'Angami science of dreaming' and thus combines the preliminary discussions on Angami dream culture in chapter 1, with a genealogy of anthropological dream research and emerging importance of local notions of 'personhood' in chapter 2, and culminates with the development of the Angami *ruopfü* and 'reversibility' as the central ideas in understanding Angami dream experience.

In chapter 2, I engage with a first set of theoretical ideas that illuminate subsequent discussions, and draw on a schema developed by Sylvie Poirier (2003) that promotes a more holistic inquiry into dreams and dreaming within a given community, including how dream experiences speak about a given community's broader philosophy of being, of life and of knowledge. In the discussion, I review the literature on the development of dream research within anthropology, and describe the many pathways taken, including important developments regarding the centrality of exploring local notions of personhood and allowing this to guide methodologically the anthropological approach to dream research within a given community.

In chapter 3, I engage specifically with Angami notions of the person, and specifically articulations of *ruopfü*. In this chapter I explore the 'reversibility' of the Angami *ruopfü*. Integral to this discussion is the idea that dreams of different kinds – symbolic, narrative plots and more lucid dream experiences – are part of an overall dreaming continuum. The always perceiving *ruopfü* thus allows us to speak of ordinary and extraordinary dream experiences in terms of degrees of insight. As notions of *ruopfü* describe a connectedness to a plurality of *ruopfüs*, as well as to *Ruopfü* as 'supernature', there is scope for describing the collective and intersubjective exchange or flow of knowledge between the person and other kinds of beings. This interconnectedness is a characteristic of 'reversibility', and following Bettina Bergo (2009, p. 52) may be characterised as 'trans-temporal', 'pluri-subjective' and 'embodied' relationality in sleeptime and in waketime dreaming.

Chapter 4 provides an account of dreaming in the intimate spaces of the domestic sphere. Here, dreams emerge in sleep and then enjoin routine as they are narrated to close kin and trusted neighbours. With this typically being done around the hearth, this chapter describes the ways in which octogenarian Atsa interprets her own dreams in relation to signs that appear around her, including the pain in her own body, which she reads as an omen. Together, the signs point towards a mostly unspoken truth about her husband's frailty and the likelihood of his approaching death. Dreams in this chapter take on a heaviness, a physicality that contrasts with more ethereal descriptions typical of dream research. Atsa's openness to strangers, her always growing 'hearthen economy' in waketime and sleeptime, offers room for coextensive kinship relations with persons human and non-human, visible and invisible. When her husband dies and she is unable to rely on the local clan for help, she turns to her motley collective of vendors who are happy to help move her belongings to her new place deep in clan territory. As the men arrive early in the morning to carry her furniture and luggage, they avoid trouble with the clan men, and she quietly defies patriarchal laws of separation.

Chapter 5 turns from the place of the hearth to the place-making of Christianity within the clan community. In this chapter, I focus on the idea of 'interference' in these dreams; namely the process of bringing private foretelling dream experiences into the interpretive community to be deliberated and blessed. In the case of ominous dreams, 'interference' aids in defusing disruptive supernatural knowledge. This dynamic of 'sieving' inspirational religious practice is fundamental in maintaining the symbiotic relationship between, on one hand, the openness to outsiders exemplified by Atsa, and on the other the clan's insistence on patrilineal purity. This dynamic is further replicated in the relationship between the domestic sphere more generally and the morality of sin predicated from the pulpit of the traditional Baptist church. Charismatic variants, however, have sought a middle ground. Recognising the ubiquitous nature of dreams and other forms of divination, the Baptist Revival Church opens its doors to clan and non-clan members seeking the 'interference' of intercessory prayer, many coming in response to an urgency about the future felt in their dreams. Yet, the kind of 'interference' required by the clan is the containment of new knowledge.

Chapter 6 takes us outside the village gates and turns from specific places such as domestic hearths, clan meeting platforms and church sanctuaries to the valleys, forests, mountains and human settlements beyond. Senyü's* visit to a sacred forest in Arunachal Pradesh precipitates what requires a shamanic-like intervention as his soul becomes disembodied and entrapped by a powerful forest spirit. The process of retrieving the lost soul, aided by the ghost of his mother, entails traversing checkpoints in a heavily militarised dreamscape. Here, my informant describes the hostile terrain inhibiting his soul's safe retrieval as one-in-the-same with the militarised landscape experienced on a daily basis as he regularly traverses a similarly policed roadway as part of his work taking him from his office in Kohima to other areas within the district.

In chapter 7, I turn to 'reversibility' in the public domain and the role of signs in political narrative, more specifically Naga nationalism. Here I highlight the oneiric quality of the funeral of Kevilevor Phizo, son of the late Zhapu Phizo, the father of Naga nationalism. Important for the discussion are the different ways in which the political narrative of Naga nationalism has been articulated by the various underground insurgent groups, especially in relation to divine calling – communicated through dreams, visions and prophecy. Most, however, follow the pattern of clan lineage obligation and patronage, and in this chapter I show how Kevilevor's funeral is illustrative of a different path taken from that of other underground groups; one that seems more in consonance with the dynamics of the hearthen economy.

Notes

1 The number of distinct Naga groups is contested, 88 being the number offered by Michael Oppitz in 'Naga Identities' (2008), citing the need to count all groups that self-identify as Naga with sufficiently distinct traditions. Nuh (2006) suggests 68 Naga tribes between Myanmar and India, while S. R. Tohring (2010), suggests 66. The 1991 Indian census recognises 35 Naga 'Scheduled Tribes' on the India side of the border, 17 in Nagaland, 15 in Manipur and 3 in Arunachal Pradesh.

2 The population of Nagaland, of course, includes numerous non-Naga communities, including a sizeable population of Indian nationals from other states, as well as long-established Nepali, Tibetan, Bangladeshi, and Burmese communities. 2011 India Census.

3 A contested albeit 'official' list that includes Kuki and Dimasa Kachari communities that generally do not self-identify as 'Naga', the '16 major tribes' include: Angami, Ao, Chakhesang, Chang, Dimasa Kachari, Khiamniungan, Konyak, Kuki, Lotha, Phom, Pochury, Rengma, Sangtam, Sumi, Yimchungru and Zeliang. The Rongmei community is often included in publications as the '17th', and in Assam are grouped with Zeme, Liangmei and Puimei to form 'Zeliangrong', given their common ancestry and cultural-linguistic affinities. The Rongmei, though having a small population in Nagaland, are largely settled in Imphal and Tamenglong districts in neighbouring Manipur state.

4 The Kohima *Tenyidie* dialect is also spoken by most adult Chakhesangs (known during British times as 'Eastern Angami') given their close cultural-linguistic affinity and wide use of the *Tenyidie* Bible in Chakhesang churches.

5 2011 India Census.

6 Nienke van der Heide, 2015, "When dreams shape our day" in Leiden Anthropology Blog, posted 15 April 2015. Online source: www.leidenanthropologyblog.nl/articles/when-dreams-shape-our-day, accessed 15 January 2015.

7 Rituals generally performed at the family level centred on food prohibitions. In order to illustrate this clearly, I quote Vibha Joshi (2012, p. 75): 'The term *natsei* and *narü* are used for any incorrect performance of a ritual or violation of a taboo. *Natsei* specifically means deviation from the correct way . . . All family members are required to be present at the time of the performance of rituals; if even one member of the family is away and the family performs the full ritual it would be considered a *natsei*. Traditionally a number of food taboos were observed by the giver of the "feasts of merit", and it is held that if these were not observed then the person, as a result of the anger of the *terhuo-mia* would become numb and mentally unstable (*kemelo*) or even die.'

8 Here I follow Sanjib Baruah's (2013) analysis of British colonial discourse in relation to 'plains' and 'hills', namely 'the hills-plains binary more or less coincided with a legal distinction made between "tribal" people that were governed by customary law and other colonial subjects that were governed by general law. However, the presence of "tribal" people in the plains or "non tribal" and non-native tribal people in the hills caused considerable difficulty for colonial ethnic classification', in "Politics of Territoriality: Indigeneity, Itinerancy and Rights in North-East India", in *Territorial Changes and Territorial Restructurings in the Himalayas,* Joelle Smajda (ed.), Centre for Himalayan Studies, CNRS, France and Adroit Publishers, Delhi, 2013, pp. 69–83

9 Hutton does not make this explicit, though this is the generally held belief. 'The dwelling place of *Kepenopfü* is always located in the sky, and the souls of those who have lived good lives, according to the Angami standard, that is, go to the sky after death and dwell with her' (1921a, p. 181). The Sumi Nagas, another tribe, also believe in a Supreme God named *Alhou or Timilhou.* The Sumi also believe in spirits of the sky, *Kungumi*, which can be equated with Tenyimia concepts of *terhuomia*. (See Hutton 1921b, p. 191; *see also* Eaton 1997).

10 On an earlier visit to Nagaland (prior to this research), I met a former soldier in the Naga Army (NNC), who described his personal experiences with river spirits, forest spirits and mountain spirits while active in the early insurgency. He spoke at length, for example, about the daughter of *Japfü* (the third-highest mountain peak in Nagaland), who was cursed by Japfü by splitting her head down the middle (a mountain near Wokha has a large slit down the middle from which a beautiful waterfall spills out). The wife of a man from Dimapur who is still living, is said to have once been in a relationship with the river spirit which was said to be *Japfü's* daughter. She would spend half of the year with her human husband in Dimapur, and the other half with her female spirit-lover in Wokha (15 January 2010).
11 J.H. Hutton, 'Haunted inspection bungalow at Baimho', 1915
12 All the quotations from Hutton in this section are from archives. Hutton, 1923, "Typscript copy of a letter from J.H. Hutton probably to C.G. Seligman", (archival), Hutton Ms. Box 3, 26, Pitt Rivers Museum Archive, Oxford. Available online: http://himalaya. socanth.cam.ac.uk/collections/naga/record/r73000.html, accessed 15 January 2015.
13 Ibid.
14 Ibid.
15 Victor Turner once observed that 'to each level of sociality corresponds its own knowledge, and if one wishes to grasp a group's deepest knowledge one must commune with its members, speak its Essential We-talk' (in Jules-Rosette 1975, p. 8). As I was not a member of the clan, and generally neither attended nor sought invitation to what were rather exclusive meetings among a small group of clan men, it could be said that I 'communed' as Turner suggests, with the 'Essential We-talk' of clan women, or what I later in the book term the 'hearthen economy' (ch. 4). To a large extent there is overlap in the general 'interpretive community', though this latter description would not be exclusively women, but includes male clan elders that interpret dreams drawing on passed-down clan knowledge.
16 Kohn, Eduardo, 2014, "What an Ontological Anthropology Might Mean", *Fieldsights – theorizing the Contemporary, Cultural Anthropology online*, 13 January, http://culanth.org/fieldsights/463-what-an-ontological-anthropology-might-mean

Bibliography

Bach, J., 2010, " 'They Come in Peasants and Leave Citizens': Urban Villages and the Making of Shenzhen, China", *Cultural Anthropology*, 25(3), pp. 421–458.
Baruah, S., 2013, "Politics of Territoriality: Indigeneity, Itinerancy, and Rights in North-East India", in *Territorial Changes and Territorial Restructurings in the Himalayas*, Joelle Smajda, ed., New Delhi: Centre for Himalayan Studies, CNRS, France and Adroit Publishers, pp. 69–83.
Bergo, B., 2009, "Radical Passivity in Levinas and Merleau-Ponty (Lectures of 1954)", in *Radical Passivity: Rethinking Ethical Agency in Levinas,* Benda Hofmeyr, ed., New York: Springer, pp. 31–52.
Bouchery, P., 2007, "Naga Ethnography and Leach's Oscillatory Model of Gumsa and Gumlao", in *Social Dynamics in the Highlands of Southeast Asia: Reconsidering Political Systems of Highland Burma*, F. Robinne and M. Sadan, eds., Leiden: Brill, pp. 109–126.
Bourdieu, Pierre, 1978, "Sure l'objectivation participante: Réponse a quelques objections", *Actes de la recherche en sciences sociales*, 23, pp. 70–69.
Clifford, James and Marcus, George E., 1986, *Writing Culture: The Poetics and Politics of Ethnography*, London: University of California Press.

Comaroff, J. and Comaroff, J., 1992, *Ethnography and the Historical Imagination*, Boulder: Westview Press.

Das, N.K., 1992, *Kinship, Politics, and Law in Naga Society*, Calcutta: Anthropological Survey of India.

Downs, Frederick S., 1986, "No Longer Strangers: An Historical Account of the Council of Baptist Churches in Northeast India 1836–1986", in *Community of God's People in North East India: The 150th Anniversary of CBCNEI 1836–1986*, L.J. Sangma, O.M. Rao, R. Keitzar, K.I. Aier and S. Serto, eds., Guwahati, Assam: CBCNEI.

Eaton, Richard M., 1984, "Conversion to Christianity Among the Nagas, 1876–1971", *The Indian Economic & Social History Review*, 21(1), pp. 1–44.

Eaton, Richard M., 1997, "Comparative History as World History: Religious Conversion in Modern India", *Journal of World History*, 8(2), pp. 243–271.

Fortes, Meyer, 1949, *The Web of Kinship Among the Tallensi*, London: Oxford University Press.

Fox, Richard, ed., 1991, *Recapturing Anthropology: Working in the Present*, Santa Fe, NM: School of American Research Press.

Goh, Beng-Lan, 2002, *Modern Dreams: An Inquiry Into Power, Cultural Production and the Cityscape in Contemporary Urban Penang, Malaysia*, Ithaca: Cornell University Press.

Graham, Laura R., 1995, *Performing Dreams: Discourses of Immorality Among the Xavante of Central Brazil*, Austin: University of Texas Press.

Gundevia, Y.D., 1975, *War and Peace in Nagaland*, New Delhi: Palit and Palit.

Hage, Ghassan, 2012, "Critical Anthropological Thought and the Radical Political Imaginary Today", *Critique of Anthropology*, 32(3), pp. 285–308.

Hamayon, Roberte, 1996, "Shamanism in Siberia: From Partnership in Supernature to Counter-Power in Society", in *Shamanism, History, and the State*, Nicholas Thomas and Caroline Humphrey, eds., Ann Arbor: University of Michigan Press.

Hammersley, Martyn, 1985, "What It Is, and It Offers", in *Research and Evaluation Methods in Special Education*, S. Hegarty and P. Evans, eds., Windsor: NFER Nelson.

Heneise, Michael, 2017, "The Naga Tiger-Man and the Modern Assemblage of a Myth", in *Anthropology and Cryptozoology: Exploring Encounters with Mysterious Creatures*, Samantha Hurn, ed., London: Routledge, pp. 91–106.

Hershman, Paul, 1981, *Punjabi Kinship and Marriage*, New Delhi: Hindustan Publishing Corporation.

Hodson, T.C., 1911, *The Naga Tribes of Manipur*, London: Palgrave Macmillan.

Humphrey, Caroline, 2008, "Re-Assembling Individual Subjects: Events and Decisions in Troubled Times", *Anthropology Theory*, 8(4), December, pp. 357–380.

Humphrey, Caroline, 2013, "Fear as Property and an Entitlement", *Social Anthropology*, 21(30), August, pp. 285–304.

Hutton, J.H., 1921a, *The Angami Nagas*, London: Palgrave Macmillan.

Hutton, J.H., 1921b, *The Sema Nagas*, London: Palgrave Macmillan.

Hutton, J.H., 1923, "Typescript copy of a letter from J.H. Hutton probably to C.G. Seligman" (archival), Hutton Ms. Box 3, 26, Pitt Rivers Museum Archive, Oxford. Available online: http://himalaya.socanth.cam.ac.uk/collections/naga/record/r73000.html, accessed 15 January 2015.

Joshi, V., 2012, *A Matter of Belief: Christianity in Northeast India*, London: Berghahn Books.

Joshi, V. and Arya, A., 2004, *The Land of the Nagas*, Ahmedabad: Mapin Publishing Pvt Ltd and New York: Grantham Corporation.

Jules-Rosette, Bennetta, 1975, *African Apostles*, Ithaca: Cornell University Press.

Kohn, E., 2013, *How Forests Think: Toward an Anthropology Beyond the Human*, Berkeley: University of California Press.

Kohn, E., 2014, "What an Ontological Anthropology Might Mean", *Fieldsights – Theorizing the Contemporary, Cultural Anthropology*. Online source. accessed 13 January.: http://culanth.org/fieldsights/463-what-an-ontological-anthropology-might-mean.

Lincoln, Jackson Steward, 1935, *The Dream in Primitive Cultures*, Baltimore, MD: Williams and Wilkins.

Lincoln, Jackson Steward and Seligman, C.G., 1935, "Introduction", in *The Dream in Primitive Cultures*, Whitefish, MO: Kessinger Publishing Co.

Marcus, George and Fischer, Michael M.J., 1986, *Anthropology as Cultural Critique: An Experimental Moment in the Human Sciences*, Chicago: Chicago University Press.

Merleau-Ponty, M., 1968 [1964], *The Visible and the Invisible*, C. Lofort, ed., A. Lingus, trans., Evanston, IL: Northwestern University Press.

Nuh, V.K., 2006, *The Naga Chronicle*, New Delhi: Regency Publications.

Oppitz, Michael, Thomas Kaiser, Alban von Stockhausen and Marion Wettstein, eds., 2008, *Naga Identities: Changing Local Cultures in the Northeast of India*, Gent: Snoeck Publishers.

Peal, S.E., 1894, "Fading Histories", *Journal of the Asiatic Society*, 63(3), p. 1.

Poirier, S., 2003, "'This Is Good Country: We are Good Dreamers': Dreams and Dreaming in the Australian Western Desert", in *Dream Travelers: Sleep Experiences and Culture in the Western Pacific*, Lohmann, Roger, ed., New York: Palgrave MacMillan, pp. 107–125.

Reed-Danahay, D., 1997, *Auto-Ethnography: Rewriting the Self and the Social*, London: Berg.

Schneider, D.M. and Lauriston Sharp, 1969, *The Dream Life of a Primitive People: The Dreams of the Yir Yoront of Australia*, Washington, DC: American Anthropological Association.

Tedlock, B., 1991, "The New Anthropology of Dreaming", *Dreaming Journal of the Association for the Study of Dreams*, 1(2). Online source: www.asdreams.org/journal/articles/1-2tedlock1991.htm, accessed 4 December 2012.

Tedlock, B., 1992 [1987], *Dreaming: Anthropological and Psychological Interpretations*, Cambridge: Cambridge University Press.

Tedlock, B., 2003, "The New Anthropology of Dreaming", in *Shamanism: A Reader*, Graham Harvey, ed., London: Routledge.

Tedlock, Dennis, 1979, "The Analogical Tradition and the Emergence of a Dialogical Anthropology", *Journal of Anthropological Research*, 35, pp. 387–400.

Tohring, S.R., 2010, *Violence and Identity in North-East India: Naga-Kuki Conflict*, New Delhi: Mittal Publications.

Van Den Brul, Gerard Nicholas, 1980, "An Examination of the Modernization Process and Ethnic Mobilization Among the Nagas of Northeastern India", Open Access Dissertations and Theses, Paper 5171, Hamilton: McMaster University.

van der Heide, N., 2015, "When Dreams Shape Our Day", in *Leiden Anthropology Blog*, posted 15 April 2015. Online source: www.leidenanthropologyblog.nl/articles/when-dreams-shape-our-day, accessed 15 January 2015.

von Fürer-Haimendorf, Christoph and Mills, J.P., 1936, "The Sacred Founder's Kin Among the Eastern Angami Nagas", *Anthropos*, 31(5/6), September–December, pp. 922–933.

2 The Angami science of dreaming

In this book, I interpret Hutton's insights regarding an Angami dreaming – namely that 'Of all forms of second sight dreaming is the favourite and the best. The Angamis have almost a science of dreaming' (Hutton 1921a, p. 246) – as an injunction, and in this chapter I sketch out a preliminary study of the cultural system of Angami dreams and dreaming. In the introduction I discussed the idea that dreams and dreaming for the Angami are recognised as central themes in the folklore and as integral forms of knowledge. They are generally acknowledged as the preferred means for divining the outcome of important life events as well as

Figure 2.1 Meya Clan Feast

Source: Author's photo

day-to-day decisions and economic exchanges. I also explained that despite the spread and changes brought about by Christianity, little has changed in regards to the importance dreams are given, and dreams and dreaming have transcended the domestic and public spaces of the clan.

Whilst early American Baptist missionaries made strong demands on new converts to relinquish old rituals and divinatory practices upon baptism and church membership, the widespread practice of consulting dreams continued, continues today and is an important medium of discernment among many Christians, particularly charismatic groups such as the Christian Revival Church, a phenomenon that I discuss in detail in chapter 5. Yet, in research on the Nagas very little attention has been given to dreams and dreaming as a system that pervades the personal and the public spheres in important ways, not least how dreams shape behaviour and attitudes towards events.

I would contend, for instance, that we cannot speak of Angami life stage events or indeed religious practice without discussing the centrality of dreams in directing the processes and sequences of their various rituals. This is directly related to consulting ancestors and opening avenues of exchange between human and non-human actors, because life processes extend beyond the human and are intricately enmeshed in a more coextensive sociality. While this book focuses primarily on the Angami, it must also be noted that there are numerous Naga traditions where dreams play a vital role particularly as they are shared, interpreted, represented and enacted.

The aim in this chapter is to explore what Hutton might have envisioned as the Angami 'science' or theory of dreaming, and to further broaden the investigation into the ways in which dreams and dreaming inscribe meaning that leads to action. This theory might then serve as a larger Angami philosophy of knowledge and consequently anchor the discussion as it develops in subsequent chapters. Following an overview of the development of dream research, and especially anthropological studies of dreams and dreaming, I will present a set of ethnographic examples that illustrate the ways in which dreams are interpreted in relation to important life events, how interpretation is informed by other signs such as waketime omens, and how dreams are tethered to everyday social life and routine practice. Using these examples, I will then examine the ethnography in the light of research on dreams and how understanding dreams as part of a continuum may assist us in finding where dreams and dreaming can be best placed within the social processes of a society.

The anthropology of dreaming

Anthropologists, though recognising the importance of dreams in many of the cultures they have studied, have rarely approached dreams as a stand-alone category meriting concerted attention. This can partly be attributed to the obvious difficulties inherent in the task of studying the phenomena – in observing the unobservable, relying on the non-replicable and trusting that informants are sincere in narrating from memory their dream sequences. Poirier (2003) argues convincingly that dominant dream theories, seated as they are in Western epistemological constructs, have been shaped by a long trajectory of historical processes that have gradually pushed dreams from the public into the private sphere. In the midst of this, in 1648 René Descartes published his *Traite de l'homme*, in which he wrote 'I see so plainly that there are no definitive signs by which to distinguish being awake from being asleep' (1998, p. 60), which challenged the prevailing wisdom at the time that sleep and waking states were fundamentally separate and different. His difficulty in relying on his senses led him to his famous methodology employing doubt as a way to achieve certainty (ibid.).

Two centuries later, Edward B. Tylor, the 'father' of cultural anthropology, sought to categorise dreams in relation to literate and non-literate societies, suggesting pejoratively that 'the entire life of primitives was nothing but a long dream' (1870, p. 137). Influenced greatly by the social evolutionist thinking of his time, Tylor posited that typological divergences of dreams and dreaming among Western and non-Western societies were a function of social evolution and suggested that 'the savage or barbarian has never learned to make the rigid distinction between imagination and reality, to enforce which is one of the main results of scientific education' (1871, p. 445). As anthropology as a discipline distanced itself from evolutionist thinking, research conducted specifically in relation to dreams and dreaming became increasingly influenced by psychoanalysis. And Sigmund Freud's seminal *The Interpretation of Dreams* (1900), circulating widely in Europe, produced an explosion of interest both in the cultural mainstream and in dream research among a new generation of scholars. Freud described dreams as 'regressive' in the sense that dream construction involves returning to sensory images in the unconscious, which was contrasted with conscious waking reality. For Freud, dreams constitute a concealed event in which the subconscious fulfils repressed wishes. Various psychoanalytical techniques such as hypnosis and the method of 'free association' allowed therapists to probe the dream content of patients without them needing to fall sleep during consultation. Moreover, an increasingly popular approach was self-analysis, in which individuals would record their dreams, and bring their diaries into the consulting room.

Freud's concepts of 'manifest' dream content ('meaningless' imagery and language as narrated by the dreamer) and 'latent' dream content (a dream's 'true' meaning, obtained only through an examination of the dreamer's past) are often used to distinguish raw dream reports from dream reports that have been psychoanalysed.[1] Freud also suggests that certain dream 'types' are universal – in other words, dream content, regardless of social or cultural setting, has the same latent meanings. This theory proved attractive to scholars studying dreams, and the spread of colonial workers and missionaries between Europe and the colonies opened up the possibility to test Freud's theory cross-culturally.

In England, C.G. Seligman (1921, 1923, 1924), a British physician and anthropologist, was greatly influenced by Freud, and in his travels in Sudan, the Torres Straits and Ceylon (Sri Lanka), and in correspondence with colonial workers such as J. H. Hutton, sought to test Freud's theory of 'dream types', collecting dream reports or fragments of dreams from cultures throughout the British

Empire. Jackson Steward Lincoln (1935), a student of Seligman's, then engaged in a similar approach in collecting and classifying dreams among the Navajo in Arizona. Comparing his findings with ethnographies conducted among other Native American Indians, Lincoln concluded that dreams can be separated into 'individual dreams' – unsolicited or spontaneous; and 'culture pattern dreams' – those sought or induced and therefore of greater importance to the community (Lincoln 1935). Lincoln thus established a 'dream typology' that differentiated between the individual and the communal that greatly influenced the way scholars began to understand dreams.

Though the concept of a dream typology is credited to Lincoln (Parsifal-Charles 1986, p. 291), he, along with Seligman, is critiqued for imposing a sociological typology without giving importance to how dreams are actually constructed and narrated by the indigenous peoples themselves (Tedlock 1987, p. 21). In the 1940s and 1950s, influenced by the school of culture and personality popular in North American cultural anthropology at the time – examining the interplay between individual personalities and overreaching culture – researchers began to collect manifest dream content across cultures that could be quantified and analysed. Similar to Freud's dream 'types', the 'culture and personality' school understood there to be universals with regard to personality types, and dream experiences were viewed to vary in important ways between personality types (Sears 1948; Eggan 1952; Dittman and Moore 1957; Griffith, Miyagi and Tago 1958; O'Nell 1965; Gregor 1981; in Tedlock 1987). In the field of psychology (especially Hall 1951; Hall and Van de Castle 1966; Hall and Nordby 1972; in Tedlock 1987; and Gregor 1981) manifest dream reports were collected cross-culturally, scored and divided up into categories – emotions, actions, settings, actors and objects – with the aim of identifying core personality traits among men and women of various ages across a variety of cultures (Tedlock, 1987; Edgar, 2015).

More recently, Stephen Catalano (1984, [1987], 1990) uses content analysis to demonstrate the difference between dreams of normal adolescents and those of emotionally disturbed adolescents. Though this method is still largely employed in psychology, anthropologists have found it de-contextualises dreams, with local dream theories, dream narration and dream discourse largely ignored. Vincent Crapanzano (1981) argues, for example, that methodologically the 'content analysis of dreams' theory is culture-bound, both employing a Western comparative approach, and confining the dreamer to a process where emphasis is placed on language and its symbolism. Whereas the dream narrative itself is subsumed into an objectification of the referential function.

Waud Kracke (1987, p. 31) argues that these practices of collecting dream reports neglects the fact that the dreamer has access to the 'spatio-sensory' aspect of the dream experience, namely dreams often 'feel' entirely real. Though the process of translation, whereby the dream experience is recast into social processes, is confined by the language and temporal categories of waking reality and can significantly alter the dream experience, some cultures do not 'filter' dreams in this manner. Discussing this division, Johannes Fabian suggests that whereas 'psychology is concerned with dreams as internal experiences, reflections of the subconscious', 'dreams as intentional messages, i.e. culturally defined means of communication, are the domain of anthropology' (1966, p. 560). In Tedlock's view, however, this is problematic:

> the trouble with dividing up the territory of psychology and anthropology so neatly is that it would leave psychologists free to ignore the fact that their study of the dreaming experience is partially dependent on their subjects' communication of such experiences by culturally determined means, and it would leave anthropologists free to ignore the fact that dream communication in other cultures is partially dependent on native theories about the dream experience.
>
> (1987, p. 22)

While acknowledging early anthropological contributions examining the importance of incorporating local dream theories into ethnographic work, Kracke (1979) and Crapanzano (1975) both developed the notion of local dream theories nearly a decade earlier. Similarly, Barbara Tedlock advocates greater incorporation of local theories with attention to the modes of representation, performativity, sociality and interpretation. These larger cultural systems operating in the space of dream communication are identified in early attempts at a crossover between anthropology and psychology, most notably in the development of ethno-psychiatry, in which cultural and ethnic dimensions of mental illness are explored.

On the other hand, the cognitive anthropologist, Roy D'Andrade (1961) examined a large collection of dreams from 63 societies in an effort to analyse their functions within each of their cultures. D'Andrade found that dreams appear as a result of anxieties related to self-reliance. Hunter-gatherers, for instance, use dreams a great deal more than pastoral-agrarian societies (Edgar 2015). Crapanzano (1975, pp. 145–158), in his analysis of Moroccan Hamadsha dreams, identifies a performative employment of dream symbols – in this case the metaphorical opposition of saints and *jnuns* (demons) – in discerning social tension and potential resolution.

Building on the assertion that both myths and dreams emerge as attempts to cope with waking reality, Kuper and Stone (1982) draw on Levi-Strauss' (1963) analytical approach to myth to demonstrate that dream content can be studied using the same binary rules structuring mythical thought. This theory suggests that humans think in pairs of opposites – up/down, far/near, living/dead, material/immaterial – and dreams may be said to provide a visualisation of how the mind seeks to resolve the tensions inherent in binary contradictions. Tedlock (1987) suggests that Kuper and Stone have uncovered 'underlying linguistically coded analytical rules' in dream narration but argues that it would be a mistake to suggest that these rules are involved in generating the dream material. Though acknowledging the important parallels that exist between narrated dreams and narrated myths (e.g. the rich thought processes; use of story line; imagery; and metaphor-rich language), Kracke (1987) argues they fundamentally differ in that dreams evolve from sensory imagery to language form, while the inverse is true of myths, moving as they do from verbal form to sensory imagery. Kracke's analysis also questions the viability of dream psychoanalysis in the interpretation of myths (Tedlock 1987, p. 27). Edgar suggests there are important limits to this analytical method:

> A structural approach, which is concerned with the analysis of the 'latent' analytical binary structure of the dream, can then be part only of the cultural understanding of dream material, particularly as it is not concerned with the importance of the communicative context of the dream report itself.[2]

Edgar points to a need expressed by many anthropologists studying dreams in the 1980s and 1990s to widen the concept of manifest dream content beyond the dream report.[3] Tedlock notes: 'Ideally it should include dream theory or theories and ways of sharing, including the relevant discourse frames, and the cultural code for dream interpretation' (1987, p. 25). Thus, the 'communicative theory of dreaming' shifts to a wider lens where dreams are more than a 'hermeneutically based text' (Edgar 2015), but part of a larger, complex social process, with a language and framework for understanding that process and its underlying cultural systems (Poirier 2003). Seeking to redefine the boundary drawn between the anthropology of dreaming and psychology, this theory understands dream narration as a communicative event consisting of three overlapping strands: the creation and act of narration; the psychodynamics of narration; and the interpretive emic community (Tedlock 1987). Moreover, Gilbert Herdt suggests that the debate could also benefit from a return to the basic fundamentals of observation; to 'return to describing what people actually do, say, and think in relation to their dreams, and interpret in context what seems public, hidden or unconscious' (Herdt 1987, p. 82). Dream theories, Herdt suggests, present their own 'metapsychologies of human existence' and have modes of sharing that are both nuanced and complex, and therefore challenging even from the local point of view (ibid., p. 82). 'But until we do that', Herdt summarises, 'we won't take seriously the propositions that culture may actually change experience inside of dreams, or that the productions of dreaming do actually become absorbed and transformed into culture' (ibid., p. 82).

While psychoanalytical approaches can illuminate dream theories and their communicative processes, anthropological approaches can illuminate language forms and complex concepts that are necessarily culture specific. Their combination points to a more cross disciplinary, and thus a more holistic, understanding of dreaming (Lohmann 2007). The explosion of ethnographic publications on dreams in the last three decades demonstrates an acceptance that dreams are social acts, but also that there exists a 'mutual causal interaction' between society, cultural systems and dreaming (Lohmann 2007, p. 38).

More recently, anthropologists such as Brinkman (2007), Edgar (2011) and Mittermaier (2011) have sought to use dream research as a lens for studying larger political processes and social change. Brinkman's work among former guerrillas in Angola's anti-colonial struggle, for instance, illuminates the way in which the experiences of war shaped dream content, and how this dream content translated into forms of agency in the case of individual soldiers. Brinkman says, 'Dreams constituted an arena in which the forces of evil and justice fought as much as in daily life' (2007, p. 79). Though her approach differs from Brinkman, Mittermaier also engages in an investigation of multiple social and material manifestations of dreams and dream theories in the highly politicised urban setting of Cairo, Egypt. Mittermaier navigates the urban terrain, religious symbolism, memory and imaginative landscapes described by her informants, to analyse notions of divine encounter among present-day Muslims in Egypt. Here, dreams are consulted to glean divine wisdom, but also because in many ways they may offer respite in counter-narratives in the midst of prevailing power structures that are difficult to penetrate and negotiate (Mittermaier 2011). Similarly, Iain Edgar (2011) traces the importance of dreams in Islam through a historical and ethnographic analysis of Istikhara, or dream incubation. Dream incubation is a process of dream narration and interpretation used to direct life decisions, its widespread use stems from the fact that all other forms and representations of divine knowledge are forbidden in Islam. In the latter section of Edgar's book, his informants, though not directly involved in Al-Qaeda, are able to share with him intimate details about noted cell leaders who employ dream imagery and interpretation to guide their actions. This research shows not only that dream narration and interpretation is present in the tradition of Islam, and therefore used in the present day, but also that its use can have widespread consequences because dreams are often perceived to be religious visions in which individuals may receive messages that may contradict the prevailing religious order. Similarly, dreams can sometimes lead individuals and communities to embrace new traditions and identities, or indeed to 're-discover' old ones, as is the case among Jewish Dalits in South India. Yulia Egorova and Shahid Perwez (2012), in a provocative study of the Bene Ephraim community in Andhra Pradesh, document the remarkable ways in which dreams are believed to supersede genealogical tradition, because they reveal the volition of the divine in seeking to disclose their true identity as among the lost tribes of Israel. In many dream accounts the actual 'place' of contemporary Israel is of great significance, and this resonates with a broader vision within the community that encompasses recognition of their Jewish identity ultimately entailing a final journey towards their rightful ancestral land (Egorova and Perwez 2012, pp. 152–158).

Though dream researchers have traditionally studied bounded cultures – such as the Kagwahiv and Xavante of South America, and Yolngu and Tiwi of Australia – where dreams and dreaming are overtly manifested social practices, present-day researchers conduct fieldwork on dreams in contexts with diffuse boundaries, characterised by steady streams of migration and cultural interconnectedness. Katherine Ewing characterises this new landscape in provocative terms:

> Effort to understand globalization and the diaspora experience has challenged anthropology's theoretical apparatus. We can no longer understand culture as a system of meanings that constitutes social reality and shapes the experience of individuals.
>
> (2003, quoted in Lohmann 2007, p. 38)

The study of dreams within the complex, fluid uncertainties of such environments as urban Cairo, war-torn Angola and troubled Pakistan produce works that contend with issues of social change in environments with overlapping cultural systems that cannot be studied as distinct and subsequently placed in comparison to others. Their co-existence or overlap suggests continuous influence, where foreign elements are negotiated, integrated, rejected or modified within the dimension of rapid temporal flux. Roger Lohmann suggests that 'dreaming aids the reception of foreign culture because when people dream about recently imported ideas, they place them in a familiar context of emotionally salient personal experience' (2007, p. 60).

Ethnographic studies (e.g. Bourguignon 1972, 1973) have for some time acknowledged that dreams may be catalysts of cultural change. The cacophonous nature of dream images functions to suspend ethnocentric strictures and judgements that arise when social boundaries or conventions are crossed or questioned in waking reality. The mind is able to join incongruent and potentially oppositional ideas and images in a realm that follows a different logic of time and space (Lohmann 2007). This approach suggests that dreaming, therefore, may be understood as a mental activity that is not bound by the conventions of waking reality, and thus provides innovative potential for studying social processes as they emerge from the unconscious towards greater lucidity and conscious sociality (Stephen 1982; Lohmann 2007). The salience of this approach relates to the notion of a 'boundlessness' within dreamtime, namely anything can happen in a dream, and, in this context, dreams are used as a way to decide action and therefore have an interesting potential for insight into actual, waketime, social processes.

Though anthropology has again taken up an interest in dreams and dreaming, there is still very little consensus regarding the specific objectives or frame of inquiry. What, for example, are the general problems or questions that studying dreams and dreaming can address? Is there a set of terms, categories or parameters that are specific to the sub-discipline? As Poirier rightly points out:

> It seems as if, since Tylor, [anthropology] has had a lack of inspiration (or imagination), at least in that domain. If the focus is on the social process of representing and enacting dreams (Tedlock 1987), or performing dreams (Graham 1995), rather than on dreams solely as objects or products (of the mind), then dreams and dreaming are likely to become a field of inquiry worthy of fuller consideration by anthropologists.
>
> (2003, p. 108)

Here, Poirier points out that rather than focusing on dreams as private experiences – by observing the set of practices, narrative forms, spaces and the composition of participants in dream narration and interpretation, and indeed the times of day and frequency of these processes – the anthropologist can gain important insights regarding the complex cultural systems enacted when dreams are transformed into social acts. Indeed, Poirier suggests:

> To the extent that dreams are capable of informing us about local notions of the person, local theories of human and non-human action, the cultural

construction of experience, and the status of the imaginary – in short, about specific modes of being-in-the-world, dreams are of interest to anthropology.

(2003, p. 108)

Though a new generation of anthropologists has recognised these possibilities, there is no general agreement on what questions, parameters and categories one would need to employ. Our aim should be to develop a set of tools and parameters that could be used across cultures, functioning equally well in ethnographies of Western as well non-Western societies. I will do this in two parts: firstly, in this chapter, I draw on categories, terms and parameters suggested by Poirier, because they pay attention not only to subjective experience both within dreamtime and waketime states, but also to various modes of socialisation. Poirier (2003, p. 108–109) suggests:

1) Local dream theories, and whatever they might reveal about the local notion of the person; 2) dream narratives as a process of translating, structuring, and communicating a dream experience; 3) modes of dream sharing – that is, where, when, why, how, and with whom one shares dreams; 4) local modes of dream interpretations, or, wherever present, local dream typologies; and 5) the mediating, revealing, and often creative and innovative role ascribed to dreams in a number of societies throughout the world.

As part 2 of this discussion, and in the following chapter, I will explore Angami notions of personhood, and in particular the notion of *ruopfü* – spirit, soul, or 'life-being' – as the fundamental idea in positing a continuity of consciousness between the self in the dream and the self in waking experience.

The next few sections will recount dream narratives told me by a variety of members of the *Meya* clan. As introduced in chapter 1, the *Meya* clan is one of 19 clans in *L-khel*, which in turn is one of four large clan groups in Kohima village. As one of the largest in the clan group, it is also dominant, in terms of both numbers and influence, within *L-khel*, and in many ways the village as a whole. In what follows I will detail narratives involving a family, starting with Ketu and moving on to his cousin, Ale. These dream narratives will contribute towards developing a set of ideas that might form a 'science' of dreaming among the Angami and how this 'science' affects their lives.

Dreaming and narrating the past

I met Avino at her house just below the clan compound where I resided between November 2012 and June 2015. Her niece had just given birth, and I was joining other neighbours in bringing gifts and offering the new parents congratulations. The youngest among seven children, Avino was very close to her own aunt Nikki, now a woman in her 90s, who did not conform to her symbolic function within the clan system by marrying an Ao Naga (i.e. outside her clan), and further by leaving the region in pursuit of a Master's degree in the United States. When she was finally expected to return to join her husband, she instead entered the Indian

Foreign Service and was soon a career diplomat serving as India's first ambassador to two Latin American countries. Avino's own perspective was firmly set on following her aunt's example, at least with regard to studying in the United States. However, she received a marriage proposal that her parents felt she should consider. It was her childhood friend and neighbour Ketu, the son of a respectable Christian family in the *Meya* clan. Ketu himself was atypical among the clan men of his generation. While most of his age-group took up work in state government offices, set up their own construction contracting businesses and bid on government development projects, or became more active in church ministry, he decided to pursue studies in veterinary medicine, out of state, in neighbouring Meghalaya. Though he was away for months at a time during his studies, which he began in 1989, he always travelled back to Kohima when on break to visit his recently widowed mother, his father having died of a heart attack early the following year.

It was 1990, and Avino was initially delighted to receive Ketu's proposal, but at the same time she was anxious given her desires to study in the United States. She knew that once she married she would be expected to fulfil a more traditional role in her new home and follow the established rhythms of domestic life in her husband's clan. Living with Ketu away at university, however, she imagined she might be able to follow a different rhythm. But what would her new mother-in-law, Ketu's brothers and the larger clan expect of her? She was doubtful that she would be as free to follow her dreams as far as her aunt Nikki, at least not until after Ketu had completed his programme. Her aunt Nikki, with whom she shared her concerns, encouraged her to seek counsel with Mrs Ledi, a woman they knew from church and known in the community for her gifts of discernment and dream interpretation. After spending some time in prayer with her, Mrs Ledi said, 'I will be praying for you, and you listen to your dreams. They will tell you what you should do'. That same week, Avino says she dreamed of her own wedding.

> Everything seemed ordinary. We were at the church, there were lots of people there, including many of my relatives and friends. I do not know whether Ketu was there, I cannot remember. But I became anxious when I noticed something out of place. My veil – the veil of the wedding dress – was not white but black.

When she awoke she knew this was a bad omen, but decided not to share the dream, at least not right away. She was aware that what Mrs Ledi was prompting her to do was to have a *mhonyü*, a specific kind of dream by an unmarried woman in which, following a serious marriage proposal, she may discern whether or not to accept. Her mother, grandmother and earlier generations had all followed this tradition in reaching a decision, and they had 'good marriages'.[4]

The busy-ness of the day and week following her dream, including household chores and visitors, kept Avino distracted, however, and her memory of the dream faded. Within a few months, the wedding preparations were underway, and her parents purchased several pigs and a cow to prepare food for the many well-wishers. Ketu's mother interpreted this as an extraordinary gesture of goodwill.

Although there is the customary agreement to a more or less symbolic 'bride price' of chickens and small livestock, it is expected that the groom's family will cover the lion's share of the wedding expenses. These expenses have ballooned since the early 1990s with the growth of the modern wedding industry and the social prestige associated with more modern arrangements, often resulting in considerable debt among the groom's family.

As it was harvest season, many relatives were spending their days in their fields, and only a few would be able to attend the Saturday afternoon ceremony at the church. But this was not unusual, and the church building would not be expected to accommodate the likely 1,500 to 2,000 attendees. The week prior to the ceremony several hundred well-wishers visited Avino's home and shared tea and a full meal of wedding food, especially the coveted local pork cooked in as many as six or seven ways, with the central feature being pork done with bamboo shoots. To accommodate the visitors, Ketu's brothers and uncles constructed a large bamboo reception area in front of Avino's home and took charge of transporting people, chairs and supplies in the days leading up to the wedding.

The November wedding went well, and Avino moved across the road to live with Ketu in his small, recently refurbished bungalow at the northern end of the family compound. They were settled in time to install Christmas lights and to receive gifts of local pork wrapped in banana leaves that are part of the gift exchange culture surrounding Christmas, coinciding also with the cold winter weather conducive to keeping fresh meat over a period of days. All seemed well for the newlyweds through the winter months of 1991, and by the time the March winds began rattling the thin tin roof on the house, it was time for Ketu to return to school in Shillong, accompanied this time by Avino. However, it would only be a few short weeks before Ketu was dead and Avino left a widow with her black veil.

I spent most of a day and evening sitting around a large courtyard fire with Ketu's extended family as I took notes on their stories about the events surrounding the tragic plane crash that had so devastated their clan 20 years ago. Of particular interest to me, and it seemed for those gathered, were ways in which omens appeared to various individuals before the crash, especially details of a dream that Ketu had while still in Shillong with Avino. He had shared the dream with his brothers and mother before he volunteered to escort his cousin Kenei to college in Hyderabad. Ketu's older brother, Abu, was the main narrator as we sat around the fire, and in retelling Ketu's dream, he seemed particularly careful about the sequence of events within it. In the dream, their father (who by the time of the dream had been dead for about one year) had arrived at their compound on a scooter. He stood with the engine running calling for his eldest son, Theja, to accompany him on his journey. Theja was unable to go because he was busy with a construction project. So his father called his next son, Abu, to accompany him, but he was also busy. The next in line was Ketu, who watched these exchanges before finally volunteering to go in their stead, so he got on the scooter and they drove off.

As everyone around the fire listened intently to the retelling of the dream, eyes staring at the flames, they began to add fragments of their own memories of the days leading up to the tragedy: 'you know, Ketu stubbed his toe about three times that week. That is not a good omen'. Another voice added, 'Ketu was in a strange mood, he was very emotional that week'. Another voice said, 'when he went down to buy his plane tickets he stopped at Tinpati market and bought a sack of fresh cabbages. He handed a cabbage to each clan family here in the compound, and then asked Avino if she would cook his favourite meal, cabbage curry'. This behaviour, it was explained to me, was peculiar as it signalled a farewell, the kind that involves an indefinite absence. Ketu, however, was to be in Hyderabad for only a week.

Ketu had shared his dream about his father on the scooter at around the time that his cousin Kenei's parents had arranged for their eldest son Ale, and Theja to accompany Kenei to Hyderabad. Just as in the dream, Theja's job responsibilities were such that he had to cancel. Theja's younger brother Abu had agreed to go in his stead, but everyone was uneasy about this as he had been struggling with an alcohol problem. A few days before the trip, Ketu and Avino arrived in Kohima on holiday from the veterinary school in Shillong. Immediately, Ketu agreed that he and Avino would accompany Kenei and his brother Ale to Hyderabad. So he rushed to the Indian Airlines office in Kohima town and booked a return ticket for him and his wife and bought the cabbages on the way home. The night before the trip, Avino and Ale became very ill – so ill, in fact, that they had to cancel their plans to travel. However, Ale and Kenei's younger brother Kevi had arrived earlier in the day on a college break, and Kevi agreed to go on Ale's ticket. Kenei was therefore accompanied to begin college in Hyderabad by his brother Kevi and cousin Ketu, but when he waved goodbye, that was the last time he, or anyone, would see Kevi and Ketu. They died on their return flight on the 16th of August 1991. Indian Airlines Flight 257 crashed on its descent into Imphal, in Manipur state, killing all 69 occupants. The family was devastated and were further distressed by the fact that few remains from the crash could be properly recovered and identified for a burial. A few weeks after the crash, a Rongmei woman arrived unannounced at Ketu's home. She spoke Bengali and said she came bearing a message for Ketu's mother, saying that Ketu would speak 'from the other side'. Ketu's mother knew immediately that the visitor was a *terhuope*, and she felt it would be inappropriate for her, as a Christian woman, to listen to a spirit-possessed woman. The Rongmei woman therefore approached Ketu's widow. Low, and barely audible, a voice in *Tenyidie* spoke: 'you will find me, but you will not be able to see my body or my face', and 'you must give me a proper burial'.

About three months after I sat around the fire and heard the retelling of Ketu's dream and the tragic plane crash, I met another family that had dreams related to the 1991 tragedy. I was invited to lunch by Mr Keza, a member of the Tatar Hoho (the parliamentary body of the Nagaland Federal Government, linked to the Naga National Council) and a respected deacon in the local charismatic Baptist church. Mr Keza and his wife belonged to one of the other Kohima village clans located south of the *Meya* clan, but lived outside Kohima, nearer to Jotsoma. Mr Keza drove a white Bolero SUV and picked me up just outside my gate along the road. Leaving the bustle of the town, we drove the serpentine road along the Puliebadze mountain ridge and arrived at his home in time for afternoon tea.

'We dream all the time', Mrs Keza said unprompted, and 'my daughter and I often have the same dream. My husband tells me you are interested in dreams'. 'Yes', I said, shuffling through my jacket for my notebook. She went on for some time talking about dream symbols – 'If you dream of snails, they say you'll come into some money. It's true! If you dream of paddy, it is a premonition for quarrel – you or someone you know will instigate a fight'. Her approach to the subject was not atypical; as with Vilhou's dream of a menacing mushroom in chapter 5 many of the people I interviewed opened up by sharing their experiences with dream symbols – snakes, blood, broken teeth, cutting hair, excrement, fish, among many other things. As I visited villages across a large area of the Naga Hills – from Longwa, a tiny Konyak village that straddles the Indo-Myanmar border in Mon District in the North, to Magulong, an isolated Zeme community in Tamenglong District in Manipur state – I developed an index of dream symbols with which I could draw comparisons. Many signs such as firewood, fish and paddy have a variety of interpretations, but a few possess meaning across the Naga groups that I visited. 'As I understand it', I interrupted, 'Many Naga communities share the belief that if you dream of a smartly-dressed person, it spells death'. 'Yes', she said 'this is the truth, and it has happened'.

That evening, she narrated two dreams in significant detail, one of which related to the 1991 plane crash claiming the lives of Ketu, Kevi and 67 others. Mrs Keza said,

> In my dream I was in the local ground in Kohima. A roll call – a list of names was being called out. The ground was full of people; it was a crowd or large gathering of sorts. In the midst of the sound of shuffling feet, I heard my name called out. My dream then shifted to a room. I was lying on my back and could see the roof. Women dressed in traditional Angami shawls circled slowly around me, as though in a ritual. I soon realised it was as though I was having a dream within a dream; an out-of-body experience. I could then see the scene from above, as if floating. I looked down and saw myself lying there, on a table perhaps; my fellow villagers had come to mourn my death.

She said that when she awoke she was shaking, overtaken by a sense of despair. A few minutes later, her eldest daughter appeared at her door, her face was flushed. She had also had a bad dream, one which was very similar to her mother's. In it, her mother's name was called out in a crowd. At this point they associated their dreams with a return flight Mrs Keza had booked to Kolkata leaving the next day. They rushed to the town to try to change their tickets, but the office was closed. Finally, they braved the three-hour drive in heavy rains to Dimapur to try their luck again and managed to change their tickets leaving several weeks later. That Friday, the day they were originally scheduled to return from Kolkata, Mrs Keza and her daughter were walking in town when a woman they knew, a Nepali woman from their church, ran to them and collapsed at Mrs Keza's feet. The woman was wailing in anguish as Mrs Keza knelt beside her to see what afflicted her. She then told them that only a few minutes earlier news that a plane from Kolkata, carrying her son, had crashed in the mountains near Imphal.

We sat in silence for a moment. Mrs Keza noticed that I had stopped writing my notes about halfway into her narrative. She asked me if I knew about Ketu and his cousin. 'Yes', I said. 'Their memorial stone is inside the gate of the compound where I am staying'. Mrs Keza then told me that they had not been able to locate the remains of many of those that were on the flight, so confirmation of their deaths was a long drawn out and painful process. Ketu had been a close friend of theirs, and before he had chosen to study in Shillong, he had been active in a vocal ensemble with them at Science College in Jotsoma. 'We used to sing often together, and our quintet toured different colleges and churches. Ketu was a talented person and had a really big heart. We were devastated to hear that he was on that flight, and I cannot imagine the grief his mother has gone through, losing so many in her family in such a short time'.

The memorial stone for both Kevi and Ketu stands just inside the gate of the family colony, and near to where I am staying. To the left lives Kezevinuo, Ketu's sister-in-law, and a young widow with two children. Kezevinuo is aided in the heavier chores by 18-year-old Wancho from Tangnyu village near the Burma border in the Mon district. A cheerful young man, Wancho is a Konyak Naga but speaks Angami well and often shares his dreams out loud across the vegetable garden, which separates his small thatch hut from my veranda. His casual approach to dreams is a source of constant irritation to Kezevinuo. On one occasion he shouted, 'Hey, Medonuo [the youngest daughter], I had a dream that you cut your hair!' Kezevinuo rushed outside almost immediately and scolded him, 'That is not at all a good dream, and you do not just shout it out like that'. She then turned to Medonuo, and said to her, 'That is not a good dream, you should go pray!' Just a short distance away is the 24 hour prayer centre run by the charismatic Baptist church where Mr and Mrs Keza attend services. Here church members and visitors meet prayer counsellors and stay a few minutes or a few days. The church itself holds large morning and evening prayer meetings in which mass prayers, or open congregational praying, and more personalised pastoral prayers are on offer to anyone in attendance, many of whom have come troubled by their dreams. Those kneeling at the front of the sanctuary often request spiritual intervention to lessen the impact of events perceived to have been prefigured in their dreams.

Like most married women in the village, Kezevinuo shares her dreams with her daughter or nieces in the early hours of the morning. Her irritation with Wancho stems from the fact that, among the Angami, dreams are commonly shared openly amongst kin and friends, but ominous dreams should be shared with discretion. Traditionally, such dreams would only be told under the covering of the kitchen hearth so as not to be heard by spirits who might attempt to manipulate the outcome they portend. An elder skilled in interpretation might be consulted, but typically this would also be done under the elder's hearth covering. However, this practice has moved now, and more often than not, distressing dreams are brought to the church to be prayed over. In the case of a particularly troubling dream, such as Vilhou's dream outlined in chapter 5, a prayer counsellor is consulted. A well-known 'prophetess' at the prayer centre was regularly consulted about dreams, though she had died by the time I was in Kohima. Her prophetic dreams became a main feature in church services, and the ministries such as the prayer centre were shaped by the messages she shared in prayer meetings.

Members of the *Meya* extended family and a few neighbours say that Kezevinuo has *mhoté* dreams, or that she is very *mhoté*. Here the word is used as an adjective and translates as 'clairvoyant' or 'premonitory'; namely her dreams come true. But, to have *mhoté* dreams or to be very *mhoté* is not as rare as I had initially presupposed. Most families claim that one or two of their members have a propensity for dreaming of future events with incredible accuracy, and as only close family members would be witness to any linkages between the dream narratives, interpretations and the waketime events that are ultimately connected with them, whether or not a person is *mhoté* seems to be a status given by close family. However, in many cases, married and older women in the neighbourhood are either *mhoté* dreamers themselves, or know who is, and are often the main person consulted for interpreting dream omens that emerge in conversation.

It was clear early on in my research that daily dream sharing is a practice most common among women, and particularly among married women, mothers and their daughters, and among female neighbours. Land ownership and inheritance patterns are shaped by the unilineal Angami kinship structure, with patrilineality and to a large extent patrilocality framing the inter-clan social landscape. This translates into married women being generally removed from their consanguines and relying on close friendships with their husband's sisters and the wives of her in-laws. Outside the home, dream sharing typically takes place among female neighbours who, following the same pattern, are also removed from their paternal clans.

Women gathering to chat informally in the early morning hours are a kind of interpretive community, namely a community that is attentive to omens both in waketime and sleeptime states, and regularly share them with their close friends, affines and neighbours. The following is a brief example of this.

Below my compound and along the road there is a tiny wooden shop where Bebei, one of my neighbours from a different village, sells betel nut concoctions, candy and other snacks in the morning hours before she goes to her regular office job. A few months prior to my arrival, I learned that she had shared a dream in which a giant tree fell rather dramatically behind her house. In the days after she had the dream, and when her neighbours would come in the morning to her shop, she not only shared her dream with them, but implored them to warn their husbands, fathers and uncles to be alert and careful. It is not an unfamiliar dream and is specific in the sense that it foretells the death of a clansman. According to one of the women Bebei spoke to, the falling tree is a particularly tragic dream as it is attached to the wellbeing of the family,

This dream of a big tree falling was also dreamt by a woman prophet when my father had a stroke in 1995 and she predicted that he would die. He died a month later. Big trees falling in dreams indicate that the male head of the house in a patriarchal society is like a big tree giving shelter to all and providing food for all.

It was only a week or so after she had the dream that Bebei's own husband died of a sudden heart attack, stunning her closest friends and ensuring that the link between her dream and her husband's death was firmly established. Within the community the lesson of remaining alert to the messages communicated in dreams was circulated among clan families and neighbouring communities.

Unmarried men also share their dreams, though not nearly with as much frequency as the women, and typically among close male friends within their age-group. Married men are perhaps the least likely to share their dreams with any kind of frequency, though it remains a topic of some interest to them, especially when the occasional sub-clan or clan gathering is held, and a dream may be used anecdotally to drive a particular point or argument, uphold a custom or tradition, or to emphasise the importance of ancestral knowledge in clan life.

I observed this while attending a *Meya* clan gathering where a dream was shared by Ale (Ketu's cousin), now one of the eldest male members and clan leader. As such gatherings are reserved for the clan males, their spouses and children only, I was able to get a unique glimpse into clan social dynamics as played out in a relatively exclusive space and in the span of about six hours. Resembling in many respects the Western 'extended family', averaging 40 to 50 members, those present at the gathering represented four *Meya* generations. I was invited by Ale's cousin Kenei (Ketu's brother) who lives most of the year in Hyderabad, having transitioned after school into full time work in civil aviation. I was reluctant to go as I understood the nature of the meeting but was urged to jump into the jeep that had driven back from the gathering nearly 45 minutes to fetch me. The gathering took place in a forest clearing on clan-owned land about five kilometres north of the village.

After a feast of rice, pork with bamboo shoots, chicken, goat and fish curries and mustard greens, Ale stood and spoke to the gathering. He began by stating that this was the first *Meya* gathering to be organised since the 1980s, and that it was important that they meet more often to strengthen their bonds, since it was clear that family, work and school responsibilities were taking everyone in different directions. He suggested that whatever unity the family had until now could only be attributed to the strong faith and prayers of the previous generations. He suggested that God had a special purpose for the *Meya* clan, and that this had been revealed to their ancestors. He then shared the story of an important dream that indicated the nature of God's covenant with the *Meya* clan:

> Before my grandfather Seyie was born, my great-grandfather died, leaving behind his wife and an only daughter. Great-grandmother was already carrying my grandfather in her womb. The cousins of my grandfather did not know about the condition of my great-grandmother and were making plans to distribute the properties of my great-grandparents for inheritance as per the customary law. But at that instant one of my great-grandfather's aunts had a significant dream. She therefore intercepted the cousins of my grandfather and convinced them to delay their distribution until the mother delivers the baby she was carrying. She related her dream that a bamboo plant had

sprouted out from inside the house of my grandfather, penetrating its way out beyond the roof of the house. Upon hearing her dream, the cousins of my grandfather hesitated and suspended their plans to distribute the inheritance properties. Consequently, after some months my great-grandmother gave birth to a baby boy and named him Menhouzakie, meaning 'to bring forth plenty'. Thereafter the cousins of my grandfather had to drop their intentions since a male child was born to the family, who becomes the rightful heir of the family. That was how the heritage possessions of my grandfather had been saved from being taken away and passed down to us.[5]

Ale's retelling and interpretation of the dream relates to inheritance, but also to what he believes is a promise or greater purpose for the clan from God – land being an integral part of this promise. Interestingly, the narrative does not include any disagreement on the interpretation of the dream, but tells it as though it is undisputed and taken seriously by those who would stand to lose a significant portion of land. The narrative suggests that the dream's meaning is patently clear, and their collective faith in the truth of dreams – regardless of gain or loss – is rewarded in its fulfilment.

Messages from the ancestors

A majority of Angami dreamers employ their understanding of symbolic meaning to interpret and act upon what has been communicated to them symbolically by ancestors in their dreams. Once awake they project the dream symbols against a lexicon of interpretations they have developed based on previous dream experiences and in listening to others tell and interpret their dreams. Based on this index of meanings, they judge the level of severity of the revelation and communicate this knowledge to close kin, and if necessary to the clan. Unremarkable dreams are usually forgotten or perhaps shared light-heartedly in conversation during morning chores. However, particularly cryptic, puzzling or troubling dreams are prayed about or brought to a more experienced dreamer for interpretive consultation.

Generally speaking, the accounts I have detailed in the previous section reflect the understanding that fragments or partial truths of a singular impending event often appear to multiple persons, typically among different family members, but even among different families from different communities. Though waketime omens may appear as messages, often the clearest messages come in dreams. Mrs Keza's dream of attending her own funeral, a dream which her own daughter also had the same night, was a personal and seemingly amplified version of the standard dream among many Naga groups – seeing a smartly-dressed person foretells the death of a family member or close neighbour. Here, as in psychoanalysis, dreams are not always to be taken literally but require skilled interpretation. In fact, there is a rare overlap between those dream theories that are progressive – i.e. 'the experience of dreaming is held to have a close, even determinant, connection with the future life of the dreamer' (Basso 1987, p. 86) – and Freudian conceptualisations of dream construction which have been so dominant in dream theory in the West, namely that dreams are regressive, looking to the dreamer's past in the interpretive process (ibid.).

Ketu's dream, which was shared with various *Meya* families before the event of the plane crash, was accompanied by a host of other signs. In fact, the *Meya* retell the narratives as if the whole cosmos had come alive in an attempt to alert or deter the *Meya*, and Keza families, and possibly others, from boarding a specific flight on a specific date. But the key recipient of the message, in many ways the main subject of the revelation, was the victim himself. In dreaming of his father's spirit, calling for the eldest, and then the next of kin, all unavailable, and finally himself, Ketu's dream was not the clear message 20 years ago that it appears now – of an ancestor calling the souls of his sons to join him in another world. Hindsight also allows reflection on the element of fate in Ketu's very name. Ketu's full name, *Ketuselie*, means 'it is good to have another male child born into the family'. Though it would be typically interpreted (prior to his death) to mean that the household is strengthened by the birth of a male child as it secures patrilineal continuity, it takes on a new meaning in the context of the crash, with an element of sacrifice on behalf of his elder siblings. The weight of this interpretation is well understood by Ale and those gathered around the fire, and following Ketu and his brother's death, Ale and his cousin Theja, both of whom struggled with alcohol, became sober.

Ketu's dream also echoes in many ways the ancestral intervention in the dream shared at the *Meya* clan gathering in the forest. Here the name of the unborn child is also an important element in the story. *Seyie*, meaning 'to prolong our nation', is not simply about preserving the clan name and the inheritance of land (Seyie would go on to have three sons, the eldest would go on to have nine sons and a daughter, and the others would have five sons each), but because the name also reflects a promise, a covenant imparted to the clan. Thus, names are chosen with a great deal of thought, a process that sometimes takes many weeks and involves dream consultation by the child's grandparents. Names become inscriptions of destiny and are recognisable any time a person's full name is called out. It is believed that if a person is unable to live up to his or her name, he or she will not simply fail, but indeed live out a life that goes in exactly the opposite direction.

A second key point here is that events entailed in dreams are believed to have an element of inevitability, in the sense that these events, like storms, are 'collective forces' exceeding the person and not necessarily directed at the person. With ominous dreams it is believed the recipient of the dream can attempt to alter or affect the outcome (Bensa and Fassin 2002, p. 10), but all a dreamer and his or her consulted kin can do is try to minimise its impact by diffusing its force. This, it is thought, can be done by sharing the dream with others, but is also accomplished through intercessory prayer or sometimes by simply staying at home and avoiding routine actions and interactions. At the local Baptist Revival Church, morning prayer requests are usually about troubling dreams, about dreams that could not be interpreted or about afflictions that were entailed in dreams.

Dreams as community events

The dreams, as described above, in which persons attempt to navigate forces that may harm them, and that are often invisible, are challenges which resemble many of the real situations of day-to-day living within the clan. They would also reflect concerns that extend beyond the clan to the problems of inter-clan relations and state violence. The uncertainties that individuals find themselves faced with on a daily basis, must be continually negotiated, and this is best accomplished, it is believed, by listening to and interpreting the messages from ancestors, or *upfutsa-nuo ruopfü* (lit. spirits of the elders, generally understood as spirits of deceased relatives that reside near or in the village with humans). Dreams, as events, can become important life history markers, or life episodes, because they indicate a potential new direction in the person's life, or for that of the clan. As the anthropologist M.E. Louw suggests,

> [dreams] are triggers of subjunctivity – a mood or form of being characterised by doubt, hope, fear, will, desire and potentiality; by the sense that one's life is changing track; that something new is going to happen for which one can hope, desire or fear, or just be uncertain about. Divine signs become a sort of cognitive and emotional scaffold that can be used for reflection.
>
> (2010, p. 280–281)

If we are to think what constitutes personhood, then we might look to events or important life episodes which people experience and help to shape them as individuals. Rather than discarding the jagged realities the person experiences for a 'kind of flattened cohabitation of all things' (Thrift 2008 cited in Humphrey 2008, p. 375), 'it is necessary to think about how a singular human being might put him or herself together as a distinctive subject by adding to, or subtracting from, the possibilities given by culture as it has been up to that point, through the very process of taking action' (ibid.). This, then, in turn brings us back to the relationships a person has with events but also with people, culture and history. Sylvie Poirier, however, takes us further, suggesting 'these relationships, that is, one's ancestral, social, ritual and territorial networks of affiliations and responsibilities are intrinsic to the bodily self rather than extrinsic' (2003, p. 110) and thus are constitutive of personhood.

Approaching dream narratives as 'dream-events' can shed light on how dream narratives become a part of the person's life story. Here there is a compounding of fragmented dream experiences which become infused with waketime experiences that the person recalls in dreamtime memory that culminate in a dreamtime zenith (and this may be a very positive or very negative concentrated moment). In other words, the 'dreamtime event' entails an unfolding of circumstances over time. The positive or negative anxieties caused by the intense process translate into a waketime reaction – hyperventilation, rapid heartbeat, etc. The central point is that the dreamtime person stands as a 'witness' to a 'dream-event' – and in turn is in a position to tell 'what happened'.

Caroline Humphrey's discussion of the 'decision-event' highlights the idea that, though events form key reflective demarcations in community and individual memory, they are best approached as markers from which to draw out the highly contingent nature of such events for the individual themselves. In other words, dreamtime events are remembered as *events* of the person, not simply as memorable dreams. Drawing from her research in Inner Mongolia, Humphrey is particularly sensitive to the role religious inspiration and divination play in 'plumping for' specific courses of action 'precisely by avoiding reasoning, by taking the state of the individual . . . at a particular time and discovering the unknown, which is the right decision for that person in the constantly changing and multifarious coordinates of the cosmos' (2008, p. 364). Though the suggestion here is that there is a need for re-examining historical and social processes through a re-assemblage of the 'decision-events' of individual subjects, there is also a recognition of the multiple forces both internal and external to the individual that shape them and their actions (Agha in Kockelman 2007). And this is an insight that is true for the Angami experience of dreams, particularly as dreams and waketime omens are believed to be pre-emptive. Here messages communicated to them, whether by deceased relatives or the divine, are intended guide them – towards or away from impending waketime events.

Moreover, events in dreams point to an important aspect of reflexivity, namely the notion of 'waking' or lucidity. This occurs as dream-events can trigger a new reality or direction, to the extent that they cause the dream-self to 'wake up' or become increasingly self-aware within the dream environment, and though this is an experience that sometimes happens in typical dream experiences, it is more the norm among 'gifted' dreamers, which later chapters will discuss in greater detail. The notion of dream-event is also linked to 'waking up' to act on information of an impending contingency in waking reality, illustrating the actions in waketime that are possible because of a new and fresh awareness (McBride 2005). The idea of dreams influencing waketime events reveals an important way that memory is structured among the Angami, as well as how this contributes to the future orientation of dreams and knowledge obtained from omens, spirits and ancestors more generally.

The realisation that dreams are event-oriented has drawn dream researchers to explore how dreams relate to a person's waketime actions and anxieties. In other words, the dream 'self' is situated in relation to some specific challenge or condition such as a situation in which one must negotiate foreignness in a highly diverse cultural setting (Heijnen and Edgar 2010). Rather than seeking to interpret a set of dream symbols in order to reveal their meaning within the grammar of a particular culture and context, the move towards considering events has sought to articulate the connection between dreams and waketime actions. Therefore, the outcome of dreams is only resolved in the everyday action rather than within the dream itself.

What Lohman and Heijnen retain from earlier approaches, as discussed above, is the dichotomy 'imaginary'/'real' (or 'unconscious'/'conscious'). This separation means dreams are relegated to a secondary status, and it forecloses the possibility of mapping the continuities between diverse kinds of dreams and 'dream-like' experiences, and their waketime connections, which are articulated in a wide range of studies across cultures. An examination of the anthropological literature in the non-Western world, whether focused on dream theories and practices or not, reveals a belief in something more akin to a continuum in which the dream-self may be placed at any given point along a gradation of perception (cf. Kohn 2007, 2013; and Poirier 2003). Some theorists have already laid the groundwork for such a continuum. Charles Peirce (1931–1935), for instance, classified dreams as either 'iconic' or 'indexical'. 'Iconic' means the dreamtime person is the focus of the experience, and symbolic imagery contains knowledge that is encrypted in metaphor. By 'indexical', Peirce suggests that the dreamtime experience is remembered because it is a re-assemblage of aspects familiar to the person, including familiar settings, people and other experiences. Most of the dream accounts and sequences considered in this book, for example, contain both 'iconic' and 'indexical' qualities, though the dream narrative indicates that the dream-self is unable to exercise agency to affect or alter the concentrated symbolic arrangement of their dreamtime environment. Peirce's semiotic classification is helpful in sorting out aspects of dreamtime experience, allowing (perhaps) for some overlap. But more importantly, this arrangement reveals a movement from abstraction towards focused imagery, suggesting a single continuum while retaining a common anchorage in the perceiving self.

This move may accommodate anything from fragments remembered by individuals that give little importance to dreams, to the dramatic flights described by shamanic healers in search for meandering or entrapped souls. In much cross-cultural research (cf. Kempf and Hermann 2003; Lohmann 2003; and Tonkinson 2003) the dream-self, regardless of its position along this hypothetical continuum, is articulated as the dreamer's 'spirit-being' – the partial 'self' that lives in dreams, but is also the partial 'self' of vitality and feeling within the integral person.

A second, equally challenging problem that has hindered attempts to draw out a 'single realm theory' is the puzzling juxtaposition of persons and images, sometimes connected directly and sometimes not with the person in the dream 'present'. Within this strange setting is the perspective of a more or less 'aware', participating, dreaming 'self'. The dream-self does not register anything unusual in this amalgamation. Though the various participants appearing in the plot may include dead relatives, childhood friends and even celebrities, it is not a timeless narrative, nor is it, from the perspective of the dream-self, at all strange or out of place. The strangeness, in other words, is only 'strange' in retrospect, from the waking perspective. Within dreams, however, there sometimes appear aberrations that do suddenly appear strange. These typically trigger a shift, eliciting a strong emotional response, and sometimes cause the person to 'wake up', whether gaining entry to a new level of reflexivity within the dream or waking up entirely from sleep. These emotionally charged 'events' serve as mnemonic devices in recalling and retelling dream narratives.

Concluding remarks

In this chapter, I have located Angami dream culture within the genealogy of anthropological dream research and shown how dreams are fundamentally social in nature. Dreams are understood as messages intended for the community, but as illustrated in the series of dreamtime and waketime signs appearing to members of the *Meya* clan, they communicate part of a larger symbolic system that reveals the interdependence of their social lives with purposes only understood in their fullness in hindsight or, it would appear, by deceased kin. As this chapter has shown, dream theorists have operated for a long time under the premise that dreams are isolated psychic phenomena that, if anything, capture some of the processes by which humans mentally negotiate social anxieties and other psychosocial phenomena, helping the mind recover, exercise, learn, memorise and generally cope with waking reality. The 'communicative theory' posited by Tedlock suggested a corrective, that though dream narratives can reveal a great deal about the person, settings, language, times, spaces, audiences and performances in the process of narration cannot be ignored. By attending to local understandings of the person, of 'self' and of such nuances as perceived social standing, one can tap into the way dreams are locally interpreted. Yet, I have suggested that this remains problematic as Tedlock's aim is to find a kind of universal application or meaning to the dreams being collected. But as Poirier has suggested in her schema, personhood or 'the self' needs to incorporate both waketime self and dreaming 'self', and this is critical if we are to take local dream theories seriously. As Hutton seemed to have recognised (as illustrated in the two different dream accounts in chapter 1), 'passivity' and 'activeness' in both waketime and dreaming need to be understood on a continuum. This continuum reflects the true nature of personhood, allowing us to understand the blurred lines between the waketime 'self' and the dreamtime 'self'. The Angami *ruopfü* corresponds to this model, and indeed if we are to understand the nature of *ruopfü* it is only by taking this model seriously that we can do so. What this book adds on to this body of literature is to take this idea of the continuum and suggest that, in the case of the Angami *ruopfü*, the continuum does not flow one way but is bi-directional, namely there is an important aspect of 'reversibility'.

As I will show in the following chapter, 'reversibility' encompasses the idea that the waketime *ruopfü* can influence the dreamtime *ruopfü* and, importantly, the dreamtime *ruopfü* can then reverse the influence to influence the waketime *ruopfü*. This is how the *ruopfü* can develop and can be understood, and importantly, becomes critical in understanding the Angami understanding of dreams and their influence on everyday action. If we dismiss the idea that firstly, the *ruopfü* is the continuum of both waketime and dreamtime self, and, secondly, that given this continuum both 'selves' form the whole personhood and the influence from each self can go both ways, then we cannot properly understand the Angami personhood.

Notes

1 The resemblances between Freud's descriptions of the unconscious and Merleau-Ponty's notion of 'flesh' are no coincidence, and with only slight adjusting, these two theoretical threads can be brought together, linking up the discussion on reversibility in this book with a rich literature that can illuminate both what is presented here, and further research on the idea of reversibility.
2 Iain R. Edgar, Anthropology of Dreams, online source, www.dur.ac.uk/i.r.edgar/, accessed 15 January 2015.
3 Ibid.
4 A 'good marriage', as it was explained to me, entails spousal faithfulness (which is largely the norm, adultery being seen as severe and often punished by eviction from the clan community. Whether the guilt lies with the clan male or his wife, the punishment is the same) and the rearing of obedient children (arguably the norm, and I gauge this by looking at school retention, which is very high. Delinquency among village youth is also quite low).
5 This version of the dream and its interpretation was furnished by Ale several weeks after the gathering and following my request. At the gathering the dream and explanation were shorter, and the explanation was less detailed as most in the audience were familiar with the dream and its interpretation.

Bibliography

Basso, Ellen B., 1987, "The Implications of a Progressive Theory of Dreaming", in *Dreaming: Anthropological and Psychological Interpretations*, B. Tedlock, ed., New York: Cambridge University Press.

Bensa, Alban and Fassin, Eric, 2002, "Les Sciences Sociales Face a L'événement", *Terrain*, 38, pp. 5–20.

Bourguignon, Erika, 1972, "Dreams and Altered States of Consciousness", in *Anthropological Research, in Psychological Anthropology*, F.L.K. Hsu, ed., Cambridge: Schenkman, pp. 403–434.

Bourguignon, Erika, 1973, *Religion, Altered States of Consciousness, and Social Change*, Columbus: Ohio State University Press.

Brinkman, I., 2007, "Dreams and Agency During Angola's War of Independence", in *Strength Beyond Structure: Social and Historical Trajectories of Agency in Africa*, R. van Dijk, ed., Leiden, Boston: Brill, pp. 62–82.

Catalano, Stephen, 1984, "Children's Dreams: Their Meaning and use in Clinical Practice", *Child and Adolescent Social Work Journal*, 1(4), pp. 280–289.

Catalano, Stephen, 1990 [1987], *Children's Dreams in Clinical Practice*, New York: Plenum Press.

Crapanzano, Vincent, 1975, "Saints, Jnun, and Dreams: An Essay in Moroccan Ethnopsychiatry", *Psychiatry*, 38, pp. 145–159.

Crapanzano, Vincent, 1981, "Text, Transference and Indexicality", *Ethos*, 9, pp. 122–148.

D'Andrade, Roy G., 1961, "Anthropological Studies of Dreams", in *Psychological Anthropology: Approaches to Culture and Personality*, F.L.K Hsu, ed., Homewood: The Dorsey Press, pp. 296–332.

Descartes, René, 1998, *The World and Other Writings*, Stephen Gaukroger, trans., London: Cambridge University Press.

Dittman, Allen T. and Harvey C. Moore, 1957, "Disturbance in Dreams as Related to Peyotism Among the Navaho", *American Anthropologist*, 59, pp. 642–649.

Edgar, Iain R., 2011, *The Dream in Islam: From Qur'Anic Tradition to Jihadist Inspiration*, Oxford: Berghahn Books.

Edgar, Iain R., 2015, *Anthropology of Dreams*. Online source: www.dur.ac.uk/i.r.edgar/, accessed 13 February 2012.

Eggan, Dorothy, 1952, "The Manifest Content of Dreams: A Challenge to Social Science", *American Anthropologist*, 54, pp. 469–485.

Eggan, Dorothy, 1961, "Dream Analysis", in *Studying Personality Cross-Culturally*, Bert Kaplan, ed., New York: Harper and Row.

Egorova, Y. and Perwez, S., 2012, "Telugu Jews: Are the Dalits of Coastal Andhra Going Caste-Awry?", *The South Asianist*, 1(1), June 14. Online source: www.southasianist. ed.ac.uk/article/view/27.

Ewing, K.P., 2003, "Diasporic Dreaming, Identity, and Self-Constitution", in *Dreaming and the Self: New Perspectives on Subjectivity, Identity, and Emotion*, J.M. Mageo, ed., Albany, NY: State University of New York Press, pp. 43–60.

Fabian, Johannes, 1966, "Dream and Charisma, 'Theories of Dreams' in the Jamaa-Movement (Congo)", *Anthropos*, 61, pp. 544–560.

Freud, Sigmund, 1900, *The Interpretation of Dreams*, A.A. Brill, trans., New York: Palgrave MacMillan.

Graham, L. R., 1995, *Performing Dreams: Discourses of Immortality among the Xavante of Central Brazil*, Austin: University of Texas Press.

Gregor, Thomas, 1981, "A Content Analysis of Mehinaku Dreams", *Ethos*, 9, pp. 353–390.

Griffith, R. M., Miyagi, O. and Tago, A., 1958, "The Universality of Typical Dreams: Japanese Versus Americans", *American Anthropologist*, 60, pp. 1173–1178.

Hall, Calvin S., 1951, "What People Dream About", *Scientific American*, 184(5), pp. 60–63.

Hall, Calvin S. and Vernon J. Nordby, 1972, *The Individual and His Dreams*, New York: New American Library.

Hall, Calvin S. and Robert Van De Castle, 1966, *The Content Analysis of Dreams*, New York: New American Library.

Heijnen, Adrïene and Edgar, Iain, 2010, "Imprints of Dreaming", *History and Anthropology*, 21, pp. 217–226.

Herdt, Gilbert, 1987, "Selfhood and Discourse in Sambia Dream Sharing", in *Dreaming: Anthropological and Psychological Interpretations*, Barbara, Tedlock, ed., Cambridge: Cambridge University Press.

Humphrey, Caroline, 2008, "Re-Assembling Individual Subjects: Events and Decisions in Troubled Times", *Anthropology Theory*, 8(4), December, pp. 357–380.

Hutton, J.H., 1921a, *The Angami Nagas*, London: Palgrave Macmillan.

Hutton, J.H., 1921b, *The Sema Nagas*, London: Palgrave Macmillan.

Hutton, J.H., 1923, "Typescript copy of a letter from J.H. Hutton probably to C.G. Seligman", (archival), Hutton Ms. Box 3, 26, Pitt Rivers Museum Archive, Oxford. Available online: http://himalaya.socanth.cam.ac.uk/collections/naga/record/r73000.html, accessed 15 January 2015.

Kempf, Wolfgang and Hermann, Elfriede, 2003, "Dreamscapes: Transcending the Local in Initiation Rites Among the Ngaing of Papua New Guinea", in *Dream Travelers: Sleep Experiences and Culture in the Western Pacific*, Roger, Lohmann, ed., New York: Palgrave Macmillan.

Kockelman, Paul, 2007, "Agency: The Relation Between Meaning, Power, and Knowledge", *Current Anthropology*, 48(3), pp. 375–401.

Kohn, Eduardo, 2013, *How Forests Think: Toward an Anthropology Beyond the Human*, Berkeley: University of California Press.

Kohn, Eduardo, 2007, "How Dogs Dream: Amazonian Natures and the Politics of Trans-Species Engagement", *American Ethnologist*, 34(1), pp. 3–24.

Kracke, W., 1987, "Myths in Dreams, Thought in Images: An Amazonian Contribution to the Psychoanalytic Theory of Primary Process", in *Dreaming: Anthropological and Psychological Interpretations*, Barbara, Tedlock, ed., Cambridge: Cambridge University Press.

Kracke, W., 1979, "Dreaming in Kagwahiv: Dream Beliefs and Their Psychic Uses in an Amazonian Indian Culture", in *Psychoanalytic Study of Society*, 8, pp. 119–171.

Kuper, A. and Stone, A., 1982, "The Dream of Irma's Injection: A Structural Account", *American Journal of Psychiatry*, 139, pp. 1225–1234.

Lévi-Strauss, C., 1963, *The structural Study of Myth*, New York: Basic Books.

Lincoln, Jackson Steward, 1935, *The Dream in Primitive Cultures*, Baltimore, Maryland: Williams and Wilkins.

Lincoln, Jackson Steward and Seligman, C.G., 1935, "Introduction", in *The Dream in Primitive Cultures*, Whitefish, MO: Kessinger Publishing Co.

Lohmann, Roger Ivar, 2003, *Dream Travelers: Sleep Experiences and Culture in the Western Pacific*, New York: Palgrave MacMillan.

Lohmann, Roger Ivar, 2007, "Dreams and Ethnography", in *The New Science of Dreaming, Vol. 3, Cultural and Theoretical Perspectives*, Deidre Barrett and Patrick McNamara, eds., London: Praeger Perspectives.

Louw, M.E., 2010, "Dreaming up Futures: Dream Omens and Magic in Bishkek", *History and Anthropology*, 21(3), pp. 277–292.

McBride, K.D., 2005, *Collective Dreams: Political Imagination and Community*, University Park(PA): The Pennsylvania University Press.

Mittermaier, Amira, 2011, *Dreams That Matter: Egyptian Landscapes of the Imagination*, Berkeley: University of California Press.

O'Nell, Carl W., 1965, "A Cross-Cultural Study of Hunger and Thirst Motivation Manifested in Dreams", *Human Development*, 8, pp. 181–193.

Parsifal-Charles, Nancy, 1986, *The Dream: 4000 of Years of Theory and Practice, A Critical, Descriptive, and Encyclopaedic Bibliography, Vol. 1*, West Cornwell, CT: Locust Hill Press.

Peirce, Charles S., 1931–1935, *Collected Papers of Charles Sanders Peirce*, Cambridge, MA: Harvard University Press.

Poirier, S., 2003, "'This Is Good Country: We Are Good Dreamers': Dreams and Dreaming in the Australian Western Desert", in *Dream Travelers: Sleep Experiences and Culture in the Western Pacific*, Lohmann, Roger, ed., New York: Palgrave MacMillan, pp. 107–125.

Sears, Walter E., 1948, "The Navaho and Yir-Yoront, Their Primitive Dreams", B.A. thesis, Cambridge, MA: Harvard University Press.

Seligman, C.G., 1921, "Notes on Dreams", *Sudan Notes and Records*, 4, p. 156.

Seligman, C.G., 1923, "Type Dreams: A Request", *Folklore*, 34, pp. 376–378.

Seligman, C.G., 1924, "Anthropology and Psychology: A Study of Some Points of Contact", *Journal of the Royal Anthropological Institute of Great Britain and Ireland*, 54, pp. 13–46.

Stephen, M., 1982, "Dreaming Is Another Power! The Social Significance of Dreams Among the Mekeo of Papua New Guinea", *Oceania*, 53, pp. 106–122.

Tedlock, B., 1992 [1987], *Dreaming: Anthropological and Psychological Interpretations*, Cambridge: Cambridge University Press.

Thrift, N., 2008, "I Just Don't Know What Got Into Me: Where Is the Subject?" *Subjectivity*, 22, pp. 82–89.

Tonkinson, Robert, 2003, "Ambrymese Dreams and the Mardu Dreaming", in *Dream Travelers: Sleep Experiences and Culture in the Western Pacific,* Roger Lohmann, ed., New York: Palgrave MacMillan, pp. 87–106.

Tylor, Edward B., 1870, *Researches Into the Early History of Mankind and the Development of Civilisation*, London: John Murray.

Tylor, Edward B., 1871, *Primitive Culture: Researches Into the Development of Mythology, Philosophy, Religion, Language, Art and Custom*, London: John Murray.

3 The phenomenology of dreaming

The incidents described by my informants in the previous chapter were interpreted in many ways as partial messages from the supernatural realm, affording only oblique views through an otherwise all-concealing veil. Behind this veil, there was presumably a fuller knowledge of the imminent event, that if it was clearer, better understood, perhaps the tragedy could have been avoided. There are individuals, however, that do in a sense breach this divide. Having developed a few underpinning general principles towards an Angami 'science of dreaming', namely

Figure 3.1 Dreaming in Kohima village
Source: Author's photo

the function of 'reversibility' as grounded in the continuum – across sleeping and waking states – of the always perceiving and experiencing *ruopfü*, I now turn to exploring the experiences of 'specialists'. Central to this discussion is the possibility of conceiving *ruopfü* as not inseparable in some way or formed from the human body. Linkages between certain kinds of dream experiences such as flight, and the disembodied soul or spirit described in human-animal transformation or therianthropy has been only of limited concern among dream researchers (some exceptions are Kohn 2007, 2013; and to some extent Lohmann 2003). Given the once widespread practice of polymorphism in the region, namely the ability of men and women to project their spirits into the bodies of non-human animals and control their movements, this linkage merits some closer attention, and I explore in greater depth the polymorphic capacities of *ruopfü* by examining Angami and broader Naga understandings of the *tekhumiavi* – 'man in the shape of a tiger' – that still exist among the Eastern Angami. Thus, in addition to elucidating dream 'reversibility' in relation to the composite 'selves' of Angami personhood, *ruopfü* as a disembodied subject can also reveal the ways in which dreams and dreaming are consonant with practices and beliefs generally associated with shamanism.

I begin with a short ethnographic illustration which helps to set up the discussion, including some of the problems that can arise in dream interpretation, but more importantly the different ways of conceptualising the 'embodied' and 'disembodied' *ruopfü* and the ensuing shift in perspectives of the person revealed in the dream.

The nature of *ruopfü*

I met Zahou, a senior leader in the Naga underground group, the Naga National Council (NNC), for an interview in part because of his connection with the political movement but also because, according to my *Tenyidie* instructor, he was 'one of our great experts on Angami traditions'. In the months prior to the meeting, Zahou had been busy. In March, he travelled to Bangkok for talks with rival underground factions. Then came the funeral preparations for Zhapu Phizo's (the first NNC President) son Kevilevor who died in mid-April in London. Accompanying the body as it was flown to India and transported to Kohima was Kevilevor's eldest sister and NNC President Adinno Phizo – Zahou's boss. Following 50 years of self-imposed exile in a quiet suburb in London, she moved back to Nagaland indefinitely, and it is unclear how her presence back in the village will affect the dynamic of the seemingly dormant NNC apparatus.

As I entered and sat down in Zahou's front room, I tried mentally to recap the set of questions I had prepared, but Zahou pre-empted me with a few of his own: 'Why are you in Nagaland? What are your objectives? What sorts of organisations are you connected with?' I gave short, concise responses taking the role of the interrogated, a role I am used to, having navigated the numerous police checkpoints along the highway. I found a moment to introduce my research questions and explained that my Tenyidie instructor insisted I approach him. Zahou was visibly perplexed. 'Most foreigners', he related, 'are only interested in talking about the war'. He laughed, relaxed in his chair, and collected his thoughts. 'Well, dreams are very much believed . . . In our daily lives we are certainly dreaming what the next day we are going to do. That is the belief – that is our people's belief'. He then followed this with an anecdote 'coming from a long back':

> One time, one young man dreamed of himself shouting from above some-body's head – howling. And he thought 'oh, this is good for me – on top of his head'. So he was relating his dream to his family. 'I can't say, but it should not be bad' – the family also thought like that. And the next day he went to war. But he was killed that day. So later on the family came to realise that it was somebody's ramei (*or feather*). He was dreaming that he was someone's ramei. If somebody kills somebody, he becomes the hero and gets a feather on his head. So the young man dreamt he was somebody's feather.

As I took down a few notes, I noted that Zahou was himself absent from the narration of this dream, and he provided neither names nor indications regarding its particular setting. The story was also short – shared, in a sense, as a parable. However, it reflected a pattern in which the interpretive framework was disclosed. In other words, the dreamer's (and family's) search for the dream's true meaning is an integral part of the story, and it is important in retelling it that the seemingly cryptic symbolic arrangement of many dream images – the howling, the head, the feather – is preserved. This then contributes to their grammatical semblance to parables in which the lesson is encapsulated in a final, unexpected twist at the end. In this case there are two conclusions to the dream – the first one is that of the dreamer, that the dream was a sign of a good outcome. The second is that of the dream interpreter, whether an individual or the community, who can see that the sign in the dream – the young man being a feather – is a bad omen. Although this might point to the idea that dream interpretation can be flawed, it is interesting to note that despite this 'flaw' whether or not dreams are portentous is never in question, neither by the young man, the community or Zahou.

The unexpected turn in Zahou's story, that the dreaming 'self' peers from above the head of the warrior who has, in the dream, killed him and likely taken his head as a trophy – the feather being the public symbol of this achievement – draws out the notion of 'self' as a phenomenon closely linked to the Angami concept of *ruopfü*. The feather does not just represent, symbolically, the young man's departed spirit, but the dream reveals where his spirit went – his *ruopfü* has taken the form of the feather – as the tiger-man takes the form of the tiger and sees the world from that perspective.

As I have touched on earlier in the book, the Angamis describe *ruopfü* as one's spirit, soul or spirit-being, and thus integral life-source, linked to feeling and emotion, as well as to ways of relating to other beings – human, and non-human. One informant, Senyü, suggested to me that 'ruopfü and nature are one', a notion that arose in the midst of a discussion in which the present relationship between humans and nature was understood to be strained or in a state of estrangement. *Ruopfü* is also expressed sometimes as having a mind of its own, of being indifferent with regard to its habitation of the human body. Parents are always mindful of forests, rivers and sacred areas as they are believed to be inhabited by powerful spirits, possibly jealous ancestral spirits, that may 'entice' a child's *ruopfü* to leave the child's body to join them. Children that fall ill after visiting such places are believed to have lost their *ruopfü*. Parents and relatives will travel to the area or home where the child is believed to have been separated from his or her *ruopfü* and the child's name will be called out – indeed also enticed – to return. Everyone will then get into the vehicles they travelled in, and the whole party will proceed slowly back to the house where the child is laying, all the while calling the child's name.

The Angami *ruopfü* closely resembles the notion of *asabeiyang* among the Ngaing of Papua New Guinea, especially the idea that it possesses a volition of its own. Kempf and Hermann, for example, illustrate that the *asabeiyang*

> possesses the ability, under certain conditions, to leave a person's body and to lead an independent existence. But even during a person's lifetime, the asabeiyang can detach itself from the body in certain situations and move as a partial self. This can happen, for instance, when a person falls seriously ill or is sleeping deeply and dreaming. Should a sick person happen to lose consciousness, this would clearly signal that his or her spirit-being had departed.
>
> (2003, p. 64)

Like the *ruopfü*, the *asabeiyang* is the source of a person's bodily vitality, and if, for example, a person does not wake from sleep when relatives first try to call him or her, there would be concerns about whether the person's *ruopfü* is outside the body, or indeed lost or perhaps trapped in a bad place having travelled there in a dream. If indeed a person is deemed to have lost their *ruopfü*, they are certain the person will fall ill, or worse. More often than not, relatives will gently call the person's name repeatedly in an effort to reunite what are seen as two halves of the person. If the person falls ill, the family will follow the same consultation route as with an ominous dream.

In dreaming, the Ngaing *asabeiyang* and Angami *ruopfü*, as a partial self of the person, enter the dream and may oscillate between the first-person perspective – 'I' or 'Ego' – and the observed third person, and thus perform the reflexive role of the person as though a performance of one's 'selves' within the dream. It remains unclear, however, how the *ruopfü* as a partial 'self' relates to mental processes. How is the *ruopfü* tethered to the mind and to thinking? Some informants have suggested that *ruopfü* guides, or indicates, direction. When a person ignores this guidance he or she 'knows it' or 'feels it' because it moves contrary to the desires of the *ruopfü*. Within dreams, this independent volition is made more clear through the way the *ruopfü* travels, encounters and relates to other entities, and often the *ruopfüs* of other dreamers. There are, again, significant parallels here with the Ngaing *asabeiyang*. Kempf and Hermann suggest that, as it travels in the dream, the *asabeiyang* meets familiar and unfamiliar persons. However,

> those encountered are naturally not the persons themselves but once again their spirit beings (cf. Stephen 1989, p. 167). When living persons are encountered, these are their dream selves; but when they are already deceased, these are their persisting spirit beings. Dream experiences therefore constitute a way of encountering spirit beings of the deceased, that is, the ancestors.
>
> (Kempf and Hermann 2003, p. 64)

What is clear is that the *ruopfü*, as with the Ngaing *asabeiyang* and similar notions described in ethnographies elsewhere (cf. Stephen 1989; Lawrence 1965), meet and encounter other spirit entities both in dreaming and in waketime without necessarily the mediation, intervention or knowledge of the conscious, thinking person. That said, there are individuals who can consciously engage in a form of 'soul-flight'. These kinds of experiences, often associated with the capacities of traditional healers, are also conducted in conjunction with healing practices. Here, the searching for a lost soul and re-possession of the soul in the sick person is described in terms of dreams and dreaming and is posited regularly as occurring within a 'dream-state'. Before developing this further, there is yet another set of experiences that merit a brief mention.

A person's dream 'self', *ruopfü* or *asabeiyang* may also encounter a host of other entities, namely 'powerful beings known from narratives of myth, trance, or dream. Like the ancestors, they too are frequently associated with sites of power' (Kempf and Hermann 2003, p. 64). This description of the Ngaing cosmology resonates with that of the Angami, and in many ways the master spirits, or spirit guardians of the forests, rivers and mountains in the region, are considered great powers, and encounters are to be avoided. In Naga folklore and mythology, they are anthropomorphised, and the contest with such powers is described in terms of great human feats. Generally, this universe is divided into specific naturally delineated domains never to be disturbed. Indeed, an exploration into the notion of sociality among spirit beings would reveal important insights regarding the ways in which humans – 'possessed' by *ruopfü* – share attributes or gain proximity to the supernatural world and supernatural volition. But what can be said about the agential capacities of *ruopfü* apart from individual human consciousness? To what extent does *ruopfü* act on its own accord? Can a person's *ruopfü* join or collect with other *ruopfüs*? Can they intervene in human affairs? I attempt to deal with these questions in this remainder of the chapter.

Anthropologists drawing from, but ultimately inverting, Levi-Straussian ideas concerning the binary relationship between culture and nature have drawn out the notion of multiple natures or worlds. Most notable are Amazonian perspectivism as articulated by Viveiros de Castro (1998, 2002a, 2002b, 2002c, 2004), and animism as revisited by Bird-David and Descola (Bird-David 1999; Descola 1994, 1996, 2004, 2009). More precisely, they attempt to show that among humans and non-humans there is a common subjectivity. Bird-David suggests this is a corrective to earlier notions regarding structural processes of human socialisation, as 'maintaining relationships with . . . other local beings is critical to maintaining . . . personhood' (1999, p. S73, cited in Poirier 2003, p. 110).

Terry Turner (2009) has argued that the responses to structuralism have been unable to discard the problematic nature-culture dichotomy. In his critique of Viveiros de Castro's 'perspectivism', Turner re-examines a series of Amazonian myths used by de Castro. Turner indicates a series of what he sees as misinterpretations of Amazonian ideas of human and non-human 'being' that have led to a privileging of anthropocentrism, complicating the relationship between bodies as vessels and identity. He questions, for example, whether animals could ever reconcile their 'human' person with their non-human bodies? Turner's central question revolves around how these bodily forms or 'envelopes' relate to and ultimately shape personhood. Furthermore, persons – whether human or non-human – must also be able to recognise the difference in bodily appearance among their own kind and outside their species. Turner suggests the internal contradictions associated with privileging the human perspective are confusing and ultimately misrepresents the various Amazonian ontological concepts it is grounded in. Turner then turns to Descola and Bird-David's recasting of Tylor's 'animism' and argues that these offer a more constructive approach – though there is a need to be especially mindful of what he terms 'bodiliness' as it relates to forming 'inner subjective identity' (Turner 2009, p. 31), namely, one's bodily form, shape, size, etc. . . ., greatly influences the person's (human or non-human) relational capacities, disposition and thus subjectivity in relation to the world. He draws on the Amazonian Kayapo notion of a 'generic identity of spirit' dwelling in different bodily forms – human, non-human, animate and in some instances inanimate bodies (ibid., p. 35). At the centre of Turner's thesis is the notion of bodily transformation through productive activity, through social relations, and the integrative relationship between bodily form and its content. Turner asserts that

> conceiving the body. . . [as] a series of transformations opens a perspective on bodiliness as a process of interaction of the physical body, social body and person, stimulated and guided by relations with other embodied actors filtered and regulated by formal treatments of their bodily surfaces ('social skins'). This process of producing subjective perspective and objectified bodily form, drawing upon the natural bodily content of senses and powers, goes through a series of stages but it ultimately enters a terminal stage of deobjectification as the natural content of bodily powers weakens to the point where it cannot sustain its integration within the frame of personal identity and social form. The dissolution of form and content continues through the physical dissolution of death and the separate disintegration of spirit and body.
>
> (Turner 2009, p. 36)

Here, 'bodiliness' describes the process of integration and disintegration between what appears as an ageless spirit and an ageing body – which is continuously transformed through social interaction, and through work – which then gradually fades in its capacity to shift, modify and deploy its various identity agencies in social relations. Following the Kayapo, the spirit remains somewhat ambivalent to the life routines, and perhaps there are important parallels to be made with the Angami *ruopfü* in this regard. However, Turner is vague about the possibility of spirit estrangement from the body during the normal course of human life, or synchronous to the life-cycle sequence of 'bodiliness' transformation he describes, beginning in birth and ending through death and disintegration. There is also no mention of multiple 'bodilinesses' following the idea that human souls can enter other bodies. The Angami generally articulate the notion of 'unattached-ness' of the *ruopfü* from the body, and in some respects, they detail its shifting out of and into multiple dwellings as both a mode of experience and a general human predisposition (or susceptibility). The importance of this 'unattached-ness' for our discussion is that it is a significant mode of experience informing local understandings of the person, and the variable 'untethered-ness' of the person's *ruopfü* to a single bodily form, and in some instances the notion that it may dwell in forms outside of consciousness, and reveal itself in dreams as a separate conscious 'self' altogether, as it did in the young warrior's dream. Turner's bodiliness thesis offers important insights into the relationship we are seeking to develop between *ruopfü* and embodiment insofar as he emphasises the ways in which material conditions and activities of the person ultimately give shape to the 'forms' he speaks of. The problem here, however, concerns passiveness and volition, if indeed we are to draw parallels between Turner's 'forms' and *ruopfü*. The agential qualities Turner attributes to 'bodiliness' are suggestive but not clearly articulated, and do not resolve the ambiguities of conscious volition – of the 'I' or 'Ego' in relation to *ruopfü* – arising from the notion of the passivity in 'forms'. He suggests, for example, that

> the forms of things immanently contain the agency or power to produce themselves, through the transformation of their own contents. The forms of things, in other words, are actually embodied processes of formation, or the potential capacity and templates for them. They contain the agency or force that impels the content of things to assume the specific characteristics and behavioural patterns proper to their species or kind.
>
> (Turner 2009, p. 34)

Here the value of 'immanence' and of the 'embodied processes of formation' are perhaps the most important contributions of Turner's thesis for our study, and as we discuss the nature of inter-corporeality, namely the connectedness of *ruopfü* to other *ruopfüs* and to what is articulated as a more all-encompassing, perhaps transcendent *Ruopfü*, we can draw on these ideas in understanding the character of their correspondence.

In the following section I explore this notion of inter-corporeal correspondence at the level of the *ruopfü* (as opposed to the level of the 'I' or 'Ego'), and how this relates to consciousness through the notion of 'reversibility'.

Ruopfü and the tiger-man

The enigmatic relationship in Angami articulations of *ruopfü* between, on one hand, an individual's *ruopfü* and other human and non-human *ruopfüs* and *Ruopfü* as 'supernature', and on the other hand, between these generally unconscious relations and human waketime consciousness are all dimensions that draw significant parallels with work of Merleau-Ponty, beginning with his concept of the pre-conceptual body-subject as developed in *Phenomenology of Perception* (1945). He suggests, for example, that the notion of 'being', as it relates to the human stance or condition in relation to the world, entails an outward extension of the body into the world, a field of relatedness that precedes our consciousness of it. It points towards the possibility that human beings can apprehend the 'other' because the 'other' or 'otherness' simultaneously apprehends human 'being'. As David Morris states:

> our passive openness to unified things is crucial to the coherence of our activity and body; dislocations and ruptures in the world dislocate and rupture us. The body inheres in the world. But this does not simply mean that the body is stuck, inherent, in some outside, alien domain, it means that the worldly domain inheres, participates, in the body and perception.
>
> (2010, p. 13)

Merleau-Ponty (1945) establishes his contrasting position to other philosophers (and to his principal influences, Husserl and Heidegger) with his insistence that the primary site of knowing the world is not consciousness but the body, or what he calls the 'body-subject' (ibid.). Though he maintains his notion of the pre-conceptual perceiving body at a more or less 'conceptual' level largely to differentiate himself from classical epistemology early in his career, later in life he takes a decisive step towards making ontological claims regarding his main ideas about 'body-subject' or 'flesh', and this is apparent in his unfinished *The Visible and the Invisible* (1964b). Here, he develops a more encompassing vision of human perception and experience, and dreams form an important part of this late development in his thinking. 'Reversibility' is one of the key concepts he develops to describe the inherence of corporeity-consciousness in perception, the 'body-subject' being something that Merleau-Ponty describes as having an intentionality of its own and a permanent 'openness' to the world (Merleau-Ponty 1964b).

The concept of reversibility is salient in relation to this book because it speaks to a series of issues that emerged throughout my ethnography challenging the passiveness of 'passivity', and the activeness of 'activity' in dreams and dreaming. This arises particularly when documenting the dream narratives of persons that describe their dreams as, on one hand, events in which they are passive participants in the dream plot, and on the other, dream-events in which they consciously interact with other dream-subjects, and breach the personalised universe of dreaming into a kind of 'invisible real', finding direct correspondence between what is dreamed and the events of waking reality.

In order to illustrate the ways in which these 'specialist practitioners' relate to the broader Angami cosmology and belief system, I will illustrate the ways in the *tekhumiavi* (man in the shape of a tiger) exemplifies the relationship between the *ruopfü* – a person's spirit, soul or life-being – and the animate landscape often described in folklore and which also features in dream narratives.

J.H. Hutton, the first to describe the Naga *tekhumiavi* at length (especially 1920 and 1921b), suggests Naga concepts and beliefs about the *tekhumiavi* are unique in the region, but also notes they closely resemble Meso-American *nahualism*, a practice among some Mexican indigenous communities in which men sleep, and in their dreams inhabit jaguars, often to guard crops and settlements and at one time for war. As with *nahualism* in the Americas, re-imaginings, embellishments and circulation of the myth of the *tekhumiavi* in contemporary urban legends and folk-tales sustains its popular fascination. Few among the younger generations in Kohima know it was once a more widespread practice and belief, and, even fewer, that it may be still practised in some areas of Nagaland today.[1] Preliminary research on the subject of tiger transformation may be found throughout Southeast Asia, with some of the most detailed ethnographic work on the subject focused on Malaysia and Indonesia (see Bakels 1994; Boomgaard 1994; Endicott 1979; Wessing 1986). In November 2009 I interviewed Dr Gam Shae, a Baptist missionary who was serving in Banjarmasin, the provincial capital of Kalimantan, Indonesia in 1998 when he witnessed a very peculiar event in his own home. A guest student, Henry,

> was on the floor again growling, gnashing his teeth, clawing the floor, resisting anyone who restrained him with super human strength. Henry did not know what transpired during this type of experience. But he knew that all of his friends became afraid of him and rejected him. As a member of his own cultural group, he shared with his friends the understanding that he was under the influence of a power outside of himself. He believed that he was possessed by the spirit of his ancestor called the tiger spirit. Furthermore, he was told by his relatives that whenever he was possessed by that spirit, he would become lucky. So while it was a frightening experience for his friends, he looked upon it as a positive experience that would bring fortune.

In Northeast India, the phenomenon has been recorded among a variety of large indigenous groups and sub-groups including the Khasis, Garos, Chins and Nagas. Instructive for this inquiry is that the widespread practice of human spirit possession of non-human animals found among these groups and in the wider Southeast Asian region is accompanied by myriad creation myths giving reverence to, and reflecting both a fascination and an affinity with, powerful feline predators such as leopards and tigers (see Abbot and Thant 2000; Elwin 1958, 1970; Norbu 1999). An ancient Ao (another Naga tribe) myth reflects this:

> [. . .] in the beginning of the earth there was no distinction between light and darkness [and] men and animals lived together in perfect understanding and

harmony [. . .] [thus the spread of] tales of girls being 'married' to tigers and lovely maidens having trees as lovers.

(Ao 1999, pp. 65–66)

Similar myths of origin are found among Native Americans in Amazonia (see for example Kohn 2007; Viveiros de Castro 1998) and among the Inuit of Alaska, whose traditions 'describe an early period when all animals and humans lived in the same community, speaking the same language, frequently changing appearance, and intermarrying' (Willis 2006, p. 31). Students of mythology would perhaps find these passages unremarkable, and indeed in nearly every way they adhere to universal ideas and symbols found in creation myths throughout the world (e.g. Lévi-Strauss 1964–1971). Yet the metaphorical quality typically associated with such origin myths is unsettled by accounts documented by ethnographers that are more consistent with the literal approach found in local understandings. Illustrative of this are ethnographies detailing the meticulous regulation of various food-related taboos, hunting practices and other rituals invested in the notion of a common kinship between humans, non-human animals (specifically tigers or leopards) and spirits. Hutton, for instance, writes:

When an Angami village kills a tiger or a leopard the Kemovo (priest or elder) proclaims a non-working day for the death of an 'elder brother'. The flesh of tigers and leopards is often eaten by Angamis (men only and under certain restrictions), that of leopards (never of tiger) by the Changs, but the Sema would not dream of eating either. It is absolutely genna (taboo) to touch it, and most Sema villages, if they kill a tiger or a leopard, leave the body to rot where it lies, though the head may be taken and brought back to the village. The fear of the tiger among all Nagas is considerable, and all regard them as beings apart from the ordinary wild animals and very nearly connected with the human race. Thus a man who is descended from one who was killed by a tiger will not eat meat from a tiger's kill, as it would be equivalent to sharing the dish of a hereditary enemy.

(Hutton 1921a, p. 208)

Ao suggests that this belief in the common kinship between humans and non-human animals extends to the notion of soul co-essence, and that this is a significant idea governing Naga ontology, namely 'the human soul can reside in forms other than the human' (1999, p. 66). Julian Jacobs, citing W.G. Archer, records the words of a Sangtam Naga *tekhumiavi* describing the process as a shifting of the soul between the human body and that of the animal:

My soul does not live in my body. It lives in the leopard. It is not in me now. It visits me in sleep. I meet it in dreams. Then I know what it [sic] has been doing . . . If anything happened to my leopard in the day, my soul would come and tell me. I would get the same wounds.

(Jacobs 1998, pp. 85–86)

The person in the time of transformation is engaged in a kind of soul-transfer with an animal, where the man's body remains untransformed, and the man's spirit or soul is channelled in a sort of deep dream state and becomes fully engaged in the actions of the animal. The body of the man (who may be lying in bed at home) moves convulsively and shifts around as the tiger or leopard moves about in the forests or fields outside. Entering the tiger or leopard during sleep, the soul usually returns to the human body with daylight. But if, for example, it were to remain in the non-human animal for a period of days, the human body, although conscious, would be weak and lethargic. Hutton states that

> during sleep the soul is the leopard with its full faculties, but when the human body is awake the soul is only semiconsciously, if at all, aware of its doings as a leopard, unless under the influence of some violent emotion, such as fear, experienced by the leopard.
>
> (1921b, p. 202)

According to Hutton, *tekhumiavi* possessions were often accompanied by swelling and severe pain in the knee and elbow joints, as well as pain in the small of the back, depending on the level of activity of the tiger or leopard (1921b, p. 202).

Regarding the acquisition of this unique ability, most accounts suggest it happens at an early age. Detailing the Sumi Naga (another tribe) beliefs on the subject, Hutton's informants suggested that the phenomenon could not be induced by external means, but that it could be acquired through close association with a known *tekhumiavi*. The ability could also be obtained by being fed 'chicken flesh and ginger . . . given in successive collections of six, five and three pieces of each together on crossed pieces of plantain leaf' by a *tekhumiavi* (1921b, p. 201). Among the Ao Nagas, the belief is that the ability can be inherited from either the paternal or maternal lines, though a generation gap may occur in the line of succession. In addition, multiple family members of the same generation with a tiger-spirit are not known to exist or to have existed. Inherited or non-inherited, predestination is necessary and those possessing a tiger-spirit can discern if others are also predestined to receive the 'gift' (Sutter 2008, p. 280). Still others suggest that the tiger-spirit can also be acquired by appealing to a person who is 'reputed to be in possession of such a power' (Ao 1999, p. 67). Ao writes that 'if the applicant's prayer is to be granted, he will be offered a cup of wine or pipe to smoke by the person to whom he has appealed' (1999, p. 67).

Descriptions of the world that the *tekhumiavi* navigates in tiger form are rare. Though there is a considerable gap in anthropological research in the Naga-inhabited areas from the 1940s through the 1990s due to the Indo-Naga War, recent fieldwork on the subject (most notably Ao 1999; Longchar and Vashum 1998; Longchar and Davis 1999; Longchar 2000; Sutter 2008) demonstrates striking similarities between current and early descriptions of the tiger-spirit world (particularly Hutton 1920, 1921a, 1921b, 1931, 1942; Mills 1922; Smith 1925). Descriptions offer considerable detail; namely, that it is organised in ways that resemble human social structures. Non-human animals in this domain are social beings – with societies, political structures and specifically designated duties – the distribution of which is based on a stratified system of ranks. Informants who have participated in this world in their transformed tiger forms describe the existence of tiger conferences, tiger battalions and companies with rules and laws – all dictated and enforced by a 'council of tigers':

> On 5th August we used to have a conference, after the harvest . . . every year. [. . .] Piyong Tenem is near the Dikhu riverbank. There is one waterfall, a very big one. This is the place. [. . .] There are also seasons . . . We use to decide in full moon nights. During full moon we hold our meetings. [. . .] And then what kind of animals we can take – all these things are discussed. We have to divide the animals among ourselves. [. . .] And then, there is also a discussion about the fields of the farmers. We have a system. We will discuss about the farmers. Whether the next harvest will be good or bad – we will decide. If the farmers face water problems, we will call the water. [. . .] But if they are in bad luck, they use [sic] to face problems from us [sic]. Means: It depends upon the mood of the Water God.
>
> (Sutter 2008, p. 272)

The laws set forth by this underworld encompass a wide range of activities for the tiger-men, including a prescribed diet. The spirit guardians indicate which animals can be hunted, and as different spirits have 'ownership' of different areas of the forest, mountain and rivers, they must be consulted before a kill (Sutter 2008, pp. 272–273). Besides the arduous tasks demanded by the 'council of tigers', and the demands of the spirits, interviewees also described a lighter side. Sutter writes:

> [It is] a complete tiger world in which they, as tigers, make jokes, fight, marry and sometimes even have families. The Ao tiger-man from Khensa even sang a song in a fictive language, which male and female tigers sing out loud in call and response form: 'Every time we meet, the male tigers used to hold their daos and then they sing: Ejem tachu yula, ejem tachu yula and the females will respond to them: Ankangkang raksha wai, ankangkang raksha wai'.
>
> (2008, p. 285)

Tekhumiavi would often spend days at a time in their darkened homes, asleep and engaged in soul travel, living and interacting with other spirits through the bodies of animals which may be hundreds of kilometres away.

As touched on earlier, Eduardo Viveiros de Castro's 'perspectivism' thesis (1998) draws from similar findings among Amazonian indigenous peoples. In these perspectival ontologies, animals and spirits are anthropomorphic, and though masked by bodily 'skins', like humans they are socially organised and possess agency. Similarly, Bird-David (1999) in her efforts to recast the term 'animism', develops the idea of 'relational epistemologies' wherein human beings co-inhabit the world alongside other people, some of whom may not be human. This recalls our earlier discussion regarding human and non-human animal kinship in the creation myths of the different Naga groups. Notions of personhood, therefore, are developed by human and non-human beings through shared, embodied interactions and seem to be maintained in relation to each other.

We might view this nature-culture continuum as necessitating a transfer of knowledge between the two, and this is usually done by mediums – individuals endowed with abilities that enable them to see the continuum and provide necessary insight to those that have greater difficulty with such perception. Oral tradition, of course, is just as important in this transfer of knowledge as the practices of skilled or gifted individuals (healers, shamans, mediums, etc.), and folk-tales and myths shared among community learners deliver a tried-and-tested classification system for carefully discerning the multitude of visible and invisible signs and actants one encounters. It is believed that a map of this vast hidden domain and a prescribed set of behaviours and rituals one must adhere to are necessary in order to traverse the terrain without provoking disequilibrium and ultimately bringing misfortune on a community.

The *tekhumiavi* phenomenon necessarily situates the *ruopfü* in the 'front seat' so-to-speak, in a give and take underworld of exchange between humans (represented by the *ruopfü* – inhabited tiger and non-human spirits that hold dominion over certain areas of the forest). Interestingly, human spirits, animal spirits and other spirits all share sufficient attributes to be partners in this exchange. Important parallels can be drawn with the 'hunting shamanism' of Siberia as described by Hamayon (1996, pp. 78–80), namely 'human actions (obtaining good luck and then killing game) must occur in the framework of an exchange relationship and must be balanced by a compensation' (ibid., p. 79). Taking on the role of mediator, the *tekhumiavi* acts as mediator between two worlds and inhabits two worlds. But may we satisfactorily classify this world as 'real'? Can it be satisfactorily classified as 'dreamed'? Both these classifications prove unsatisfactory, and yet both worlds are inhabited by the conscious *ruopfü*, while, in any case, the person's body must remain more or less immobile.

Following Charles Peirce's 'iconic' and 'indexical' categories (chapter 2), I am claiming that the different kinds of experiences of specialists such as the *tekhumiavi*, the tiger-man and, as I discuss in the next section, *mhorüvemia*, or dream traveller, can be plotted along a continuum, allowing us to engage a broader set of dream and dream-like experiences employing the same categories.

Mhorüvemia dreaming

Mhorüvemia – or 'dream traveller' – describes the experiences of a handful of my informants, and I include some of the more detail-rich narratives of Senyü in order to illustrate the ways in which the *ruopfü* as dream 'self' resembles the movement of the *ruopfü*-inhabited tiger. Moreover, as will be made clear, dream symbols (indexical) and vivid dream experiences (iconic) are not mutually exclusive, but can be experienced by the same person and sometimes simultaneously.

The experiences I will detail in this section were shared by several of my informants and form, in some sense, a middle way between shamanic gifts, including the practices and experiences of the *tekhumiavi*, and the normal everyday dreams typical in community life. It must nevertheless be stated, that gifted dreamers do exist in small numbers, and are usually well known in their communities. The first that I came across was a woman, a 'prophetess', working in the local Baptist Revival Church. The other four were men, two of whom were healers, one claiming to have a leopard spirit living nearby in the forest. This particular healer lived in a village several hours east of Kohima, and I met him while accompanying a medical team for a weeklong visit. The third was a college student in Wokha (a town several hours north of Kohima), who, according to close relatives, had raised a man from the dead by rushing home to sleep, and subsequently pursuing in his dreams the wandering soul of the dead man and successfully enticing it to come back. The young man awoke, rushed to the old man's house, and 'woke' the old man up – to the astonishment of the gathering family. The fourth, Senyü, a software developer and architect in Kohima, gave me the most detailed dream accounts, and I include these in this chapter (and in chapter 6 in the discussion on space and landscape).

Senyü was consulted regularly by close friends, and sometimes his employees approached him regarding their dream experiences. My interview with Senyü was set up by one of my research assistants and was held in the second-floor dining room at his office in Kohima town. It is a busy place with about a dozen computer stations and as many employees – Nagas from various parts of Nagaland and mostly in their 20s – busily shifting through symbols and icons on their screens, entering lines of code, and creating a cacophony of mouse-clicks. Senyü knelt by one of the younger female web developers sitting by the entrance, and in pencil marked out tiny corrections on a printout – 'this line of code is separate so that this command is not obstructed' – while a second employee waited patiently in the doorway.

Senyü tells me that when he was growing up with his mother and brother they spent a lot of time listening to elders telling their dreams. 'They were stories to us – like storybook fantasies, we loved to hear them'. It wasn't until he was a teenager that he began to take dreams and dream signs more seriously.

> If I see dogs it translates to relationships with girls, or something with the opposite sex. Snakes would translate to enemies. If I see meat, or see myself eating it means bad health. If I see ceilings it means prayer – I need to spend more time in contemplative prayer. If I see walls it has something to do with the future – challenges that will affect my future. If I see schools – schools are very important. When I see myself going back to school and studying or trying to give an exam, for the next one month there will be a test, and I have to be really prepared. If I see the police, these are about events in the next few days I should avoid. It might be a party, but whenever I see police in my dreams, if people call me to a party, I have to avoid it.
>
> 'Really? Even now?' (me)
>
> 'Yes, even now.'
>
> 'What happens if you ignore your dream?' (my assistant)
>
> I'll go there and get too drunk, or I'll just mess up everything. And if I dream of our underground militant terrorists, it will be something that comes

to me, like some situations that I can't avoid, it will come and hit me. If I see certain people, based on my reading of those people, it may not be exactly about that person, but someone similar. If I see friends that have passed over, it's because they have a warning, they have come to warn me.

One interesting aspect of his work at the firm is that he has found a need to engage in a kind of spiritual mediation when dealing with 'cursed' land upon which he is asked to build. On one occasion the state government contracted him to design and build a structure about ten kilometres northwest of Kohima along the Dimapur road. The roadside land and adjacent fields were remote and not claimed by any village. State officials feared that the Indian Army would try to use the land if there was no presence there. They also knew, however, that it was 'cursed', that it was indeed inhabited but by spirits, and that Senyü would need to negotiate with the spirits before he could build anything.

Senyü sent three of his employees down to camp by the road and instructed them to watch the land until they could construct a permanent roadside structure – a rest-house for travellers. On the first night, however, the men had trouble sleeping, and they refused to stay a second night.

The spirits were relentless in harassing the guys. The place was clearly cursed, and with voices hollering and ghosts marching up and down the field wielding their daos – I can't imagine anyone being able to sleep no matter how brave. So I had to go down to check it out and see what I could do.

Senyü says he went down to try to deal with the issue by speaking with the spirits in his dreams. At around three or four in the morning he says his dream-self can wake up and move, and he can roam around his room, go outside and see the world with different eyes. While at the camp, in his dream, he walked along the perimeter until he came to a fence. On the other side was a small terraced field with several farmers tilling the soil. He spoke to them about the land, and they agreed that if he respected that field and did not cross the fence, he could build a structure by the road. When he woke up he walked the perimeter and prayed Christian prayers that the land would not be haunted or cursed by evil spirits. Senyü says it worked, and as the spirits no longer tormented the three men, they were able to continue with the surveying and construction.

About mid-way through the interview, Senyü calls someone downstairs to make tea for us. 'I actually didn't grow up here, but was brought up with my mother and brother in Dimapur, near the airport'. He mentions having a dream a few years back where a nurse had told him that his land in Dimapur was once used to set up a makeshift field-hospital next to the air-strip to receive casualties coming down the mountain from Kohima.

One time I dreamt that a young British soldier came and requested me to dig a portion of my land saying that there was something buried there. It was something like a pendant or a necklace. He narrated a story where he said that he was going back to England with a promise to return some items from two friends whom he had promised. These two friends passed away in Kohima. In my dream he told me that, on reaching Dimapur he fell sick and passed away and that those items were buried in my land.

In the dream, the soldier took Senyü to a section of his own field and pointed to a spot where the items were buried. Senyü ignored the dream for many years, but it was a recurring dream, and he began to suspect that perhaps it was a spirit. One morning he woke up and decided to see if there really was something to it.

I sent my boys to dig and surely they found some rusted grenades, some metal pieces, pieces of bones and a small jeep piston. Now my boys sent the piston to me and that night I got a second dream. There was this young boy maybe 17 years or slightly more who said that the piston came from his vehicle and he went on to explain his interest in design. He told me that he had been designing a vehicle that can run on compressed air. It consists of three cylinders of compressed air below the seat. One is attached to the suspension and also the seat mechanism by a hydraulic method so that as the vehicle moves, all the vibration is converted to mechanical energy to charge the compressed air tank. The second tank runs the vehicle and the third is kept as reserve. He told me his design developed a problem because the mechanism under the seat raised the level of the seat too much and that the centre of gravity of the vehicle was too high. He asked me to improve the design.

Senyü's boys did not, however, manage to recover a pendant. The grenades they found raised safety concerns, as similar discoveries in and around Kohima – especially by small children – had ended in horrific tragedy. He told them not to dig further until he could excavate safely. Similar encounters he has had over the years have involved other ghosts, including a Japanese soldier 'who wants to be buried again with a proper headstone', and visitations by his own grandmother whom he calls 'my guardian spirit'.

The reversibility of *ruopfü*

In Senyü's accounts, there is correspondence between different modes of dream experience. At the beginning of the interview he details the ways in which signs appearing in dreams correspond with impending realities, as if appearing to warn him. If he ignores the signs, he then potentially faces the consequences. In subsequent accounts, there is a move from passive observance, to conscious activism within his dreams. These two modes of experience, which echo the two accounts Hutton details in his correspondence with Seligman, blur a series of assumed binaries separating dream experience from experiences typically associated with shamanic-like abilities. Here waketime and sleeptime, real and imaginary, bleed one into the other. These are indeed fields of correspondence, and Senyü's dream-subject and his *ruopfü* are one-in-the-same, able to remain passive in one instance, and in another, consciously interact with other spirits that appear to him. What do we make of this blurring of trans-temporal, inter-corporeal experience?

We can speak of a form of inter-corporeal sociality at the level of the *ruopfü* in examining the ways in which human and other spirits relate to each other, which, at any rate, is an ongoing activity for which there is little conscious awareness. We can understand how this works by drawing on Merleau-Ponty's concept of *chiasm* or 'flesh' and in many respects on Levinas' late conceptualisations of *trace*,[2] both of which speak of a sub-level, of the work of the unconscious in spite of the 'I' or 'Ego'. Exploring these questions can give us further insights into the function of *ruopfü* in dreamtime, particularly as the notion of a form of intentional relationality between one's dream-self with other 'selves' is regularly registered in dream narratives. Interestingly, Merleau-Ponty draws a great deal from Freud. In particular, he draws on his notion of the unconscious and develops his ideas of the body-subject, or *flesh*, by freeing the unconscious from the confines of deep psychic interiority, and placing it as a kind of perceptual organ. This move enables him to articulate the activities of memory sorting and immanence, of making sense of the ubiquity of dreams and outward-directed precognitive perception, employing the singular concept of the *flesh*. He writes, for example,

> The dream is begun by that which, in us, receives events and classifies them relative to our acquired intersubjective dimensions – [there is therefore] a thin thread of oneirism in all awakened life – 'this shadow', this germinative production . . . of my psychic life . . . this automatism that moves in me, this is 'the unconscious'.
>
> (Merleau-Ponty 2003, p. 208)

Here, Merleau-Ponty follows Marc Auge in being careful not to immediately equate the dream weaver, so-to-speak, with the dreaming subject. It is clear that dreaming entails a plurality of subjects and is indeed 'inter-subjective'. He then interprets dream symbolism in line with corporeal immanence, indexing this inter-subjectivity, such that it 'consists in corporeity and the relation with the other person [*avec autrui*]' (Merleau-Ponty 2003, p. 205). Indeed, he resists the temptation to isolate the dream, setting it apart from perception, and suggests that '[t]he passage to the dream is not a passage to an absolute nihilation of pure signification. It is the partial functioning of the signifying machine, the living apparatus, *reduced above all to interpersonal relationships*' (emphasis original, ibid., p. 199). In fact, Merleau-Ponty goes to great pains to articulate the continuity between dreaming and waking states. He suggests, for example, that '[t]he dream dissolves in awakened life like the monocular image (the "phantom") in binocular perception' (ibid., p. 198). He continues,

> The relationship imaginary-real is not [between] the empty and the full, the unobservable and the observable, two incomparable universes. . . [it is] entirely as species with a different structure. [I]s the 'visual' thing (the

reflection) 'real'? . . . the 'pre-spatial field' of touching as touching, is it 'real'? . . . It is not unreal. . . [The] fantastic symbolism [of dreams] disappears in the waking consciousness of this symbolism, but . . . its prestige was not simple irreflection; its capacity to represent something else with itself [autre chose avec soi] was not simple impotence.

(Merleau-Ponty 2003, cited in Bergo 2009, p. 49)

Here Merleau-Ponty's insights point to a characterisation of dreaming, as a mode of perception, that resembles the always perceiving nature of the Angami *ruopfü*, but also that dream significations are a form of registering relations with other persons. Indeed, what dreams are suggestive of is the deep-seated ethical predisposition of the human being towards others.

Merleau-Ponty offers an 'anchorage' which would ground these experiences in what Peirce would term the 'indexical' and 'iconic' directional propensities (discussed in the previous chapter) along a singular continuum. Here dreams shift up a scale to one of primary status, alongside conscious awareness in human experience. Merleau-Ponty's notion of *flesh* reflects the idea of 'reversibility', that perception is multi-directional and reciprocal so that dreams are a form of perception as much as waking states are and that each can influence the other. As with the Angami *ruopfü*, 'flesh' is always perceiving, and thus never ceases to be relational and is necessarily transcending waking and sleeping states (Morley 1999; see also Merleau-Ponty 1962b, 1964a, 1964b, 1968, 1969, 1970).

A second argument for employing Merleau-Ponty's concept of 'flesh' is in regards to its 'openness' to the world. We can draw some parallels here with the notion of 'immanence', in which we can speak of past experiences sedimented in the present and embodied in quotidian practices and everyday routines and relationships. Immanence, in this sense, is also open to the inter-corporeality of the *'flesh'*, and thus there can be the continuous indexing of relations with otherness, in addition to the relationship to memories of the past. The multifarious ways in which these sedimentations – past and present – are registered, in all their odd juxtapositions of time, people and places, are perceivable, Merleau-Ponty would argue, only in dreams (Küchler in Ingold 1996, p. 230; see also Bergson 1998 [1907]; Olivier 2005; Deleuze 1991).

Auge's (1999) study of dreaming in relation to spirit possession is also of relevance here. We can bracket the full set of possession-related practices that are significantly elaborated in relation to divinities, ancestral spirits, healing and other practices in many cultures, while accepting the rudimentary logics that appear to parallel Angami spirit-mediated traditional healing (cf. Joshi 2013), as well as the disembodiment and soul-projection illustrated with the example of the tiger-man or *tekhumiavi* (cf. Sutter 2008). I suggest that these experiences are not divorced from the myriad experiences that mirror possession described in dreams, such as in the case of Senyü. Here, it is important to remember that in dreams external actors do seem to exert themselves on the dreaming subject in a way that reflects a form of volition external to the dreamer.

Following Auge, we might say that an aspect of 'reversibility' may be found in the idea that a not altogether familiar self can be constitutive of personhood; in a sense an embodied unfamiliarity or otherness which might take the first-person perspective in the dream, or at least in some way appears before the dreaming subject and takes the form of the dream 'self'. Here the 'self', indeed *ruopfü*, may show an ambivalence to the dreaming subject, and if we follow Auge, resonates in many ways with the 'otherness' identified by spectators in spirit possession:

> For the dreamed subject who acts in the dream is not fully identical to the dreamer (to the dreaming subject) and the possessing power is not completely alien to the person who is possessed (a return will be made). Nor is it totally alien to the spectator to the degree that, in systems where possessing powers are clearly distinguished, the spectator recognises and locates it in relation to other figures of possession.
>
> (1999, p. 32)

In the case of dreams, as well as in possession, the 'selves' that are responsible for the performance of the event are 'intermediary figures' which, not opposed to the person, 'arise rather from a series of transformations' (ibid., p. 33). Beyond the volitional independence of the dream-self, what is also of significance is the capacity of the dream-self to generate a series of relations that exceeds the conscious person, and yet is fundamentally integral to personhood. Put differently, the capacities to relate to other 'selves' at the level of the 'flesh', body-self or *ruopfü* are greater than the relational capacities of the 'I' or 'Ego' in conscious, waking social interaction. Merleau-Ponty's notion of 'flesh', he suggests, can be understood as a 'connective tissue of exterior and interior horizons' (1968, p. 131). David Abram articulates this in the form of an inter-corporeality entailing a kind of reciprocal dependence:

> The Flesh is the mysterious tissue or matrix that underlies and gives rise to both the perceiver and the perceived as interdependent aspects of its own spontaneous activity. It is the reciprocal presence of the sentient in the sensible and of the sensible in the sentient.
>
> (1997, p. 66)

Here, the relationality and indeed interdependence characteristic of this 'connective tissue' is suggestive not only of a kind of 'inter-corporeal' relationality, but of a relationality with an intention independent of the 'I' or 'Ego's awareness. Going from the kind of passivity entailed in perception, towards a kind of 'unconscious intentionality' on the part of the 'flesh' or *ruopfü*, we can now in many respects conceptualise the relationship between *ruopfü* and the broader notion of *Ruopfü* as 'supernature' – or as Senyü suggested '*ruopfü* and nature are one'.

Auge follows Tedlock in acknowledging the importance of drawing out local understandings of 'self' and how these are constitutive of personhood, while also illuminating the relationship between real and imaginary. This is important not because the integral 'selves' of a person may or may not assume the first-person 'I' or 'Ego' simultaneously, but because they can elucidate the nature of symbols and their cultural deployment. This would illustrate a primordial form of pluri-subjective bond within personhood that prefigures intersubjective ethical engagement (Auge 1999, p. 40). Indeed, as Auge suggests,

> On at least three points (the plurality of the self, the non-dualistic conception of the real, the interpretation of the event as a sign and incidentally of the dream as an event) African, Amerindian, Oceanian and other cosmologies provide us with room to reflect on the precise extent to which, whether it be as anthropologies or cosmologies, they correspond to hypotheses which focus on the nature of individual reality and relations between individuals.
>
> (1999, p. 39)

Auge suggests that there is room to reflect on a form of ethics, and indeed a kind of politics that assumes a coextensive kinship with other persons, human and non-humans. The claim here is that the relationship between the subject and 'other' is a precognitive relationship, one that occurs at the level of the deepest being, of *ruopfü*, and indeed that this is an integral characteristic in the broader Angami philosophy of life. Auge's aim is essentially to break down the dualisms that would create undue differentiation at the level of the 'spirit', among different kinds of beings – human spirits, ancestral spirits, animal spirits, spirits of the forest – beings which are in fact ontologically connected by the same 'tissue'. When conceptualising transcendent beings or deities that are of a different order, Auge argues they are indeed different, but not different in nature:

> From the moment when they are individualised and singularised (objects, in a sense, of a work of supplementary symbolisation in relation to pure, diffuse forces and energies, which are identified with a receptacle that is simultaneously specific and reproducible, with a 'fetish', but which nonetheless lack the form and status of a person), those beings which for the sake of convenience we call 'gods' are usually presented by mythologies as ancient men or, at the very least, beings who in ancient times lived on earth.
>
> (1999, pp. 39–40)

Auge thus argues that the logics behind human-divine interaction in possession resemble the experiences of dreaming in significant ways. His aim is certainly to dispense with unhelpful binaries, but he also aims to accentuate the significance of articulating the composite nature, and indeed the plurality of selves within the person. As Merleau-Ponty puts it, dream significations are 'precipitates' of intersubjectivity. This relationality, within and without the person, connects the person with others. Auge's illustrations of possession indicate that this relationality can extend to the spirits of dead ancestors.

Concluding remarks

In the ethnographic section of this chapter, two main dream categories emerge: the first is a form of dream shared by a majority and understood to convey symbolic meaning that can be interpreted and acted upon. The other main category, namely *mhotékezhamia* dreaming, involves conscious volition during the dream. In other words, the dreamer is aware of their own agency, and in particular their ability to gain knowledge through interaction with other conscious entities – dead relatives and in some instances the *ruopfüs* of other dreamers – that appear to them in their dreams. These tendencies along the spectrum of dreaming experience are also found in early anthropological accounts recorded by Hutton in the second decade of the 20th century. Tedlock's call to focus on cross-cultural notions of 'self' has spurred the discussions of this chapter both into a broad spectrum of ideas about the nature of personhood in relation to alterity, but also helped illuminate some underlying object of Angami articulations of *ruopfü*, including the notion of *fluence* which I suggest can aid in articulating the inter-corporeal nature of *ruopfü*, thus laying the theoretical groundwork for 'reversibility' as it is explored in subsequent chapters. In the following chapters, I show how these theoretical ideas inform the quotidian routines of everyday life; become grounds for dispute with church and clan hierarchy; and form the basis for understanding new spatial orders – of clan domains threatened by non-clan outside forces, replicating the distance between village boundaries and threatening outside forces. These ethnographic discussions then culminate with a discussion on the ways in which omens can invade the quotidian public with the oneiric, with the potential to conjure a powerful nostalgia for nationalist resistance.

Notes

1 These accounts are drawn from a series of interviews conducted among mostly teenagers in Kohima in January and February 2013.
2 Here I follow Bertina Bergo in that Levinas' generally esoteric metaphysics in Otherwise than Being, namely his elaboration of Said, Saying, and Il y a concepts, gain clarity when read through the works, especially in Visible and Invisible, of Merleau-Ponty (Bergo 2009).

Bibliography

Abbot, G. and Thant, Han K., 2000, *The Folk Tales of Burma: An Introduction*, Handbuch der Orientalistik III, Volume 11, Leiden, Boston/Köln: Brill.
Abram, David, 1997, *The Spell of the Sensuous: Perception and Language in a More Than Human World*, New York: Vintage Books.
Ao, Temsula, 1999, *Ao-Naga Oral Tradition*, Baroda: Bhasha Publications.
Augé, Marc, 1999, *The War of Dream: Exercises in Ethno-Fiction*, London: Pluto Press.
Bakels, J., 1994, "But His Stripes Remain: On the Symbolism of Tiger in the Oral Tradition of Kerinci, Sumatra", in *Text and Tales: Studies in Oral Tradition*, J. Bakels and J. Oosten, eds., Leiden: Netherlands Research School CNWS, pp. 33–51.
Bergo, Bettina, 2009, "Radical Passivity in Levinas and Merleau-Ponty (Lectures 1954)", in *Radical Passivity*, Benda Hofmeyr, ed., Dordrecht, Germany: Springer, pp. 31–35.

Bergson, Henri, 1998 [1907], 'Introduction' and 'On the Meaning of Life – The Order of Nature and the Form of Intelligence', in *Creative Evolution*, New York: Dover.

Bird-David, N., 1999, "'Animism' Revisited: Personhood, Environment, and Relational Epistemology", *Current Anthropology*, 40(S1), pp. S67–S91.

Boomgaard, P., 1994, "Death to the Tiger! The Development of Tiger and Leopard Rituals in Java, 1605–1906", *South East Asia Research*, 2(2), pp. 141–175.

Deleuze, Gilles, 1991, *Empiricism and Subjectivity: An Essay on Hume's Theory of Human Nature*, New York: Columbia University Press.

Descola, Philippe, 1994, *In the Society of Nature*, Cambridge: Cambridge University Press.

Descola, Philippe, 1996, "Constructing Natures: Symbolic Ecology and Social Practice", in *Nature and Society: Anthropological Perspectives*, Philippe Descola and Gisli Palsson, eds., London: Routledge, pp. 82–102.

Descola, Philippe, 2004, "Le Sauvage Et Le Domestique", *Communications*, 76(1), pp. 17–39.

Descola, Philippe, 2009, "Human Natures", *Social Anthropology*, 17(2), pp. 145–157.

Elwin, V., 1958, *Myths of the North-East Frontier of India, Volume 1*, Shillong: North-East Frontier Agency.

Elwin, V., 1970, *A New Book of Tribal Fiction*, India: North-East Frontier Agency.

Endicott, K., 1979, *Batek Negrito Religion: The World-View and Rituals of a Hunting and Gathering People of Peninsular Malaysia*, Oxford: Clarendon Press.

Hamayon, Roberte, 1996, "Shamanism in Siberia: From Partnership in Supernature to Counter-Power in Society", in *Shamanism, History, and the State*, Nicholas Thomas and Caroline Humphrey, eds., Ann Arbor: University of Michigan Press.

Hutton, J.H., 1920, "Leopard-Men in the Naga Hills", *The Journal of the Royal Anthropological Institute of Great Britain and Ireland*, 50, pp. 41–51.

Hutton, J.H., 1921a, *The Angami Nagas*, London: Palgrave Macmillan.

Hutton, J.H., 1921b, *The Sema Nagas*, London: Palgrave Macmillan.

Hutton, J.H., 1931, "Lycanthropy", *Man in India*, 11, pp. 208–216.

Hutton, J.H., 1942, "Lycanthropy Correspondence", *Folklore*, 53(1), pp. 79–80.

Ingold, Tim, 1996, *Key Debates in Anthropology*, London: Routledge

Jacobs, J., Macfarlane, A., Harrison, S. and Herle, A., 1998, *The Nagas: Hill Peoples of Northeast India: Society, Culture, and the Colonial Encounter*, Bangkok: River Books.

Joshi, V., 2013, *A Matter of Belief: Christianity in Northeast India*, London: Berghahn Books.

Kempf, Wolfgang and Hermann, Elfriede, 2003, "Dreamscapes: Transcending the Local in Initiation Rites among the Ngaing of Papua New Guinea", in Roger Lohmann, ed., *Dream Travelers: Sleep Experiences and Culture in the Western Pacific*, New York: Palgrave Macmillan.

Kohn, E., 2013, *How Forests Think: Toward an Anthropology Beyond the Human*, Berkeley: University of California Press.

Kohn, Eduardo, 2007, "How Dogs Dream: Amazonian Natures and the Politics of Trans-Species Engagement", *American Ethnologist*, 34(1), pp. 3–24.

Küchler, Susanne, 1987, "Malangan: Art and Memory in a Melanesian Society", *Man* (N.S.) 22, pp. 238–255.

Lawrence, Peter, 1965, "The Ngaing of the Rai Coast", in *Gods, Ghosts and Men in Melanesia*, P. Lawrence and M.J. Meggit, eds., Melbourne: Oxford University Press, pp. 198–123.

Lévi-Strauss, C, 1964–1971, *Mythologiques*, 4 vols. Paris: Plon.

Lohmann, Roger Ivar, ed., 2003, *Dream Travelers: Sleep Experiences and Culture in the Western Pacific*, New York: Palgrave Macmillan.

Longchar, Wati and Vashum, Y., 1998, *The Tribal Worldview and Ecology*, Jorhat: Tribal Study Centre.

Longchar, W., 2000, *The Tribal Religious Traditions in North East India: An Introduction*, Jorhat: Eastern Theological College.

Longchar, W. and Davis, L.E., eds., 1999, *Doing Theology With Tribal Resources*. Jorhat: Tribal Study Centre.

Merleau-Ponty, M., 1962a [1927], *Being and Time*, J. Macquarrie and E. Robinson, trans., New York: Harper and Row.

Merleau-Ponty, M., 1962b [1945], *Phenomenology of Perception*, C. Smith, trans., London: Routledge and Kegan Paul.

Merleau-Ponty, M., 1964a [1947], *The Primacy of Perception*, J. Edie, ed., Evanston, IL Northwestern University Press.

Merleau-Ponty, M., 1964b, *Le Visible et l'Invisible*, C. Lefort, ed., Paris: Gallimard.

Merleau-Ponty, M., 1968 [1964], *The Visible and the Invisible*, C. Lofort, ed., A. Lingus, trans., Evanston, IL: Northwestern University Press.

Merleau-Ponty, M., 1969 [1960], "'Preface' to Hesnard's L'oeuvre de Freud", in *The Essential Writings of Merleau-Ponty*, A. Fisher, ed., New York: Harcourt, Brace World.

Merleau-Ponty, M., 1970 [1968], *Themes From the Lectures at the College of France: 1952–1960*, J.O'Neill, trans., Evanston, IL: Northwestern University Press.

Merleau-Ponty, M., 2003, *Nature: Course Notes From the Collége De France*, Evanston, IL: Northwestern University Press

Merleau-Ponty, M., 2006, *The Structure of Behavior*, Pittsburg: Duquesne University Press.

Mills, J. P. 1922. *The Lhota Nagas,* London: Macmillan.

Morley, James, 1999, "The Sleeping Subject: Merleau-Ponty on Dreaming", *Theory and Psychology*, 9(1), pp. 89–101.

Morris, Brian, 2000, *Animals and Ancestors: An Ethnography*, Oxford: Berg Publishers.

Morris, David, 2010, "The Enigma of Reversibility and the Genesis of Sense in Merleau-Ponty", *Continental Philosophy Review*, 43, pp. 141–165.

Norbu, K., 1999, "A Ritual Winter Exorcism in Gnyan Thog Village, Qinghai", *Asian Folklore Studies*, 58, pp. 189–203.

Olivier, Bert, 2005, "Lacan and the Question of the Psychotherapist's Ethical Orientation", *South African Journal of Psychology*, 35(4), pp. 657–683.

Poirier, S., 2003, "'This Is Good Country. We are Good Dreamers': Dreams and Dreaming in the Australian Western Desert', in *Dream Travelers: Sleep Experiences and Culture in the Western Pacific*, Lohmann, Roger (ed.), New York: Palgrave MacMillan.

Smith, W.C., 1925, *The Ao Naga Tribe of Assam: A Study in Ethnology and Sociology*, London: Palgrave Macmillan.

Stephen, Michele, 1989, "Self, the Sacred Other and Autonomous Imagination", in *The Religious Imagination in New Guinea*, Gilbert Herdt and Michele Stephen, ed., New Brunswick, NJ: Rutgers University Press, pp. 41–64.

Sutter, Rebekka, 2008, "Shadows and Tigers: Concepts of Soul and Tiger-Men", in *Naga Identities: Changing Local Cultures in the Northeast of India*, Oppitz, M, eds., Gent: Snoeck Publishers, pp. 275–292.

Tedlock, B., 1992 [1987], *Dreaming: Anthropological and Psychological Interpretations*, Cambridge: Cambridge University Press.

Turner, Terrence, 2009, "The Crisis of Late Structuralism, Perspectivism, and Animism: Rethinking Culture, Nature, Spirit, and Bodiliness", *Tipiti*, 7(1), pp. 3–40.

Viveiros de Castro, Eduardo, 1998, "Cosmological Deixis and Amerindian Perspectivism", *Journal of the Royal Anthropological Institute*, 4(3), pp. 469–488.

Viveiros de Castro, Eduardo, 2002a, *A inconstância da alma selvage (e outros ensaios de antropologia)*, Eduardo Viveiros de Castro, ed., São Paulo: Cosac & Naify.

Viveiros de Castro, Eduardo, 2002b, "Imagens da natureza e da sociedade", in *A inconstância da alma selvage (e outros ensaios de antropologia)*, Eduardo Viveiros de Castro, ed., São Paulo: Cosac & Naify, pp. 317–344.

Viveiros de Castro, Eduardo, 2002c, "Perspectivismo e multinacionalismo na America indígena", in *A inconstância da alma selvage (e outros ensaios de antropologia)*, Eduardo Viveiros de Castro, ed., São Paulo: Cosac & Naify, pp. 345–400.

Viveiros de Castro, Eduardo, 2004, "Perspectival Anthropology and the Method of Controlled Equivocation", *Tipiti*, 2(10), pp. 3–22.

Viveiros de Castro, Eduardo, 2009, *Métaphysiques Cannibales: Lignes D'anthropologie Post-Structurale*, Paris: Presses Universitaires de France.

Wessing, R., 1986, *The Soul of Ambiguity: The Tiger in Southeast Asia*, DeKalb: Northern Illinois University and Center for Southeast Asian Studies.

Willis, Roy, ed., 2006, *World Mythology: The Illustrated Guide*, Oxford: Oxford University Press.

4 The corporeality of dreams

Atsa's body is an omen. Or at least this is how some of her family members put it. When her niece Agu said 'she gets pains in her knees and we get so worried', she was concerned at one level for her aunt's unfortunate ailment. Undoubtedly she has significant pain in her legs and knees and often struggles to walk from her small house to her outdoor kitchen. She also consults a traditional healer on occasion, who comes and speaks with her and gently massages the swelling away. Agu continued: 'When Atsa's knees swell up badly, and she is in great pain, everyone has the sense that someone in the village is going to die'.

In this chapter I posit that waketime and dreamtime omens are indeed corporeal, and as such have substance and are manifestations of the 'body' as conceptualised

Figure 4.1 Atsa's hearth
Source: Author's photo

in the previous chapter with reference to the Angami term *ruopfü*, in light of Merleau-Ponty's *chiasm* thesis. In order to explore reversibility in relation to ordinary lived experience, I now trace the oneiric in quotidian domestic life in and around the kitchen hearth, in light of our explorations of Angami personhood. Corporeality may also be approached as the various 'selves' of personhood 'incarnate' in the world, a condition of experience and of precognitive 'openness' to the world (developed as 'generosity' in Diprose 2012; and 'subjecting the body' in Garcés 2013).

Hearth as materiality of *ruopfü*

The notion of the body as 'being toward the world' (Csordas 2011, p. 139) is helpful in elaborating the 'corporeality' of the Angami concept of *ruopfü* which I will develop in this chapter. In the first instance, corporeality as an aspect of *ruopfü*, indeed as 'self' in dreamtime, although describing something akin to the human soul, is possible because it retains the identity and outline of the 'physical' body in dreamtime experience. When one of my informants (Senyü, introduced in chapter 2) suggested that '*ruopfü* and nature are one' he suggested something akin to 'consubstantiation' of visible and invisible, of physicality and consciousness, and an extension between the particularity of the subjective *ruopfü* and a 'materiality' that is also not differentiated from the natural world – animals, trees, mountains, rivers, all participating in this 'oneness'. So we may say that *ruopfü* shares substance and sense with this animate/inanimate oneness, and is thus able to 'know' or perceive the world. In the sections that follow, I develop this further by organising the discussion around three characteristics of the hearth. I thus suggest that the concept of *ruopfü* as corporeal is consistent with the ethnographic data, and I intentionally employ the term 'hearth' and 'hearthen economy' to firstly turn our attention back to 'material' things (in relation to the last chapter), but more importantly, to define 'hearth' as *ruopfü* extended from the body into the world materially.

Contrasting significantly with lineage group membership, which is primarily concerned with clan security, disallowing the use of clan settlement property by non-clan members, and finding ways to discourage extended stayers, it is important to note that the domestic sphere is oriented in the opposite direction. As the hearth is the primary sphere of food production and labour, it is not automatically coerced, and various techniques of acquiescence and rejection are employed in order to broaden relations beyond the clan domain, where they trade, exchange and negotiate a better price for goods, including the various ingredients necessary to maintain a productive hearth.

Secondly, the hearth is the centre of omen interpretation, whether those omens are observed in waketime or in dreams. The hearth is where they are shared and discussed before they circulate beyond the household. Here new information obtained in dreams can often override the clan laws, and thus is a form of emergent authoritative knowledge that does not necessarily correspond with clan genealogical knowledge. The alternatives that new forms of knowledge and information contribute form a dialectic to the conservatism of patriarchy, and this back-and-forth dynamic plays out daily in community life.

Thirdly, by stating that 'hearth' is *ruopfü* manifested corporeally, or a partial, material manifestation of *ruopfü*, then the notion of openness is broader than material exchange. This 'openness' may be characterised as a disposition towards the world that recognises an existence in which humans share a world in common with other kinds of beings. In this world 'in common' non-clan members, human and non-human, are not at first instance adversaries, but unknown extended kin, as the natural world is also extended kin. Indeed, we might say 'otherness resides within us' (Merleau-Ponty 1969, p. 120), and this openness is encapsulated in the activities going on around the hearth. Moreover, *ruopfü* as hearth is to consider that the relation between the activities of domestic work and the wider world is one of inter-corporeality, it is 'a world in common' (Garcés 2013, p. 11), and what I term the 'hearthen economy' for the duration of the book. This is new territory, in part, because it enables the recognition of *ruopfü* as corporeal and inter-corporeal, but also because it pushes back on the dogma of clan self-sufficiency.

Before turning to the ethnography, I turn very briefly to a few studies that have looked at the 'hearth' as a category meriting attention. Anthropological discussions in the literature on the idea of the 'hearth' suggest it to be a pervasive symbol throughout cultures and antithetical to centralised power, though paradoxically also remaining the hub of food cultivation and production activities in clan life. Indeed, the division between public and domestic social spaces and institutions has been an enduring theme in the anthropological literature, and in many studies (cf. Carsten 1995; Weismantel 1988) the hearth has proven a salient metaphor, particularly in kinship studies, in examining marginality and subjectivity, but more importantly, how these are transformed into forms of agency through an admixture of day-to-day routine, child rearing and creativity in food preparation. The hearth is an intimate hub around which these practices are performed and can index the gendered division of labour that these practices entail. This is particularly true when the hearth is juxtaposed to public spaces which, in most societies, are male dominated and are typically a forum for patrilineal clan members to assert political influence in the community and in relation to outsiders. Women, by extension, are generally not welcome in these spaces, thus articulating further the gendered division in public institutional membership, and participation in community discussion and decision making more generally.

The hearth as a symbol of intimacy and nurturance, and at the same time hospitality to outsiders, is articulated in the work of Janet Carsten (1995, 1997). She offers a more complex picture than the dichotomy portrayed in theories that articulate the hearth in terms of resistance (e.g. Weismantel 1988; Counihan 1999). Here, the symbolic potency of the hearth posits it as a remnant of a fuller (or idealised) pre-industrial significance in relation to labour. It serves as a metaphor for quotidian resistance, elaborated as unsurveilled productive and reproductive labour, unyielding to hierarchical regimes – men, clan, state, corporation – that would seek to coercively control it and extract rent from it. There is much here that resonates with the Angami context, and the archaic Naga notion of females as 'cultivators' and males as 'warriors' contains much truth. Indeed, it is a pattern found replicated in much of the lower Himalayas in and around the Assam plain (see for example Chatterjee 2013).

Moreover, 'the heat of the hearth', writes Carsten, 'is a source of life. The dapur [hearth] and its food sustain those who live together in one house; they are the source of their unity' (1997, p. 56). And the endurance of this life-giving crucible, as creative and indeed as procreative, is not conceived as political, but as generative; historical because it was firstly natural: 'When a new house is established, its hearth must be lit so that cooking can begin. It is mothers who provide their daughters with the means for this to occur. As mothers generate daughters, so dapur generates dapur' (1997, p. 80). In this light, the hearth reflects the ways in which the human body and bodily activity extend outward; the repetitive motions and routine activities endowing the spaces in and around the hearth, and its various stocks and instruments – such as the baskets storing grains, cooking utensils and firewood – with the same generative capacities and qualities one traces in the hands, feet and indeed wombs of mothers, and nurturing practices of other family members.

But, the hearth is physically a very simple thing, and it is a place or indeed more of a 'happening' than it is a thing or place. In other words, as the above sections have suggested, it is 'substantially' more, bringing together more than what appears to be present. It certainly serves a mnemonic purpose, its routines and activities eliciting memories of things, past gatherings, family visits on holidays or persons long lost. But it is also the 'presence' of all of those things *there* and *then*. The phenomenological 'body' that extends outwards into the world can be flipped around to describe the extended 'presenting', the immanence of all these things 'happening' in the ambit of the hearth.

In the following sections I introduce Atsa and her husband Apfutsa, both octogenarians, residing just outside the clan area (see Figure 1.2). Much of this ethnographic material was recorded in conversations over tea – Atsa often preparing tea for me while I worked – and during occasional meals in Atsa's kitchen, some in the early morning and some in the late afternoon.

Atsa's contingency

Atsa's home sits on the northwestern slope of Kohima village, just below one of the many roads crisscrossing the hill. A small room on the southern side at the end of the corridor served as my study space during much of my fieldwork. The small structure which she and her husband rent has sunk down about 12 inches on the downslope side and looks as though it will plummet down the steep 50 ft. cliff with the next heavy rainfall. A detached outhouse is a patchwork of tin roofing scraps wired to a wooden frame and straddles an open ditch that joins a larger canal taking the sewage down towards the national highway.

Atsa's neighbourhood is on Lhisemia clan land (Lhisemia are one of four clans in Kohima village) just below the old American Baptist missionary compound. The large hillside plot was donated in the Indo-Naga peace effort in the early 1970s, becoming the Transit Peace Camp following the Shillong Accord signed between leaders of the Naga National Council and Indian government in 1975. Bounded on all sides by a high fence, the Peace Camp resembles a cloister – a community of Naga Army veterans waiting patiently for India to fulfil its half of the deal. The northwestern slope of Kohima village, and surrounding Atsa and Apfutsa's rented home, is a settlement made up largely of Khonoma villagers, a village higher in the hills 15 miles away. Khonoma is the home of members of Zhapu Phizo's (the first NNC President) *Merhema* clan. Having fled when the Indian Army laid siege to Khonoma village in 1956, the repeated targeting of Phizo's clan members throughout the war dissuaded them from returning to Khonoma.

Atsa, aged 27 at the time of the 1956 siege, was separated from her family in the chaos that ensued and fled south towards Manipur. She, along with a few clan members, lived in the forests on the southern side of the Dzükou valley for several months, receiving food and help from members of a Zeme village just over the Nagaland border. This Zeme village had a long history of aiding refugees from Khonoma, most notably following the infamous 'Battle of Khonoma' in which British-led forces attacked, burned and dispersed the village in 1880 (see chapter 1). Atsa was eventually taken in by a Kuki village in the Senapati district of Manipur where she stayed for several years. After a couple of years, she returned to Kohima in search of her family and found them and many of her fellow clan members living as refugees under the temporary protection of the Lhisemia clan.

I first visited Atsa in early April, just at the start of the heavy winds. She was troubled by a dream she had had a few nights before and shared her dream as she prepared tea. I had come, in part, to mend a window that had shattered in the high winds a few nights before. In the dream all seemed fine at first:

> I could walk like I always have from the house to the kitchen; up and down from Vonuo's kitchen down the hill. But in an instant it felt like everything had changed in my dream. I suddenly could not support my own weight. My knees began to buckle. Apfutsa called me and I couldn't come. I was dragging myself along the floor. When I woke up I found the broken window and that is a very bad sign.

The following morning, Atsa's niece, having heard about the broken window, asked her: 'Who do you think will die now?' In his 80s now, Apfutsa struggled with a lung infection over the winter, and everyone was aware that it might just be his time. Apfutsa is originally from a Rengma Naga community in Manipur and is a former footballer who learned to play from American soldiers while they were stationed in Imphal during World War II. He loved the game and was good enough to play professionally as a left-fielder for the Manipur Eleven in the '50s and '60s – touring the Northeastern states and reaching the championships in Calcutta. This old athlete seemed to weather this most recent storm, and though he had a rough winter, he regained his strength. The sense at that point among Atsa's family and neighbours was that the sign of the broken window – plainly visible to anyone entering the living room – communicated something that had not yet taken place. But what could it be? 'What then', some of the family members were asking, 'will befall Atsa?'

The waketime omen – the shattering of the window – had overshadowed a potentially important, clear message in the dream. Atsa's niece Agu mentioned to me that the dream seemed to be about Atsa herself and probably related to her increasing incapacity to care for Apfutsa, given their age and frailty. Agu's expression was shared by several other family members, the feeling of inevitability of Apfutsa's death. His death was, in many respects, not the tragedy itself – though it certainly was lamentable even though he was now quite elderly. It was because Atsa had lost so many close family members in such a short period of time.

Atsa's knees began to swell a few weeks after her dream, and she now used a walking stick to get around. But her knee problem seemed to be more than an ailment, and indeed there were moments when, having just heard news of someone falling ill or a death in one of the neighbouring clans, she would say something to the effect of 'oh, I felt it in my leg, I knew that someone in that neighbourhood was not good'. In one of our earliest conversations she told the story of her meeting her mother after she had died. The house had been locked, and she and her two sisters, herself in the middle, had gone to bed. It was in the very early morning hours that she heard a sound and awoke to see her mother at the foot of the bed. The ghost reached out and touched her leg, which she felt, and then left the house through the front door. When they were all awake, her sister found that the latch on the front door had been opened at night.

I had difficulty understanding whether she connected the memory of her mother's ghost touching her leg and her present condition. Traditional healers such as the Ao healer she consults for massaging her leg share the common experience of being called by a spirit, in the context of a dream, while in their teenage years. In the dream, they are invited to receive the gift, and if they agree they are tutored in becoming, in a sense, a 'vessel', as the power to heal channels through them. Indeed, Atsa's regular comments regarding her capacity to 'feel' invisible forces, perhaps the flow of spirits now coming to entice living human spirit kin to come with them, the logic accompanying shamanic 'calling' seemed to be at play as well.

Though I encouraged her to consult a doctor, she showed little interest. In a series of side comments, she indicated that she distrusted the shiny new medical facilities in town, the treatments, the confusing pharmaceuticals. She critiqued what she saw as opportunism, as these facilities seemed to pop up out of nowhere in recent years and were expensive. Consulting a physician invariably led to a string of additional expenses, consultations seemed rushed and at times she felt they were too eager to write drug prescriptions for any and all physical discomforts, with little, if any, physical examination. For almost a decade her daughter Roko had complained of severe migraines, and there seemed to be no agreement among the various medical practitioners she visited of what exactly afflicted her. However, they were unanimous in prescribing strong drugs which, in the end, proved fatal. At 47 years of age and caring for five children, Roko was first bedridden and could no longer work. The dialysis treatment she needed for her damaged kidneys was not available locally, so a makeshift bedside system was devised in her home, and her daughter – 10 years old at the time – learned to use a syringe and administer the treatment. Despite her family's best efforts, however, Roko drew her last breath in the summer of 2011.

As with her neighbours clustered around her, Atsa is acutely aware of her precariousness. Roko's father (Roko means 'abundant with luck') was an officer temporarily stationed in Kohima, who later transferred to Shillong, never to return. When Roko was a teenager, Atsa married Apfutsa who was a close neighbour and accountant in the new Nagaland State bureaucracy. Following his career in sports, he was able to earn a decent wage as a government servant and was able to save while also supporting his seven sons from his first marriage.

Since Atsa did not marry into a local clan, she had no land of her own to cultivate and believed it was foolish to place her hopes in finding employment in the offices of the government administration, to which many other immigrant families to Kohima were drawn. After all, her husband, having served for nearly four decades in government offices, received a monthly pension of 10,000 rupees, covering only their basic needs. This seemed evidence enough of the moral bankruptcy that Atsa felt characterised government institutions, institutions that she remembered at one time as being more honest and fair.

Atsa's sense of belonging centres on her relationship with the 'hearthen economy' which she continuously nurtures. Her relationship to her father's clan, for example, was violently interrupted. She left the protection of her clan not as a clan woman typically does through the ritual of marriage to her husband's clan. She left running as her home burned, due to an attack by Indian forces. There has scarcely been an opportunity to materialise continuities in, for example, the way that clan lineage members can. Her relationships were not mediated by her father's clan, and in fact were not officiated by the church. She thus forges her own way, following a logic of survival and non-dependence on the clan. Atsa's son-in-law once said 'girls are only free during the first two years of their lives', reflecting on the reality of girls and women as the main producers of the crops of consumption and exchange; a reality and expectation that accompanies them throughout their entire lives. The activities of cooking, of preparing *akhuni* (a traditional dish of fermented soya), are more than about generating a little side income, and are indeed more than the social value of their exchange (as in Mauss' 1925 seminal study of *hau* in 'The Gift'). The preparation of *akhuni* allows Atsa to generate, to create, to bring into being an aspect of her past, possibly a trace of her mother, that is there for her, just that it is something she can make visible and tactile through her techniques. For example, Atsa is often caught unawares talking aloud to no one in particular. She will sometimes get quite irritated at the interruption, but the words reveal it to be conversations with her mother, who has been dead since she was a teenager. Her regular preparations of *akhuni* are 'processes of materialisation', as John Harries (2010) articulates, which are 'attempts to arrest the ambivalent movement between presence and absence' of that which the *akhuni* itself embodies. In other words, she is seeking to be 'haunted by the thing itself, which is both insufficient to, yet in excess of, these materialisations' (ibid., p. 403). Severin Fowles suggests, for example, that

> When absences become object-like, when they seem to exist not merely as an afterthought of perception but rather as self-standing presences out there in the world, they begin to acquire powers and potentialities similar to things. Object-like absences (or what Fuery (1995: 2) refers to as quasi-presences), in this sense, become full participants in the social characterized by their own particular politics and, at times, their own particular emotional and semiotic charge.
>
> (2010, p. 27)

As discussed above, the patrilocality of clan homes and their kitchens forecloses the possibility of female home or land ownership. Only in the rarest of circumstances will ownership pass to a daughter or be sold out of the clan to an external buyer. When a woman marries she leaves her father's home and moves into a newly constructed house, typically in the sub-clan area of her husband. If the husband is the only son, or the youngest son, he and the bride will reside in the husband's father's home, though the bride will construct a separate hearth. In every case, marriage entails a new hearth, and the hearth will likely accompany the bride all her life and often until death. Men rarely outlive their wives, so the hearth is finally extinguished when the bride dies in old age.

If one were to identify a space or setting where dreams are told the most, a space *par excellence* for dream narration, the Angami hearth, according to Visakhonü Hibo, was 'where the whole family was allowed to sit together along with friends, visitors from neighbourhood or even visitors from other villages. Taboos were often interpreted, shared and warned from these kitchen talks' (Hibo 2013, p. 4). One way to approach this bi-sedimentation is by conceptualising the hearth as representative of the domestic sphere, and thus removed from clan laws and surveillance. It is the space where dreams are most often heard and where omens generally incubate. Public clan spaces, in contrast, might then be represented by the image of the *morung* – men's dormitories and quasi war lodges. These structures are no longer used in Kohima, but remain a symbol of the education of clan boys and men in the clan genealogy, supplanted in important ways by new community organisations such as the Angami Youth Organisation, an age-group institution much like a club, where clan interests are discussed, frequently accompanied by heavy drinking.

The activities of the hearth are situated but unsettled, gendered but non-exclusive, non-public but nodal and 'plugged in' to a broad informal network that includes other married women in the clan, but extends to vegetable and meat vendors from other communities, many of whom are from beyond district and state borders. This hearthen economy is decidedly non-hierarchical, with no centre, and mixes bargaining and buying with socialising. The 'hidden transcript' of Atsa's hearth and the broader hearthen economy is not 'rage' against clan violence or violence from the state, but constitutes a carefully performed set of techniques that reflect a general ambivalence towards clan institutions. These might emerge as techniques of contestation in some instances and of complicity in others (Scott 1990, 2009). Put differently, a community of non-inheritors, married clan women constitute a 'horizontal' collective (Thomas and Humphrey 1996), but this 'collective' is not always clearly in opposition to the pervasive vertical structures of power within the clan. This paradox is only a contradiction if viewed outside of the long durée of genealogical temporality. Hearthen practices are situated in in-betweenness, engaging in both sustaining vestiges of traditional conservatism through old recipes and food preparation, but also creatively incorporating new ways of doing things through ongoing interaction with a larger 'hearthen economy'. Indeed, Atsa frequently receives advice from her various contacts regarding possible alternative treatments for her knees. In fact, the traditional healer she now sees was recommended through her network of vendors, and she says she always feels better afterwards. Her family has not discouraged her from seeing the healer but has stated that only proper medical treatment can help her. She finds this difficult to stomach given her daughter's death linked to overmedication. Indeed, caught up in a medicalised landscape, Atsa believes the experts are just unknown salesmen and untrustworthy. Within the pragmatism of the 'hearthen economy' there is a more ambivalent stance always at play, the kind of ambivalence deployed in the facial expressions in everyday petty bargaining in the marketplace. Indeed, this operative stance, of pragmatism and ambivalence, is underwritten by the knowledge that, as Ian Harper suggests, 'other orders and rationalities exist and circulate', and an over-reliance on the 'best' is simply too high a risk to take, and possibly fatal (2014, p. 71).

So the idea of the 'hearthen economy' that I develop here is about all the material and immaterial 'things', 'people' and exchanges that become entangled in the body, that are the formations that give birth to 'subjectivity' of the person. Atsa's mother and her recently deceased daughter are therefore 'non-absent' (Harries 2010, p. 403), thus 'present' and in very powerful ways. The pain in Atsa's knee is a corporeal manifestation of 'non-absences', a kind of 'weather vane' registering this 'fluence'. Her dreams, likewise, are events in which these non-absences 'materialise' and become tactile. They become 'present' in a different way from waketime reality. It is in a way that reflects the complex entanglement of non-absences that make up Atsa's 'subjectivity' – a jumble of disjointed times, places and peoples that make up who she is and how she experiences the world.

These embedded practices of in-betweenness also involve the circulation of knowledge that wider relations bring to the table. This sometimes comes in the form of dreams and omens communicating knowledge about the clan from outsiders. Moreover, the engagement with this kind of spirit-mediated knowledge may be said to be an extension of this outside community. Ancestral knowledge, for example, is also a negotiation with otherness, and often entails beings that can be named and have genealogical histories both in dreamtime and in waketime reality. The cultivation of this 'hearthen economy' of coextensive relations thus follows a fundamentally different logic than the isolationism and protectionism that is characteristic of clan patriliny. Cultivation of the fields and of herbs, the collection of firewood and of water, remain the activities of women. Women thus, through their labour, sustain and nurture the clan. But these are resources produced in surplus and employed in broader exchange, with other clans, other villages, other peoples. And these relational capacities encourage different forms of knowledge sharing, broader notions of consensus and encompass a vision that extends beyond clan and village.

These processes stand as a first order of push-back or critique of clan dominance of social and cultural affairs. In the next section the presence of critique will be highlighted in the wide variety of practices that violate normative patriliny, but only to an extent, and rarely beyond the threshold of critique towards revolt.

Atsa's sharing and remembering

Atsa was good at concealing her thoughts behind a quiet demeanour and measured movements. Despite this, she had always appeared to me to be intensely perceptive of her surroundings. She could also be light-hearted and was known for her vicious under-the-breath comments on one's personal appearance, particularly among her grandchildren when they sat inside her kitchen for a meal and a story: 'oh, you didn't shave'; 'you should cut your hair'; or 'you are thin – is your wife not feeding you properly? I will speak to her'. One by one each person present would hunch towards the collection of kettles on the wood fire and serve themselves rice and Atsa's famous pork curry. Invariably, she would share an incident of that day, and sometimes would insert a dream experience she had remembered from the previous night, as side comments in casual conversation:

> This knee aches more than the other, but right now I am alright. I had a silly dream last night. I was visited by a man that told me I could make some extra money if I put photographs of myself in one of those calendars. But this man said I would have to dance too. How funny, imagine me dancing – I can hardly walk up those steps.

Atsa felt strongly about her faith in *Kepenuopfü* and spent several hours every day reading the Bible and praying, but was at the same time increasingly weary of the revivalist rhetoric at her church which would have her renounce her 'worldly condition' – her day-to-day struggle. After all, though it is an existence largely caught up in a thankless routine of cooking, hauling water, cleaning floors and washing clothes, these are aspects of her life over which she is mostly in control. Her orientation away from influential community or state institutions was accentuated following a string of recent and successive tragedies in her life: the death of her son-in-law in 2011; the death, only four months later, of her only biological child Roko; and then the sudden death of her dear sister and next door neighbour the following year to cancer. These were unbearable losses, which caused her to become increasingly insular in her attitude towards the world. While conducting fieldwork, I found she would leave her home only in the most exceptional circumstances. Her sliding, rented home – with a small bedroom, a room to receive guests, a second bedroom which I sometimes used as an office and a little outdoor kitchen – is a space she understood and could muster the strength every day to manage.

In August 2013, as the monsoon rains subsided, the pain in Atsa's knees had worsened, and she began consulting a traditional healer. As she reclined in her room, the slightly built man gently massaged her knee and encouraged her to be careful not to stress her sensitive joints by climbing the steps. I was surprised to see Atsa consulting a traditional healer given her strong loyalty to her local church, a traditional Baptist church in the centre of town. She had been a member of the same church for most of her life and always refused to entertain invitations to attend other Baptist churches with virtually identical services situated nearer her home. Moreover, Apfutsa was a strict Seventh Day Adventist, a markedly more conservative church that prohibited the use of traditional divinatory practices. This made the massage session all the more perplexing. But Atsa frequently expressed interest or curiosity about spirit activity, particularly in the nearby forests, and about the power of spiritual forces generally.

At around that time, I visited Rev. Zakie*, a leader in one of the old Angami traditional churches, and, I was told, an expert on Angami old beliefs and traditions. Rev. Zakie's home is on a congested hill on the southern side of the village, and I was only able to reach it via a tangled system of concrete stone steps running up from Choto Bosti (little village) road that circles the village barrier below. His newly constructed masonry home had a large meeting room where he receives his guests with ample space and chairs for prayer meetings and Bible studies. We stepped inside and exchanged a few words about the recent State Assembly elections before turning to the strangeness of the weather. The unseasonably heavy rainfall two months prior to monsoon had been greeted with a mix of reactions, as water shortages had driven the price of 1,000 litres of river water from 300 to 500 rupees among private water trucks. It had also caught local farmers off guard as it complicated their cultivation timings. Originally from the Chakhesang areas east of Kohima, Rev. Zakie suggested there were individuals in each village that still practised the old custom of reading the phases of the moon and setting the timings for cultivation, harvest and festivals.[1]

That the moon-phase readers were otherwise ordinary individuals with no specific privileges or elevated status seemed to be a common characteristic among a few old specialists. As was discussed briefly in chapter 1, the office of the *Kemovo* – the hereditary village head – identified by the British as being the de-facto village chief was given a red blanket as a uniform to wear, symbolising his loyalty as a British subject – likewise was not a king or powerful political chiefs, but largely of equal status with other respected elders. Well into the 1950s, the *Kemovo* (or *Thevo* among the Eastern Angami or Chakhesang groups) received special portions of food and special places during feasts and were expected to be versed in the ceremonial traditions and genealogies that the village held dear. They were the oldest living descendants of the original village founder and entrusted with transmitting the village's treasured knowledge. In many respects, the *Kemovo/ Thevo* represented the life-source of the community, and thus was to be protected.

Interestingly for our discussion on the corporeality of *ruopfü*, Christoph von Fürer-Haimendorf, on a short visit through the Eastern Angami areas prior to the outbreak of World War II, observed that the person of the *Kemovo/Thevo*

> is the vessel that holds the magical 'virtue' of the village, and as such is more important for the welfare of the community than anyone else. To understand his functions in the social life of a village it is necessary to take into consideration the psychological factor. The Angami holds a firm belief in the influence of magical forces on the success or failure of all his activities, and, above all, on the growth of his crops. He therefore gains confidence from the conviction that one man of his village, qualified by descent and office, is somehow in especially close contact with those forces.
>
> (1936, p. 931)

The behaviour of the *Thevo* and that of his wife were scrutinised by the village elders as any violations would anger the spirits and potentially bring harm to the village. He was also the only individual in the settlement that officiated at the village level, and thus served as a link among sometimes quarrelling clans – 'the living symbol of the essential unity of the village in a tribe where the ordinary social and political life exhibits individualism in the most extreme form' (Fürer-Haimendorf, Christoph and Mills 1936, p. 931). The *Thevo* did not, however, preside over agricultural rites, funerals or rain-making rituals, as these were the responsibility of other specialists such as the *Pitsu* – always the oldest member of the village; the *Chekrü* – a male member from any clan who might be trusted not to break any taboos; and the *Lidepfü* – an elderly widow of any clan, who is least likely to engage in sexual intercourse, and thus able to follow the ritual through (Hutton 1921, p. 189; Fürer-Haimendorf, Christoph and Mills 1936, p. 932).

All Angami settlements trace their migration back to the small village of Kezhakenoma just on the north side of the present Nagaland-Manipur border, and as settlements at the time spread northwards, westwards and eastwards from this point, they followed specific strategies to safeguard the safety and prosperity of each new settlement. For one, to avoid consanguinity, two individuals from separate clans were sent to settle a new area. One of them, the principal settler, had to be either the *Kemovo/Thevo* himself or a descendent of the founder of the village of origin (in which case probably the *Thevo's* brother or son), thus carrying with him the knowledge and history of that village. Most Northern, Southern and Western Angami settlements have a *Thevoma* clan, and it is from this clan that each clan family acknowledges the position of the *Kemovo*, generally the oldest living relative of this clan at any given time. Thus the Northern, Southern and Western Angami equivalent of the Eastern Angami or Chakhesang *Thevo* is the *Kemovo*, a direct descendent of the village founder and member of the *Thevoma* clan. His dwelling traditionally sits on the spot where the original settler first built his house, and he was responsible for transmitting the treasured knowledge and officiating all the rituals and ceremonies in the village.

Though the office of the *Kemovo* may be traced back to the older eastern tradition, a series of changes associated with the line of descent transformed the office to what might be associated with a religious 'priesthood', and Kohima offers the most 'advanced' stage of this innovation. Whereas most other Northern and Western Angami villages have a *Thevoma* clan, Kohima does not. The original settler established the *Tsieramia* clan, and though the present *Kemovo* is still a hereditary office – always the oldest male descendent – he traces his lineage back to *Whinuo*, from which *Ke-whira* or *Ke-whi-mia* (the people of *Ke-whira*) are drawn. The most important innovation, however, is that the *Kemovo* passes on most of his responsibilities associated with performing rituals and ceremonies to a clan council ordained *Pitsu* (or ritual practitioner). Each clan in Kohima village elected a *Pitsu*, and often from the *Pfuchatsumia khel* (*P-khel*). In the process of electing a *Pitsu*, a chicken is throttled to see whether it will cross its legs properly (right over left); if the man passes the first test, the old *Kemovo* will then consult his dreams that night. If he has bad dreams the candidate would be passed over and a second candidate would be identified until the omen and the dream lined up.

Though there were many restrictions associated with the office – as with the Eastern *Thevo* – the title offered an opportunity to influence clan and village affairs. Presiding now over individual, clan and village ceremonies and rituals, the *Pitsu* gained a considerable position of authority, though his powers were always checked and balanced by his counterpart in the old *Kemovo* and a council of elders (always the oldest members of the village). An example of the development of this office is the elaborate liturgies such as those performed at rain-making rituals:

> Ukepenuopfü! I do not want bad things. In [this] great distance [hear my voice. That] good things may come to us; make everything in the house be good. We killed very clean, good things in your name. Your meat be cut and may be doubled. Your meat should be like the hills of white ants. May it take as long and it be hard to cut it up [as] a big tree-trunk. When meat will be given to all the village, and what remains should fill all your house and it should be distributed to all the neighbourhood. Also your madhu should come out like a spring, and like a river. It should not be finished. Your rice-beer given [to] all the village, the village, the remainder should be distributed as you want. All your tame animals should grow inside and outside of the house. Whoever lives on your house-site should become old and be rich and wise. And your seeds given to the good large earth, should grow very strongly and it should be all over the stones and woods. Today is the day to begin to be very lucky, by the grace of Ukepenuopfü, and your relatives should be just as good.[2]

Directing individual ceremonies and public rituals and fashioning the annual schedule for them in consultation with the *Kemovo*, moon-phase reader and the village elders, the *Pitsu* was a conservative public figure concerned with order in the village as a whole. At the more individual level, community members themselves played the leading role in reading omens, listening to dreams and directing their actions based on this knowledge. In Khonoma, while the *Kemovo* (like the Kohima *Pitsu*, he directs public rituals) and the *Zhevo* (the oldest member of the village) participated in the stone dragging ritual, they took a secondary role to that of the man and his wife who led the ceremonial aspects of the ritual and discerned the will of the spirits throughout the process.

In these details, we can see the gradual shifts and innovations taking place in the office of the *Kemovo* and particularly a move away from a shamanic role of mediating between human and spirit worlds, to a ceremonial role that requires knowledge of ritual practices but not shamanic abilities, and is elected and operates under clan laws. Interesting for this discussion, however, is precisely the kind of corporeality of the early *Kemovo* as 'vessel' detailed in Fürer-Haimendorf's descriptions based on his travels in the Eastern Angami areas in the 1930s. He observes the *Kemovo* to be holding 'the magical virtue of the village', and that the *Kemovo* is 'in close contact with those forces', not necessarily defined by his healing or shamanic mediatory practices as by consultative 'work' on behalf of individuals. It is likely that he was also consulted by individuals, but his primary work was associated with his body; his corporeality encompassed the purity and righteousness of the village. Indeed, Fürer-Haimendorf in the same passage is precise in using the term 'embodiment', namely,

> He knows that the 'virtue' of the village, embodied in that man, is well guarded by numerous tabus – tabus which this one man observes as a representative, as it were, of the whole community, and for the general benefit. Tabus which the ordinary villager could never observe, though he clearly sees their importance, are thus observed on his behalf.
>
> (1936, p. 931)

I cite these early observations because they very distinctly illustrate the physicality or materiality of *ruopfü*, to which the term 'vessel' seems to allude because it articulates an 'openness' or, as quoted earlier, a 'being toward the world' (Csordas 2011). The various restrictions associated with the office, as described by Fürer-Haimendorf, already assumes the *Kemovo* has lost some of his function as 'village-head' as the hereditary position would entail. One could also surmise, however, that there is indeed a shift in the way communities orient themselves towards the world as they grow, cultivate more and more lands, and develop more central institutions. Increased complexity would likewise seem to require greater regularity of rituals associated with appeasing the spirits, thus side-lining the importance of original forms of exchange agreed upon with spirit owners in earlier periods of village establishment.

But in the idea that corporeality is both visible and invisible, that indeed *ruopfü* is spirit but it is also substance (as I have already discussed, my informant Senyü suggested that '*ruopfü* and nature are one') and that because *ruopfü* is also inter-corporeal, then the reading of pain in Atsa's knees as omens – as messages or of movement elsewhere – makes sense. This is particularly the case if we take Angami articulations of personhood at face value. And besides reverting to the polymorphism of the *tekhumiavi* discussed in chapter 2, the Eastern Angami *Kemovo* as observed by Fürer-Haimendorf, helps to provide some ethnographic precedent for this contemporary phenomenon.

There are other kinds of openness associated with the hearth and with Atsa's activities, and I turn now to her principal pastime and the kind of relations that are mediated through the products she generates in and around her hearth.

Making *akhuni*

Atsa's friendships with vendors, construction workers and other individuals not connected in any way with the Kohima clan family, indeed her connection with the broader 'hearthen economy' of relations, is mostly through her homemade dish, *dacie*, or what is more widely known as *akhuni* (or 'akhone' – a term borrowed from the neighbouring Sumi Naga dialect). The fermented and smoke-dried soybean paste is used as a condiment in Angami food and is a variant of a product made in kitchens throughout Asia. Atsa's *dacie* is legendary according to some of her customers. And though in recent years she has shifted to using a pressure cooker and a gas burner to save on the cost of wood and time (boiling takes 30 to 40 minutes), any change in taste has gone unnoticed by her loyal clientele within the Lhisemia, another Angami clan. The small 50 to 100 packets of lemon-yellow coloured paste, which she stores inside the chimney or behind the fire within the hearth, can fetch her 10 rupees per packet, and through word of mouth she often gets customers from outside Kohima Village to buy her product in large quantities of 10 to 20 packets.

The process is simple. Atsa washes and then soaks locally available soybeans in water and boils them until they are soft. She then drains and wraps them in banana leaves in a bamboo basket placed near the hearth to dry and ferment. After three days, she tastes them, and if ready they are mashed with a wooden pestle, tightly wrapped in banana leaves or paper and tied with a thin strand of bamboo. The income she receives, however, is not enough to make any significant home improvements or help her grandchildren with school expenses. In fact, the cost of living in Kohima far exceeds the income capacity of many poor households. All meals, therefore, are simple and vary little – rice, dal, mustard greens and occasionally chicken or pork, often brought by a relative – and 'living simply' is, and has always been, a matter of pride for Atsa. My own offers to up the rent, to fix or replace the outhouse or to pave the sidewalk were always brushed aside with one comment – 'not necessary'. There were times when Atsa used her earnings to purchase *zu* (rice beer), which numbs the pain in her knees and generally helped her and her husband sleep. Throughout fieldwork I would pop into her small kitchen to share a cup or two of *zu* with her husband, Apfutsa.

But the true value in the *dacie* is in maintaining her linkages with her neighbours in the clan, other villagers and non-Naga traders. These interactions would oscillate with the changing rhythms and circulation of the seasons and seasonal ingredients coming from rural villages that are far too costly, if available at all, in the Kohima market. Traders that she had not seen in a long time would be greeted as old friends. When someone visits, she might get fresh mushrooms picked from the forest above Khonoma, or home-grown Raja chilli peppers from Peren, southwest of Kohima, or fresh bamboo shoots from Tuli, further north. These are highly sought-after and occasionally brought by her birth clan relatives in Khonoma, but more often by relatives of her neighbours or clients who come carrying a bundle and stop first at Atsa's kitchen so she has the first choice, sometimes for a small price or in exchange for a fresh packet of *dacie*. With these exchanges, Atsa is able to recreate the traditional dishes she and Apfutsa are accustomed to, that are reminiscences in themselves, with ingredients that are now increasingly scarce. The best of these special dishes are reserved for weekends when nieces, nephews and grandchildren typically show up. What is possible on weekends with family visitors is a reification of familial gatherings of the past and of old memories; old recipes served up for at least two generations that have few other ways of relating to the village practices that closely followed the changing seasons.

One of Atsa's many customers, Kezevinuo, is a widow, her garden ending just a few metres below my window. Her husband was a heavy drinker and eventually died of liver disease roughly five years prior to my arrival. His tomb is a few feet from those of his brother Ketu and cousin Kevi who both died in the plane crash in Imphal back in 1991 (as detailed in chapter 2). Kezevinuo rears pigs, which is technically prohibited by the village council because of its generally unpleasant smell. She has moved the pig enclosure away from the road, shifted it around the compound several times, but is almost entirely dependent on the pigs for income. Her vegetables and herbs and small shop help, but the high school fees for her son and daughter keep her on her toes. She is a survivor, though had she not had a son the property her home is built on would revert to the clan. Her son, a shy 8-year-old boy, studies before and after school and somehow the monotony of work seems to lighten when he arrives back home to feed the pigs and help cook dinner.

Unlike Atsa, Kezevinuo lives inside the village boundary of the clan and inside a clan compound. She is therefore protected from the harassment and taxation by underground political groups that accompanies owning a small shop or convenience store in Kohima town. But at the same time, she is doubly-bound – with her husband dead, she is stuck in an in-between place where she has little say in how the world around her is organised. She shares her dreams with the other women in the vicinity, believing that they will come true. She shares them frequently while watering the garden and boiling scraps for the pigs. Her busy day of buying and selling food items, her pig rearing and great interest in omens and dreams seem to come together as a form of struggle, but also of gentle but unyielding resistance to clan restrictions.

This notion of survival, of getting through, tends to emphasise both the present and the need to understand what comes next – that which is forthcoming. The anxiety is to understand the future, what it might bring, since memories and dwelling on the past are not things any of the married women living within the clan have the luxury to worry about at any rate. But this is not to say that memories – memories of childhood, of familial relations in the father's clan – are not intensely felt and continuously a strongly felt absence. The past creeps in and disturbs waketime and sleeptime, and is thus ever-present. The consequences of the past haunt their existence and shape their every capacity to act in the unfolding present. The confined spaces, though offering room to work, to plan and perhaps to contrive, are also spaces that make them aware of their limits (Merleau-Ponty 2006; Trigg 2013).

For Atsa, despite her appearing not to care very much sometimes whether or not her guests would want to hear her complain about her knee or about some piece of news she heard from a neighbour, nonetheless cherished fellowship. She would not speak about her past unless asked specifically about particular years or life events. It was not because she could not remember or did not want to relive painful memories, but because she did not want to place herself in the centre of a narrated plot – she indeed sought constantly to depersonalise her own story. Very often, Atsa's revealed in her retelling of her own stories of survival, the process which she undertook of absorbing, negotiating and transforming personal loss and separation into fragments of experience that then could be the ingredients of what Carsten calls 'creative refashionings, in and through everyday processes of relatedness' (2007, p. 24). Her generally light-hearted demeanour spoke volumes about her capacity to cope with loss and instead to divert her attention to her grandchildren, to her friends, including the vegetable vendors and other workers that she welcomed regularly to sit for tea and conversation, and to her faith.

Carsten suggests that these kinds of memories, including traumatic memories and memories of escape, can help elucidate 'everyday forms of relatedness in the present', as well as 'subjective dispositions to the past, and in the imagination of possible futures' (2007, p. 1). In studies of intimate settings in relation to political violence, memory can be 'a source of negotiation and conflict in society, perpetually open to revision and effectively rendering past and present consubstantial' (Schramm and Argenti 2010, p. 7). However, when we speak of trans-generational forms of memory, we also acknowledge that such transmission is conditioned in that it is 'constrained by what constitutes a compelling narrative and the available materials for reconstruction' (Cole 2005, p. 4). Moreover, as is also the case with dream sharing, there is a significant element of depersonalisation in sharing memories, and though one could very well have done or experienced an extraordinary thing, he or she will go to lengths and search for words in an attempt to de-emphasise her or his role or responsibility in relation to the achievement (cf. Graham 1995, pp. 137–174).

I regularly requested Atsa to speak about her past, about her childhood in Khonoma and perhaps about such things as seeing the British or the Japanese in her village during World War II. One of Atsa's nieces, 17-year-old Zaza, would listen in on our conversation while playing games on her smartphone, and on occasion showed great interest, asking follow-up questions, and then stating in amazement that she had never heard these things before. Atsa would chuckle and simply shift to the next activity. But Atsa's experiences seemed, at times, entirely foreign to Zaza and the younger generation. Though Atsa's dramatic escape from her burning village as it was under attack suggests she undoubtedly experienced some of the worst moments in the war, Zaza's age group appeared scarcely to know there had been a war at all. Certainly indicative of the way different generations converge and diverge in terms of their own constructions of identity in relation to friendship groups, familial and other affiliations, there was a sense in which the different generations '[embodied] different temporal dispositions' (Carsten 2007, p. 24).

Ultimately, the politics of memory are linked to the complex, but more nuanced and personalised terrain of kinship, relatedness and constructions of self (ibid., p. 5). This linkage leads towards subjective, often intimate, individual circumstances that 'point to the myriad articulations – of temporality, memory, personal biography, family connection, and political processes – that are manifested in subjective dispositions to the past, and in the imagination of possible futures' (ibid., p. 1). In some sense we could say that there exists a continuum where subjective particularities in terms of memory recall are most marked in contexts where notions of the self are less clear. Moreover, a more decisive separation and/ or alienation from kinship relations correlates with a more fragmented notion of temporality and space in memory recall. Here, rootedness and continuity in kinship relations is believed to affect directly the condition of the self (ibid.).

Atsa's sharing, including her sharing of dreams, albeit fragmentary most of the time, was done recognising that loss and suffering were productive in sourcing restorative reconfigurations in day-to-day relatedness. Atsa's ability to develop new relationships wherever she shifted next was predicated on the ability to consciously acknowledge loss. Carsten suggests that 'in this sense, we might say that a work of memory is the necessary counterpoint to kinship relations in their broadest sense' (2007, p. 24). Indeed, ways of remembering that, due to present circumstances, are rendered difficult or indeed not possible at all, constrain the ability to relate to others in new ways. In contexts such as Nagaland where changes in the community appear to be symptoms of large economic, political and religious shifts on an entirely different scale, more intimate, subjective, familial processes of negotiating, refashioning and remembering are overlooked. Indeed, very little work has been conducted in recent times on Angami kinship, subjectivity or relatedness outside of a few recent works of fiction (see for example Kire 2011a, 2011b, 2014).

These attentive observers, who give credence to the significance of dreams, shift between two modes of perceiving a single space. Two possible approaches to understanding one's position in a given context are thereby offered up. It is in that locality that I came to better understand Atsa's experiences and the way she negotiated the challenges faced. Atsa's 'agency' in the midst of this enclosure is an experience shared by Kezevinuo, and individuals in similar circumstances and exemplified by widows. As with many in the community that reside at the margins of the 'enduring pattern', they are enmeshed in repetitive, often arduous routine, but also aware of their situation and more attentive to knowledge that may transform their condition, whether in waketime reality or in dreams.

Concluding remarks

Two months before I finished my fieldwork, Atsa's husband, Apfutsa, died. He had suffered a bad lung infection earlier in the year and had declined rapidly in the months leading up to his death. Atsa asked her relatives to allow her to stay at the old house, but she eventually agreed to live with her nieces up the hill. She now lives within the clan boundaries, and in some respects her living conditions have improved. Her relatives set up a makeshift stove outside so she could cook *dacie*, and she continues to receive her customers, selling the packets for 25 rupees each, often in large bundles.

The pain in her knees has also subsided, and her family has not pressed her so much on getting an operation or taking painkillers. Her nieces say her knee sometimes flares up and she says she feels someone is either very sick or going to die – her pain serving as an omen, her body extending outward and absorbing and becoming absorbed into the sentient landscape.

Atsa's continued participation in the 'hearthen economy' of relations also allows her to distribute her marginality. She shares her dreams, her daily annoyances with a physical handicap, and by doing so she joins an anonymous multitude of other individuals negotiating day-to-day uncertainties. By inviting non-clan and very often non-Naga vendors and shop owners to join her and her husband in the kitchen by the hearth for hot tea or a meal, she decided not to participate in the kind of elitism that seemed to pervade in the village. The village council had, for instance, banned Muslims from working within the village boundary, with hefty fines and possibly physical assault if the new law was not followed. The Hindu day labourers now working construction sites throughout the village – typically from Bihar, Uttar Pradesh, and neighbouring Assam – still face the possibility of physical assault if they make mistakes or are seen to take too long on a project.

By hosting guests generally unwelcome beyond their labouring hours, she seems to lift her chin a bit in defiance and in some respects to assume part of the guests' marginality by not pretending to be anyone except a guest herself. When the small army of non-Naga labourers and traders appeared in the early morning hours to carry a few large boxes, kitchen pots and kettles and cabinets on their heads to help her move house, they walked steadily up the hill and into the heart of the clan neighbourhood with an air of pride. They were giving back the way they could, and this move was a testament to her capacity to make friends among a motley group of ragged men and in this way showed her own air of pride in the face of what she felt to be unnecessary snobbery. Her challenge to boundaries, to what seemed like unfettered and unnecessary levels of consumerism within the village, and her more recent ambivalence with regards to the morality of the church, did not preclude her from a deeply felt responsibility for everyone she received in her kitchen. According to one of her nieces, the pain in her body and the signs and omens that appeared to her in her dreams and in her increasingly fragile, tactile environment, only become more acute with old age. The insights – *kesi* – that she gleaned are not simply warnings of impending events or troubles, but were a much more dynamic patterning of aspects of the unfolding present that may yet be in a fragile assemblage, malleable, not-irreversible; pathways that were not foregone conclusions or resistant to re-direction, but which existed in an expanded temporality, emerging from a broader universe of hidden possibilities, which could potentially be apprehended, or altered through one's own creative intervention. The more attentive she was, the more capacity she had to think through the patterns – in dreamtime and waketime – that emerged and informed her. These very 'real' absences, as Severin Fowles suggests 'perform labor, frequently intensifying our emotional or cognitive engagement with that which is manifestly not present' (2010, p. 27). When Atsa shares her dreams or the signs she has gleaned from her ambit of work and routine, she speaks *for* and *with* the messages, because they are not absent or in the past. They are present and part of a long succession of interpreted, acted upon messages that have altered her life course. She no longer shares *kesi*, but *kesikele* – 'insights with knowing'.

Atsa lives at the tail end of a complex history of personal and familial challenges. Though her birth clan in Khonoma is Christian, the very first Christian converts were banished and their houses burned. These homes were reconstructed and then burned again by Indian forces given the clan's kinship proximity to Zhapu Phizo, the leader of the underground nationalist movement. Apfutsa served as a government servant for most of his adult life, and so Atsa's clan would have viewed him with suspicion, clan members working in the Nagaland Government were viewed and treated as traitors. Ironically, though Atsa is closely related to Phizo – he was her maternal uncle – she is landless and rented a house on land away from the village of her birth. Atsa's contingency can be said to contribute to the openness of her lived experience and to her willingness to host members of the vast hearthen economy of relations she is connected to – individuals that would not find the same reception within the clan. Levinas posits that at the heart of subjectivity is 'the one-for-the-other' and not a 'for itself' (Zeillinger 2009, p. 107). Atsa and many of her neighbours express an ethical disposition, not because it is sacrificial, nor even intentional, but because otherness is at the heart of subjectivity, 'this way of being, without prior commitment, responsible for the other (autrui), amounts to the fact of human fellowship, prior to freedom' (Levinas 1996, p. 91).

In the following chapter, this notion of 'openness' and the ethical disposition that this entails, extends beyond humans to the supernatural. The signs and omens that Atsa and others glean are intended to be shared because they are ultimately for the community. As we shall see, sharing entails forms of regulation, of sieving through deliberate 'interference' in regards to foretelling signs. And this 'interference', though originating in the ambit of the hearth, spills out into other important ambits, including the Christian church.

Notes

1 In his 1936 field notes on the Eastern Angamis Fürer-Haimendorf makes reference to this specialist: 'There is a special calendar-expert in an Eastern Angami village who finds out which month it is at any time of the year. The gennas are then fixed automatically according to the lunar months.' Online source: http://himalaya.socanth.cam.ac.uk/collections/naga/record/r70001.html, accessed 22 April 2014.
2 Fürer-Haimendorf's unpublished 1936 field notes. Online source: http://himalaya.socanth.cam.ac.uk/collections/naga/record/r70001.html, accessed 23 April 2014.

Bibliography

Carsten, Janet, 1995, "The Substance of Kinship and the Heat of the Hearth: Feeding, Personhood, and Relatedness Among Malays in Pulau Langkawi", *American Ethnologist*, 22(2), pp. 223–241.

Carsten, Janet, 1997, *The Heat of the Hearth: The Process of Kinship in a Malay Fishing Community*, Oxford: Clarendon Press.

Carsten, Janet, ed., 2007, *The Ghosts of Memory: Essays on Remembrance and Relatedness*, London: Routledge Press.

Carsten, Janet and Stephen Hugh-Jones, 1995, *About the House: Lévi-Strauss and Beyond*, Cambridge: Cambridge University Press.Chatterjee, Indrina, 2013, *Forgotten Friends: Monks, Marriages and Memories of Northeast India*, New Delhi: Oxford University Press.

Cole, Jennifer, 2005, "Memory and Modernity", in *A Companion to Psychological Anthropology: Modernity and Psychocultural Change*, C. Casy and R.B. Edgerton, eds., Malden, MA: Blackwell, pp. 103–120.

Counihan, Carole M., 1999, *The Anthropology of Food and Body: Gender, Meaning, and Power*, London: Routledge.

Csordas, Thomas, 2011, "Cultural Phenomenology", in *A Companion to the Anthropology of the Body and Embodiment*, F.E. Mascia-Lees, ed., Oxford: Wiley-Blackwell.

Diprose, Rosalyn, 2012, *On Giving With Nietzsche, Merleau-Ponty, and Levinas*, Albany: State University of New York Press.

Fowles, Severin, 2010, "People Without Things", in *An Anthropology of Absence: Materializations of Transcendence and Loss*, M. Bill, T. Sørensen and F. Hastrup, eds.,New York: Springer-Verlag, pp. 23–41.

Fuery, P., 1995. *The Theory of Absence: Subjectivity, Signification and Desire,* Westport: Greenwood Press.

Fürer-Haimendorf, Christoph von and Mills, J.P., 1936, "The Sacred Founder's Kin Among the Eastern Angami Nagas", *Anthropos*, 31(5/6), September–December, pp. 922–933.

Garcés, Marina, 2013, *Un Mundo Común*, Barcelona: Edicions Bellaterra.

Graham, Laura R., 1995, *Performing Dreams: Discourses of Immorality Among the Xavante of Central Brazil*, Austin: University of Texas Press.

Harper, Ian, 2014, *Development and Public Health in the Himalaya: Reflections on Healing in Contemporary Nepal*, Oxford: Routledge.

Harries, John, 2010, "Of Bleeding Skulls and the Postcolonial Uncanny: Bones and the Presence of Nonosabusut and Demasduit", *Journal of Material Culture*, 15(4), pp. 403–421.

Hibo, Visakhonü, and Chumbeno R. Ngullie, (eds.), 2012, *Tapestry,* Dimapur: Heritage.

Hibo, Visakhonü, 2013, "Naga Movement: Alternative Perception of Naga Women", presented at 2013 Hutton Lectures Symposium, 4th December, Kohima, India (unpublished).

Hutton, J.H., 1921, *The Angami Nagas*, London: Palgrave Macmillan.

Iralu (alias Kire), E., 2011a, *Bitter Wormwood* (A novel covering the period 1937–2007 dealing with the Indo-Naga conflict using the story of a small Angami family), New Delhi: Zubaan.

Iralu (alias Kire), E., 2011b, *Life on Hold* (A novella of Kohima in the 1980s and 1990s, using the story of star-crossed young lovers as a metaphor for the Naga story), Kohima: Barkweaver.

Kire, Easterine, 2014, *When the River Sleeps: A Novel on the Spiritual Universe of the Tenyimia*, New Delhi: Zubaan.

Levinas, Emmanuel, 1996, *Emmanuel Levinas: Basic Philosophical Writings*, A.T. Peperzak, S. Critchley and R. Bernasconi, eds., Bloomington, IN: Indiana University Press.

Mauss, Marcel, 1925, "Essai sur le don: Forme et raison de l'échange dans les sociétés archaiques", in *L'année sociologique,* July 1923–July 1924, 31–186.

Merleau-Ponty, M., 1969 [1960], "'Preface' to Hesnard's L'oeuvre de Freud", in *The Essential Writings of Merleau-Ponty*, A. Fisher, ed., New York: Harcourt, Brace World.

Merleau-Ponty, M., 2006, *The Structure of Behavior*, Pittsburg: Duquesne University Press.

Schramm, K. and Argenti, N., eds., 2010, *Remembering Violence: Anthropological Perspectives on Intergenerational Transmission*, New York: Berghahn Books.

Scott, J.C., 2009, *The Art of not Being Governed: An Anarchist History of Upland Southeast Asia*, New Haven: Yale University Press.

Scott, James, 1990, *Domination and the Arts of Resistance: Hidden Transcripts*, New Haven: Yale University Press.

Thomas, N. and Caroline Humphrey, eds., 1996, *Shamanism, History, and the State*, Ann Arbor: University of Michigan Press.

Trigg, Dylan, 2013, *Memory of Place: A Phenomenology of the Uncanny*, Athens: Ohio University Press.

Weismantel, Mary, 1988, *Food, Gender and Poverty in the Ecuadorian Andes*, Prospect Heights: Waveland Press.

Zeillinger, Peter, 2009, "Radical Passivity as the (Only) Effective Basis for Ethical Action. Reading the 'Passage to the Third' in Otherwise than Being", in *Radical Passivity: Rethinking Ethical Agency in Levinas*, New York: Springer-Verlag.

5 The authority of dreams

The *Meya* clan, as with the other clans in *L-khel*, finds ways to maintain a sense of unity despite the fact that its five lineages are more or less scattered within the larger *L-khel* vicinity and beyond the village boundary. The growth of Kohima town and the myriad roads and national highway below have obscured what are traditionally the *L-khel* lands and paddy fields, all stretching to the north and northwest of the village. Clan unity in the absence of residential congruity was once achieved through combined community rituals organised by the lineage elders. But the few ritual practices that remain are mere re-enactments, having shed their original magico-religious purposes – an eligibility requirement for church membership. The old men meet more often to discuss the ever-present

Figure 5.1 Angami Clan men in full ceremonial dress
Source: Author's photo

problem of land encroachment, or perhaps to agree on a common law marriage in the case of a teen pregnancy. Occasionally, clan meetings involving women and children are organised to rekindle ties, and in chapter 2 I detailed the occasion of a gathering in a forest clearing in which the preservation of lineage lands and thus the unity of the *Meya* clan was attributed to a prophetic dream. Disruptions, whether due to the lack of a male heir, the unlawful sale of clan lands or a major inter-lineage dispute, are a regular preoccupation among primarily clan men. But the old laws also encompassed disturbances that were not so material in nature, and this chapter traces the ways in which attentiveness to waketime and dreamtime omens, although once more public and associated with spirit propitiation, remains an active practice in the domestic sphere. Moreover, they are one way in which clan lineage and domestic kin collaborate.

As illustrated in the previous chapter, the principal locus of daily interpretation of signs in dreams and waketime omens within the clan are gendered domestic spaces. Herein lies a fundamental tension. On one hand, clan authority is underwritten by passed down ancestral knowledge and deliberated through the clan councils. On the other hand, insights received by spirits of deceased relatives in dreams, or waketime omens, can constitute another form of authoritative knowledge in the clan, foretelling events that can potentially affect the whole community. Interpretation, thus, is a community affair that intersects domestic and clan spheres of influence. I posit in this chapter that these constitute a set of practices, though now mainly rooted in dream interpretation, that can be traced to the general preoccupation with sieving spiritual power and volition in human social life.

The informal collective of generally clan women I call the 'hearthen economy' in chapter 4 regularly share their insights and are keen to pass on any warnings or potential blessings the fragmented messages may be suggesting. But the interpretive process involves a form of 'arrestment' and 'enhancement' of the imparted messages, and here I draw on insights developed by Nienke van der Heide (2015a) in her use of the term 'interference' in describing dream culture in post-soviet Kyrgyzstan, namely that 'a foretelling dream can only materialise after it has been explained and blessed by people of importance . . . The idea that daytime interference influences the actual outcome of a dream is all-pervasive'.[1] Resembling the Angami experience of approaching clan elders in the case of particularly enigmatic dreams, 'interference' articulates the notion of interpretation as involving a form of 'plumping for' a desired outcome, and its assimilation into the group context through a form of 'submission' to an elder or recognised interpreter becomes a requirement for its materialisation.[2] Although dreams may possess great potency to influence daily life, as van der Heide suggests, 'they can only do so when they are integrated into the social world'.[3]

Another significant feature in this process of interpretation is the 'depersonalisation' of knowledge and narrative, and this is illustrated convincingly by Laura Graham (1995) in her seminal ethnography among the Brazilian Xavante. Graham suggests that, whereas the dominant Habermasian theory of 'communicative action' (Habermas 1984, 1987), namely that collective work towards reaching mutual understanding is a process of consensus-building among rationalising individuals, 'the Xavante organize discourse to be the product of multiple selves in the form of multiple voices' (Graham 1995, p. 140). In other words, the Xavante engage in a 'de-coupling of individual authorship', and thus legitimacy, for example, in clan council deliberations, is conditioned on 'negation of self' (ibid., p. 143). As touched on earlier, Angami clan councils follow a very similar decision-making logic, and downplaying or limiting charisma is a virtue and significantly an Angami social norm more generally. Moreover, this norm also informs the 'interpretive community' in the way it approaches information received in dreams and believed to derive from the spirits of deceased relatives and the divine. Indeed, once circulated, dream sequences begin to lose their necessary proximity to the dreamer, and indeed sometimes become but an ingredient in a large soup of signs and omens already at play. Similarly, Joel Robbins (2003), drawing on his ethnographic work among the Urapmin in Papua New Guinea, has observed that, while dreams certainly are influential in local political processes, spurring charismatic leadership, the same dream report, as it spreads, is also now interpreted by a community that has little interest in recognising this newfound charismatic authority. Robbins suggests, then, that 'the absence of charismatic leadership in Melanesia becomes not a simple fact to be registered but rather a social accomplishment to be explained' (ibid., p. 23).

In order to illustrate the way these various moving parts inform the ethnography and our understanding of the Angami ways of making sense of dreams, I will explore three key historical developments in which the processes and dynamics of 'interference' may be observed. Firstly, I briefly explore the office of the village head or *Kemovo/Thevo* in relation to pre-Christian religious practices; secondly, I explore practices that take place in the sanctuary and prayer centre of the Baptist Revival church; and finally, I look briefly at the early years of the Naga conflict and the emergent charismatic movement. I organise these discussions employing, as a trope, the dream and dream-related experiences of one of my informants. In this way we may observe the processes employed by the 'interpretive community', namely *narration, interference, disruption* and *regulation*.

I thus begin with the story of Vilhou, a man who ignored advice he received having shared a particularly troubling dream and found himself faced with the consequences. He recognised it was a serious dream, sought 'interference' – so in a sense the full weight of the event is understood to have lessened – but did not observe *genna* (lit. 'prohibition') – the Angami traditional notion of taboo requiring abstention from physical labour. Traditionally, a *genna* pronouncement by the clan or village head would accompany any serious omen, and there are ways in which this important prescription has been transformed, yet continues to be prescribed by elders.

The dream as omen

When dream reports circulate widely, like gossip, news of its signs and possible meanings tend to travel particularly quickly around the *khel*. This is especially the case if, like the symbol of a falling tree, they are about the impending death of a clansman. Dreams of a person dressed in new clothes, for instance, or of black birds, one's teeth falling out or the roof over one's house being blown off are dreams associated with death – the latter two specifically about the approaching death of parents.[4] Their particular novelty, however, is bolstered by the identity of the dreamer him or herself. And though authorship, as I have argued, generally is blurred once the dream report has been circulating for a few days (which I attribute to the general social more of 'depersonalisation'), some individuals, or *mhotékezhamia* (lit. 'person with true dreams'), are coupled with their dream messages like a kind of dream 'branding'. A person may have a terrible dream, but if that person is also known to be *mhoté*, that dream is, in many ways, his or her prophetic word about what is coming.

Just down the road from the Baptist Revival Church lives a man who many believe is *mhotékezhamia* – or simply *mhoté* (lit. 'has true dreams'). Vilhou lives just below a cul-de-sac of homes belonging to the *Meya* clan on the northern slopes of the village. Unusual for the village as a whole, the small compound has three traditional Angami 'long houses' still largely intact and in use. They are made of sturdy log frames and, instead of straw and bamboo, are covered with corroded metal sheets made from flattened barrels and recycled roofing materials – some of them bearing the scars of shrapnel. In the village, at least some of the structures along the northern slope remained intact following the 1944 Battle of Kohima, and roofing pulled to shelter the trenches would have been recycled by the villagers during reconstruction. Walking through the village today, the few remaining traditional Angami structures are still bandaged with these holey scraps, and while most dwellings are now rectangular and wooden, masonry or multi-storey reinforced concrete structures are now present, such as the rather imposing four-storey house by the road of the small compound belonging to Vilhou's younger brother Sazo. When one enters the traditional long houses, the entire structure converges on the kitchen hearth at the back. Indeed, the hearth has always been the heart of domestic activity, as I have shown in chapter 4. In the new architectural designs, the hearth is no longer centrally situated, and though families try to accommodate what they can in the new spaces, they usually resort to erecting a separate wooden structure outside that is entirely dedicated to cooking, drying meats and other activities associated with the hearth.

The youngest in the family, Sazo, inherited his father's plot and cares for their elderly mother. Opposite Sazo's house is a *tehuba*, an elevated, circular space with sitting stones along the circumference where elders gather for clan meetings, and from there stone steps descend to a small patio with a separate kitchen structure on the south side facing a modest, single-story wooden house belonging to Vilhou, his wife Kevi and two toddlers.

'Your brother Sazo tells me you've had some really interesting dreams. Is that true?' Vilhou nodded as he folded a fresh paan leaf with betel nut, lime and tobacco and placed it inside his left cheek.

'Last year I had a terrible dream'.

At the end of March, the weather is pleasant at mid-day so we sat outside in his patio with his outdoor kitchen to our backs. A few months into fieldwork my

Tenyidie proficiency consisted of greetings and phrases I had picked up on short visits over the course of the last decade. I could usually pick out words, but the five possible tonal inflections were taxing. Vilhou's betel nut chewing muffled his consonants making it all-the-more frustrating. Most young to middle-age men in the village chew tamul or paan with tobacco throughout the day and only suspend the habit to eat or sleep. As long as the tones are distinguishable, there is no particular exertion to enunciate clearly, so speech often sounds like a kind of exercise in muffled, atonal Sprechstimme. I resigned and placed the recorder on the ground. Vilhou continued,

> You know, when you dream of mushrooms it's a bad omen. In my dream I was in my bed and I saw a mushroom under my bed growing beneath me. It was growing slowly, but soon was so large, it was like a giant boil in the floor. It kept growing and growing until I thought it was going to consume me. It was diseased, bubbling and spewing fumes – a terrible sight! I'm not really a church-going Christian, you know . . . so you'll hardly ever see me at Khedi or Baptist Revival, but I was so frightened by my dream. A dream like that is very ominous, and may spell death! So as soon as I woke up I went to the prayer house just down the road here.

The prayer centre that Vilhou visited after his terrifying dream is about a five-minute walk from his house and is constructed beside the village road opposite the Baptist Revival Church and dug into a steep slope below the road. The prayer centre is open 24 hours a day, 7 days a week, and is staffed around-the-clock.

> When you have a dream like that you need to be really careful. I knew I had to stay out of trouble – to avoid trouble that whole week. At the prayer house they prayed for me, and I decided I would just stay calm and go about my business. At first, I wasn't sure I should go to work, but I thought that it shouldn't be a problem so I just went down to my shop later that morning.

Waketime interference

It was a first for him, and though he attended a traditional Baptist church as a child, as an adult he rarely set foot inside of a church. As has been mentioned previously, any dream, particularly an ominous one, will be discussed with close family members. If this is not believed sufficient in disarming its destructive potential, then the dreamer will approach a knowledgeable clan elder or church elder for prayer. Vilhou decided to skip these first two steps, preferring instead to head straight to a prayer counsellor.

The Baptist Revival church and prayer centre is located inside the clan neighbourhood, and prayer services are held twice a day in the sanctuary above the road, across from the centre that Vilhou and Senyü (chapter 3) visited. The prayer services last for about 15 minutes. The building sits on a slope above the road, but appears too large for the hill and juts out over a lower road suspended in the air by a series of reinforced concrete pillars. During my first visit, I accompanied 31-year-old schoolteacher Vonuo to an evening service in the earlier part of June. Single, and having lost her father ten years earlier, the recent death of her mother to cancer was devastating, and she had been attending prayer services regularly ever since, despite her heavy workload at the school. We access the main entrance via the upper road and down a long set of concrete steps. About 200 people attend the evening session, filling about a quarter of the massive sanctuary. In the midst of a power outage, the space is lit by a clear sky as we prepare to begin. After a few words from a prayer leader, the whole congregation speaks in unison,

> Jihova thse, Jihova thse, Jihova tshe. Shiro, pelekezhamia gei zasi hako tuo-tuo, uko a za nunu terhuo kesuoko whuolietuo . . . Jihova thse, Jihova thse, Jihova tshe

It is a passage from the New Testament book of Mark 16 verses 17 and 18: 'And these signs will accompany those who believe: In my name they will drive out demons; they will speak in new tongues. . . ' After the 'Jihova thse, Jihova thse, Jihova tshe' refrain – literally 'Praise Jehovah' – the whole place suddenly erupts into a mass prayer, with at least half of the congregation shouting. This lasts for about 35 seconds, followed by a unison 'Amen' and another unhurried 'Praise Jehovah' refrain leading again into mass prayer. This time it lasts 40 seconds, followed again by the refrain. The congregation sits, and the pastor invites individuals to come forward and kneel before the platform for the laying on of hands and pastoral prayer. As he walks and kneels in between four individuals that have come forward, he listens to their specific requests. He then stands before them, and the congregation repeats the refrain as the pastor then prays for the specific needs mentioned. This is the half-way point of the service, and the second half is nearly identical, ending with a prayer of thanksgiving in place of the pastoral prayer.

After the service, Vonuo led me outside where her friend Razu was greeting attendees. A prayer counsellor working in the church's 24-hour prayer centre across the road, Razu stated that many of the attendees coming for the morning and evening prayer meetings do so because they have had powerful dreams. In fact, he said,

> people from all over Nagaland come here to the Prayer Centre. Many of them are troubled by their dreams; by bad spirits; they have tried other things, but sometimes nothing works and finally they come here to the Centre.

The Baptist Revival church is more accommodating to people from outside the village, compared to the traditional Baptist church that sits at the highest point in the village – Khedi Baptist Church. Preserving the order or service, the hymns and preaching style of the American Baptist missionaries who first arrived in Kohima in 1878, Khedi Baptist is a large 5,000-member church with a small primary school, large women's, youth and men's groups, and a global missions programme with a dozen or so missionaries serving in other parts of India, as well as in Southeast Asia. The team of pastors at Khedi regularly attend Baptist World Alliance conferences overseas, and their mixed choir toured the United States in 1999, sponsored by the American Baptist International Ministries in Valley Forge, Pennsylvania, the agency that originally sent the first missionaries to India's Northeast from the 1830s onwards.

Community disruption

Vilhou runs a small butcher shop on clan-owned land near High School Junction just north of the village. His shop is adjacent to a large encampment of the Border Roads Organisation (BRO), a paramilitary road labour corps with encampments throughout Nagaland and the Northeast region, and in charge of both maintaining and securing national highways. Vilhou had been at the gate of the encampment for some time attempting to get the commander's attention. The drainage ditch he agreed to let out to them to build on his land was now overflowing with rubbish. In the hot sun the stench and swarming flies rendered his nearby butcher shop inoperable. The pollution was just a step too far in a long history of tension. The encampment is on clan land and based on old leases agreed on generations ago. One of the main tensions between villagers and the Indian paramilitary is that the clan land occupied by the various bases in town is done so with little in the way of adequate compensation. It is ultimately against clan will and they have no recourse.

Being ignored entirely, Vilhou was fuming and suddenly started climbing the fence of the encampment. He was immediately tackled and beaten by the soldiers who were manning the inside of the gate. Some of my neighbours up in the village stated that the whole of the village was alerted, and it started when a local passer-by recognised that the bloodied figure bent over with a dozen rifle barrels aimed at his head was in fact Vilhou from *L-khel*. One by one, then in trucks, and then in the dozens, rushing along the national highway towards the encampment, the swelling crowed shouted for Vilhou's release. The encampment commander had gone inside, having approached the gate to tell the crowd to disperse. One informant suggested that he went back inside and phoned the Major General of the Assam Rifles, because in what seemed like a matter of minutes heavy military trucks carrying fully armed paramilitaries were negotiating their way through traffic towards the encampment, while the Major General had sped ahead in an attempt to avert an outright confrontation. According to an Indian Reserve Battalion officer who was a close neighbour in the village, the Indian paramilitaries, from inside the encampment, can 'lawfully' shoot anyone who trespasses the camp gate or fence. And, in hindsight, Vilhou surmises that the full weight of the event was lessened by the fact of his approaching the prayer centre about his dream, citing the fact that the guards showed restraint and did not shoot him or any of his clansmen. Indeed, shooting Kohima villagers – Kohima itself being the epicentre of the Naga conflict – would have undoubtedly escalated quickly, shattering the fragile 1997 ceasefire.

> All these lands are Angami lands . . . and up there [pointing northwards] those are our clan's lands . . . and we lease them out. The Assam Rifles wanted to lease part of my land to build a sewer for the BRO. At first I was not happy with that, but I said they could build it if they kept it clean – that was the condition – that I would take it back if they did not keep it clean. When I was down there that morning the stench from the sewer was unbearable – I could not get any customers! It made me so angry, that they just did what they wanted, with no respect for us. I went to the BRO gate and called the commanding officer, but he did not want to come out. I shouted for the officer in charge to come clean the mess. I admit I was really angry and shouting at the BRO officers in the camp. No one was listening so I climbed the gate. The officers that were there rushed at me, threw me on the ground, kicked me, and pointed their rifles at my head. They were shouting all kinds of obscenities at me, and saying they were going to shoot me for trespassing. I was so angry, I shouted 'shoot me then, you always do what you want, you have no respect, even though you are not welcome here, and so on'. Some of my fellow clansmen passing by saw what was happening and they came to the gate and started to argue with the officers. They also called people in the village, so the Angami Student Union came down, and in a short time it seemed the whole village came down. Everyone was venting their anger, and in a short time the Major General of the Assam Rifles had to drive down from Kohima headquarters to try to calm everyone down. It was really bad – and it could have led to shooting, and probably end the ceasefire!

Vilhou then shifted his tone and looked up – 'these dreams always come true – it's inevitable – once you see something in your dreams, it becomes true no matter what you do'. In subsequent months, I approached a dozen or so people and asked them about the events at the BRO camp in 2012. All of them confirmed, more or less, the details that Vilhou's narrated to me. One gentleman who had come to dehusk several sacks of rice in the mill below my fieldwork residence remembered the events clearly: 'Yes, I remember that day – it was very tense. The Assam Rifles commander had to rush down from the town with his security personnel to keep it from starting the war again!' In another interview, I asked a distant relative of Vilhou's, who is serving as an officer in the Indian Reserve Battalion, about the incident.

> Vilhou is crazy, he is lucky to be alive – he should never have tried to climb the fence like that. You know that we have the order to shoot and kill anyone who trespasses the IRB base. Yes, the BRO was irresponsible for not keeping the ditch clean, but you have to be crazy to confront them like that – Vilhou is crazy.

Visiting the prayer centre several months after that initial interview with Vilhou, I asked a counsellor if he knew about the BRO camp incident. The counsellor said he was new to the staff, but that he had heard about the event and Vilhou's connection to it. 'Actually, we get a lot of people coming for the early prayer service asking for prayer because they have had a bad dream'. But, in addition to being known as *mhotékezhamia* around the village, among his clansmen he is known for his bad temper. Sober for several years now, when Vilhou used to drink he was entirely belligerent in the community, and the *Meya* clan men had pressured his brothers to intervene. But in many respects, the incident at the BRO camp was about the significantly unwelcome presence of a paramilitary force on clan land, and one more event justifying the clan's longstanding anger towards what most view as the excessive military presence in the heart of clan residential areas.

These kinds of outpourings, whether of anger or grief, are rare in what can only be described as a generally insular, conservative society. One exception is in the context of funerals. The village community is sufficiently densely populated that funeral wakes can waft through the air from this or that direction, indicating that someone has died, if someone had not called, or indeed the news of a dream message portending the death had not circulated first. A second exception is, of course, the outpourings occasioned in the midst of the admittedly tightly structured charismatic services at the Baptist Revival church. The mass prayers in particular of religious inspiration mixed with grief. But these expressions have their roots in the events that followed the exit of the American missionaries, who were asked to leave the country in the 1950s. And in the following section I briefly examine the context within which these expressions emerged, a context to which the birth and character of the revival movement can be traced.

The sudden departure of the American missionaries and the leadership void this created coincided with the political turn of events of the Naga nationalists in Naga nationalism following the 1951 plebiscite, the 1952 all-Naga boycott of the Indian general election and the visit of Prime Ministers U. Nu of Burma and Jawaharlal Nehru in 1953 to Kohima (discussed in chapter 1). Up until that moment the Naga National Council (NNC) had led a non-violent movement of resistance to Indian rule. When Nehru refused to meet them during his visit, the crowd of 15,000 Nagas he was about to address from the podium turned their backs on him and slapped their behinds in defiance before exiting the ground en-masse. Within hours, orders were to hunt down the leadership of the NNC, and they were forced underground and began to take arms. The deployment of tens of thousands of Indian military and paramilitary forces throughout the Naga areas further exacerbated the tension, and stories of atrocities began to circulate, creating an increasing sense of despair.

During this time, women both Christian and non-Christian began to meet regularly to share information, to bury their dead and to comfort families caught up in the conflict. Itinerant preachers would visit the women's groups and share news of other similar meetings – often news that God was moving in powerful ways to protect people from the violence (Angelova 2014). The intensity of feeling surrounding the secret meetings – catalysed by their sense of being surrounded by hostility – led to a revitalisation of practices that had become subdued for some time as the behaviour expected in Baptist churches increasingly became the accepted norm.

This intensely pressurised environment in the heat of war also translated into religious outpourings involving Christians and non-Christians, and the rate of Christian conversions continued to accelerate. In the 1961 Indian census, out of a total Naga population of 369,200, 195,588, or 53%, were registered as Christians. Linyü describes the typical revival meeting:

> Though they were aware of the reality of a powerful God, the Nagas, regardless of their faith . . . were still living in a world of spirits. So, to begin a service, the evil spirits would have to be driven out first. This, they would all do together, shouting, stamping their feet, telling evil spirits to go away. After this they would confess their sins in the same manner. The third stage is to ask or pray for 'power' or 'blessing'. This would begin by singing songs, which they had memorised, and clapping. The singing would continue until it turns into a melody without words. Then this would go on faster and faster, assuming the pattern of *Kewhu*.[5] Then this would lead the whole congregation to burst into a frenzied mass prayer. After the 'Amen' is said the whole congregation would shout 'Jihova thse! Jihova thse! Jihova thse!'. Almost like saying Wi Wi Wi, after the completion of *Kewhu*. This ends the prayer. But then there would be persons either rolling on the floor, making strange utterances or acting like in a trance. Those rolling on the floor and moaning and crying in utter agony were said to be going through the baptism of fire. Those who were like in a trance, either lying on the floor or sitting would be seeing 'visions' or prophesying. Especially those who would be lying on the floor would appear like the *Terhuope* [literally 'bridge of the gods' referring to individuals that use trance to communicate with ancestors and spirits]. And they would convey messages on behalf of God or see 'visions' which they would relate the contents later.
>
> (2004, p. 134–5)

The various spirit-mediated expressions, though recognised as older practices, were interpreted in Christian terms: those speaking unintelligibly were said to be speaking in tongues – drawing on New Testament texts associated with Pentecost.[6] In the Chakhesang (Eastern Angami) areas, a Baptist pastor remarked,

> Miracles were performed, revival songs were heard everywhere, reconciliations were made, Christian love was restored, visions, prophecy, ecstasy and glossolalia (languages) were phenomenal, non-Christians rushed to see the miracles and became Christians in individuals and in groups. Churches were all packed. Food, sleep and farming were all forgotten, but the believers lacked nothing; Church extensions became necessary in so many places.
>
> (Dozo 1983, pp. 15–16)

Though Dozo paints a positive picture, the revivals created a number of aspects that were antagonistic to each other. On the one hand some revival gatherings – especially in the earlier movements – sought a clean break from what they viewed as a dark past of blood feuds and headhunting, and that this required the destruction of all vestiges of the old customs. Traditional weavings, jewellery and ceremonial dress used in festivals and material culture, seen as polluting their newfound faith, were broken or destroyed in huge fires. On the other hand – and this was characteristic of the later movements in the 1970s – the gatherings believed that many pre-Christian beliefs and practices were consistent with Christian teachings and found ways to blend traditional forms with Christian worship.

The increased brutality at the hands of the Indian forces seemed to fuel all variants equally, as they responded with ever-increasing converts and accelerated evangelistic efforts. By the early 1960s large groups of local missionaries were sent to work in remote Naga areas further east and into Burma, even as the political violence had escalated considerably in their hometowns and villages. The unstructured nature of the revival movement was such that a visiting British clergyman at the time, Rev Michael Scott, remarked,

> Out of the religion brought by American Baptist missionaries, who loved them and were welcomed amongst them as friends, they have made something of their own and in no way incompatible with their own zest for life and for the songs and dances, animated by beings and beliefs which they have not discarded and see no incongruity in retaining along with their beliefs in the powerful reality of God, the driving force of creation and purpose in their lives and all life – yet no one could possibly describe them as a pious or even a moral people.
>
> (Linyü 2004, p. 37)

From the very beginning of the nationalist movement, the NNC had linked the political cause with Christianity. As early as 1952, the NNC's newly formed Federal Government of Nagaland (FGN) had used the slogan 'Nagaland for Christ' in an effort to, according to Linyü, 'galvanise the Nagas to stand united against the "Hindu" Indian Army' (2004, p. 142). Indeed, Linyü suggests that it was a mistake to suggest that Christians were theologising violence and rebellion:

> the opposite was true. It was during this period that the Government of India, represented by the Indian Army, that expelled the missionaries, killed church leaders like Rev. Pelesatuo, raped women, burnt church buildings, that came to be viewed as opposite to everything that is Christian that made the Naga Christians to work with more vigour.
>
> (Linyü 2004, p. 142)

Regular meetings to share news and count the casualties had the effect of casting a new rhythm on collective village activities, and this fed into the nationalist ideal of forging a more unified Naga identity. Indeed, the violence in the jungle strengthened solidarity in village communities, generating a recognition of what and who the Nagas, as a whole, were as a people and who they were not. In the event that traditional Baptists were reluctant to accommodate revivalists, spaces to gather were acquired, and remained neutral among clans. They put aside their differences in order to coalesce around common ideals. Some church buildings were also built as joint community efforts on donated community land. Moreover, the ambiguity of the gatherings – as un-invested in clan laws, clanic histories and genealogies – allowed it to be a new vessel for identity formation at the village level. The simple liturgies of regularised services held in common throughout the Naga areas allowed for communication between villages that bypassed fraught inter-village histories and rivalries. Here, the sense of solidarity, mediated through liturgical ritual, also increasingly defined those that did not identify with the new ritually-mediated symbolic and institutional repertoire.

By the early 1960s aerial bombardments were being deployed by the Indian Armed Forces, leading to desperation and a refugee crisis. At this juncture the Nagaland Baptist Church Council, representing the various Naga Baptist associations, recruited two respected politicians and a British clergyman – well-recognised for their views on non-violence and peace – and brokered a ceasefire between the FGN and the Indian Government in September 1964. The ceasefire brought some calm to the region, but the heavy militarisation of the region kept tensions high, and occasional skirmishes always threatened the fragile agreement.

By this time, Christians were increasingly split, and many Baptist leaders resented losing members to the revival movement and at times retaliated against what they saw as out of control, unbiblical and borderline pagan meetings. One of my informants stated that his house was burned down by his Christian neighbours in the early 1950s because his family was non-Christian. They had to settle in Kohima town while his home was rebuilt. The neighbours who burned their house down still live across the road. In another recorded instance a Baptist pastor burst into a rage and sent members of his congregation to burn the temporary structure being used by the revivalists. The occurrence of these incidents is cited by some as a factor that led to conversion and also to movement from one Christian tradition to another (Joshi 2013, p. 199).

The interpretive community

As with the de-escalations and ceasefires with as yet no permanent resolution of the past, the incidents at the encampment where Vilhou was being held also followed this logic. Tensions were high when village leaders met the Major General of the Assam Rifles at the gate and entrance to the BRO camp, but in time the parties agreed to stop the shouting and accusations and not to pursue the matter further. Everyone seemed to stand their ground for a few minutes, but the realities of work, of family and of other responsibilities crept back into peoples' minds. The authorities released a badly beaten Vilhou, and the crowd gathered by the gate was persuaded to disperse. Still conscious he was carried to a neighbour's vehicle and taxied to a local hospital. All that Vilhou could think about, however, was that his dream had become a reality.[7]

The tensions could have easily flared out of control, and many of the villagers that had come down had lost family members in the war – many at the hands of the Assam Rifles itself – and several that I spoke to had fought in the early NNC insurgency. In fact, in the 1950s, able-bodied Naga men joined the early NNC insurgency in large numbers, and women stayed back and took over many of the responsibilities that the men left behind, including town clerical responsibilities, the management of schools and churches, postal services and transportation. However, they also organised support for the insurgency, stocking food supplies, facilitating communications and sharing news.

By this time, Christianity had spread through most of the Naga areas, so the women also gathered as they had learned from missionaries, to pray for loved ones fighting in the insurgency and sometimes hosting itinerant evangelists. As the atrocities of the war came to affect local families personally and communities directly, these women's groups were at the centre of an intensification of religious fervour that then erupted in what are generally termed the 'revivals' – first in the 1950s and then in the 1970s – and spread quickly throughout the Naga-inhabited areas.

The sense of being surrounded by hostile forces, forces that had proven capable of violence, recalled earlier times when the typical Naga hilltop settlement was generally more isolated and always attentive to attack – whether from a raid by a rival village or from *terhuomia* or harmful spirits. The 'interference' that accompanied inspirational religious practices reflected pre-Christian concerns to propitiate potentially harmful spirits. Hutton (1921) observed, for example, that Angami public rituals accompanying threats perceived in bad omens were fastidious and indicative of a deep-seated concern that, for example, entire harvests may be lost due to some unforeseen or unchecked imbalance in human relations with the spirits governing the land. An intense vigilance was necessary, and much of this could be accomplished by distributing attentiveness through the community to the signs given by ancestral spirits, acting as spirit guardians of their human kin.

This general insecurity and defensive disposition was reflective of the increasing marginality of the *Kemovo* or *Thevo*, once prominent individuals who played the central mediating role between human and non-human spirit worlds, perceiving imbalances and pre-empting any spirit-precipitated events that might be interpreted as anger towards the community. The move towards propitiation, more or less side-lining the shamanic function of mediation, was also a shift towards regularised ritual practices. This shift had the effect of shifting power among clan and village decision makers. With the advent of Christianity, and shortly after the Indo-Naga conflict, old and new traditions, namely domestic dream divining and Christian practice, which had grown close together with the clan patriarchal tradition, came together in what was essentially an outcry against the cruelty and violence.

Yet, today these distinct Baptist traditions co-exist within Kohima Village despite their theological differences regarding inspirational religious practices.

Though the traditional Baptist leaders follow the logic of and in a sense morally support clan patriarchy, the charismatic Baptists are less hierarchical and appear concerned about sufficient attentiveness and faithfulness in interpreting divinely imparted knowledge received in its services. Moreover, they are also concerned about keeping the peace with the clan and village by, in a sense, 'containing' the charisma that emerges in their services. The spontaneous outpourings that characterised the early revivals do appear in fragments, but only because they now occur in the midst of carefully planned service programmes, in controlled service timings and in specific spaces within the church sanctuary. I suggest here that, like the 'interference' of the interpretive community with regards to everyday dream experiences in the community, these controls and regulated rhythms now instituted as part of Baptist Church Revival services reflect the dynamic of 'interference' and thus regulation or 'sieving' of charisma.

Within the liturgical tradition of the traditional Baptist churches, dream experiences are largely deemed to exceed the already final narrative of evangelical theology. There is, in a very real sense, an in-built 'regulation' pre-empting the potential disruptions that new knowledge might introduce. That is to say, there is no room for new knowledge because the knowledge expressed as 'Biblical' is final. Traditional Baptists invoke the supernatural *Kemesa Ruopfü* (lit. 'Clean Spirit' or the Christian 'Holy Spirit') in so far as it produces a general or distributed manifestation, as opposed to, as Robert Tonkinson suggests, 'inducing radically altered individual states' (2003, p. 90). The 'depersonalising' general manifestation is more orderly and translates into what is believed to be a greater consciousness of the hidden truths about the 'signs of the times' deeply coded in the Bible (Tonkinson 2003). The parallels between this mode of worship and clan council deliberation are not coincidental and in many respects are at the core of the 'grafting' that occurred between the traditional Baptist churches and the clan leadership throughout Nagaland.

Members that feel this approach constricts their broader vocabulary of spiritual experiences will shift to other congregations they feel are more open and accepting. On the other hand, charismatic congregations offering accommodation, such as the Baptist Revival church, tend to privilege religious inspiration catalysed through performance. Here knowledge obtained through dreams is valued, but typically relegated to a lower rung in relation to the more public acts of spiritual healing, glossolalia and prophecy. Though they search for clues through extra-textual manifestations such as prophetic messages, visions and dreams as they are potential channels for God's voice to her people, there are caveats tagged to such manifestations, and there are warnings of false messages, false prophets and the conspiring motives of demons and Satan (cf. Stewart and Strathern 2003).

Increasingly, the traditional Baptists have begun articulating themselves according to the principles of prosperity theology, the belief that faithfulness leads to material wealth in the present (as opposed to postponed heavenly rewards). More and more, participation in evangelical mission efforts that have a broad international scope has meant that attention is diverted from many of the growing local concerns of urban poverty, a significant HIV/AIDS problem, and other community concerns where the great accumulation of resources that churches now have could be used more effectively. It is in the domestic sphere, however, that the psycho-spiritual pulse of the community is monitored, and women play the leading role in mediating the efficacy of inspirational religious experience and practice relative to the wellbeing of their kinship relations and close neighbours. The gender divide here is not absolute, as church attendance and participation are still largely sustained by women, women's prayer groups and voluntary service in the numerous church programmes and activities. And some men, especially teenagers and into early adulthood, are largely averse to the codes of practice meted out by the church, and thus create communities of shared experience among friends and close kin. Most, however, find a way to manage both by attending to the minimum requirements of church attendance while remaining open and pragmatic about a broader set of religious possibilities. This is easily facilitated through memories of their own life experiences, by dreams, by participating in dream sharing among close kin and neighbours, and by drawing on the few fragments of old customs that may be gleaned from older members.

This broader sphere of experience is akin to a horizontally oriented collective, and here I draw on Stephen Hugh-Jones' concepts of horizontal and vertical shamanism and some of the nuances that Caroline Humphrey teases out with her similar description of patriarchal and transformational tendencies within inspirational religious practice (Thomas and Humphrey 1996). The horizontal collective extends beyond individual specialists and operates as a sort of informal community watch that at its most organised is vigilant of the signs and omens that emerge from a world where everything means something. Its informal character, however, makes it fluid and more practical to daily living and has the added the bonus of having no controlling centre.

Concluding remarks

When one shares a dream, there are several levels of appeal, several stages that one traverses if indeed the dream communicates a message. Vilhou, despite his lack of interest in church or Christianity, understood that he was dealing with a dream-imparted message that only the highest level of mediation could contend with. Indeed, he was appealing for the highest level of 'interference' in order to defuse the full force of harm it portended. In present-day Kohima, daily 6am and 6pm prayer services held at the Baptist Revival Church continue to welcome all those seeking 'interference' in the foretelling dreams they have brought to the gathering, dreams of fortune and of disturbance alike. It is not uncommon for individuals to say that they pray right after waking up in the morning, seeking God's intercession. This kind of prayer is similar to prayers made for other concerns, and this is a practice that is well accepted by traditional Baptists. That the Baptist Revival Church is witness to such a significant gathering of people seeking to share and pray over their dreams points to the enduring need to bring dream knowledge to a community space. It is indeed striking that a multitude assembles twice every day, and it is a multitude from various backgrounds, socio-economic levels and a multitude of understandings about the divine. In a single space, congregants chant in unison and then speak in their own voices – as loud as they please – and then they come back to chant in unison. The prayer meetings certainly play a role in defusing and regulating the influx of new forms of knowledge into the community, but they are also providing a space for these forms of inspiration to be voiced publically.

When narrating dreams, the practice of consulting a trusted interpreter entails a form of 'interference'. Dreams that foretell fortune are narrated, interpreted and sometimes blessed, because these steps are necessary to ensure that the good fortune will indeed materialise. On the other hand, as seen in the story of Vilhou, a bad dream, if not taken seriously, can significantly disrupt the community and beyond. I have suggested that the informal practices of dream interpretation, among married village women and primarily in the domestic sphere, serve as the central loci for this 'interference'. I then suggested that this dynamic of interference is also present among charismatic Christians, and there are some very specific historical processes associated with the Indo-Naga conflict that allow us to trace this development. In the local Baptist Revival Church such practices as spiritual healing, glossolalia, prophecy, dreams and visions – practices generally frowned upon by the traditional Baptist churches – are both encouraged and carefully regulated. Sitting well within one of the main village clans, church leaders at the Baptist Revival Church ensure that potentially disruptive inspirational religious practices emerging in their services do not disrupt the village peace. It is, after all, in their interest to continue to provide an important outlet for outpourings of inspirational religious expression in the community. In the living memory of many elders, unregulated inspirational practices have been shown to prove disruptive. Indeed, when they do disrupt the village peace they are no longer compatible with the structures of clan patriarchy.

It is difficult to say whether the revivals, the ecstatic eruptions of inspirational religious expression in the midst of considerable suffering and uncertainty, would have been less explosive if villages had not been so fragmented by the war. Christianity at any rate was fairly new in the 1950s, and older practices would have still been fresh, especially in the domestic sphere where divining, through reading dream and waketime omens, remained, as compared to public rituals. In many ways the domestic sphere spilled over, and old and new faith expressions came together in what was essentially an outcry. But ecstatic appeals that they were, they lacked order – they were spontaneous, with no centre, no rules to ensure a minimal level of composure – and so they were attacked by traditional Baptists that interpreted them as wholly disruptive. The revival meetings had the capacity to undermine community cohesion as governed by the clan, and indeed they lacked 'interference'. The Baptist Revival Church and other charismatic churches of today have sought a middle ground so as to be able to cohabitate within clan laws. So they have strict worship timings, a regular schedule of services, and are led by trained clergy.

Notes

1 Nienke van der Heide, 2015, "When dreams shape our day" in Leiden Anthropology Blog, posted 15 April, 2015. Online source: www.leidenanthropologyblog.nl/articles/when-dreams-shape-our-day, accessed 15 January 2015.
2 Ibid.
3 Ibid.
4 The Naga writer Easterine Kire was instrumental in helping me with key terms, as well as filling out the lexicon of dream symbols and their meanings – often consulting her mother on my behalf just to confirm the precise translations.
5 The Kewhu is a traditional ritual chant pronounced in unison during certain old purification ceremonies and particularly during Sekrenyi.
6 The main text used comes from the New Testament book of Acts, chapter 2: 'When the day of Pentecost came, they were all together in one place. 2 Suddenly a sound like the blowing of a violent wind came from heaven and filled the whole house where they were sitting. 3 They saw what seemed to be tongues of fire that separated and came to rest on each of them. 4 All of them were filled with the Holy Spirit and began to speak in other tongues[a] as the Spirit enabled them' (New International Version)
7 Field notes, Vilhou, Kohima Village, 12 April 2013.

Bibliography

Angelova, Iliyana, 2013, 'Something like wind, unusual thing came': the Great Evangelical Revivals of the 1950s and 1970s in the memories of some Sümi Naga', in *Passing Things On: Ancestors and Genealogies in Northeast India*, Michael Heneise, ed., Dimapur: Heritage Press, pp. 90-102.
Dozo, Phuveyi, 1983, *The Cross Over Nagaland*, Dimapur: Christian Literature Centre.
Graham, Laura R., 1995, *Performing Dreams: Discourses of Immorality Among the Xavante of Central Brazil*, Austin: University of Texas Press.
Habermas, Jürgen, 1984, *The Theory of Communicative Action*, Thomas A. McCarthy, trans., Boston MA: Beacon Press.
Habermas, Jürgen, 1987, *Theory of Communicative Action: Vol. 2: Lifeworld and System: A Critique of Functionalist Reason*, Boston MA: Beacon Press.
Hutton, J.H., 1921, *The Angami Nagas*, London: Palgrave Macmillan.
Joshi, V., 2013, *A Matter of Belief: Christianity in Northeast India*, London: Berghahn Books.
Linyü, Keviyiekielie, 2004, *Christian Movements in Nagaland*, Kohima: Self-Published.
Lohmann, Roger Ivar, ed., 2003, *Dream Travelers: Sleep Experiences and Culture in the Western Pacific*, New York: Palgrave Macmillan.
Robbins, Joel, 2003, "Dreaming and the Defeat of Charisma: Disconnecting Dreams from Leadership among the Urapmin of Papua New Guinea" in *Dream Travelers: Sleep Experiences and Culture in the Western Pacific*, Roger I. Lohmann, ed., New York: Palgrave Macmillan, pp. 19-41.
Stewart, Pamela and Andrew, Strathern, 2003, "Dreaming and Ghosts Among the Hagen and Duna of the Southern Highlands, Papua New Guinea", in *Dream Travelers: Sleep Experiences and Culture in the Western Pacific*, Roger I. Lohmann, ed., New York: Palgrave Macmillan, pp. 43–60.
Thomas, Nicholas and Caroline Humphrey, eds., 1996, *Shamanism, History and the State*, Ann Arbor: University of Michigan Press.

Tonkinson, Robert, 2003, "Ambrymese Dreams and the Mardu Dreaming", in *Dream Travelers: Sleep Experiences and Culture in the Western Pacific*, Roger I. Lohmann, ed., New York: Palgrave Macmillan, pp. 87-105.

van der Heide, N., 2015a, "When Dreams Shape Our Day", in *Leiden Anthropology Blog*, posted 15 April 2015. Online source: www.leidenanthropologyblog.nl/articles/when-dreams-shape-our-day, accessed 15 January 2015.

van der Heide, N., 2015b, *Spirited Performance: The Manas Epic and Society in Kyrgyzstan*, Bremen: Rozenberg Publishers.

6 The landscape of dreams

By taking into account dreamscapes, we have a better understanding of how the Angami negotiate space. A simple example is that physical boundaries to physical space are set as much by spirits (or spiritual influence) as they are by physical features or clan (i.e. men) decision. In the previous chapter I discussed the ways in which the community receives and interprets spirit messages in dreams and in charismatic Christian worship and how this interpretive process involves 'interference', entailing the social 'regulation' of spirit knowledge in order that it may

Figure 6.1 Terraced paddy fields below Khonoma village
Source: Author's photo

be integrated into community life while avoiding any unwelcome 'disruption'. I also traced 'interference' to pre-Christian practices associated with ritual spirit propitiation. Village founders and heads, the *Kemovos*, negotiated with the original spirit owners of the land, and in this process delineated where the domain of the living ended and where the domain of spirits began. This practice influenced clan ideas of space and how, partly due to concern for preserving the contiguity of lineage property, it is a practice that remains, though the original settlement perimeter has significantly expanded (see Figure 6.2). Thus today, as in the past, ancestral spirits have as much a say about space as living clan members, and this is taken very seriously and does indeed affect everyday life and everyday understanding of the clan's place in the world. To dismiss these ideas is to misunderstand the Angami. Moreover, this relationship with space may be indexed in dreams. As with the *Kemovo* of old (chapter 4), dreams open the possibility for new negotiations over land, and in this chapter I give an example of such an exchange, one which is particularly salient given that it was a dream-mediated negotiation with spirits over land, on behalf of the state.

I begin with an example of how clan ideas of space play out in village life by discussing an ultimatum that my host family received and also circulated among households throughout the clans in *L-khel*, demanding that clan families leasing

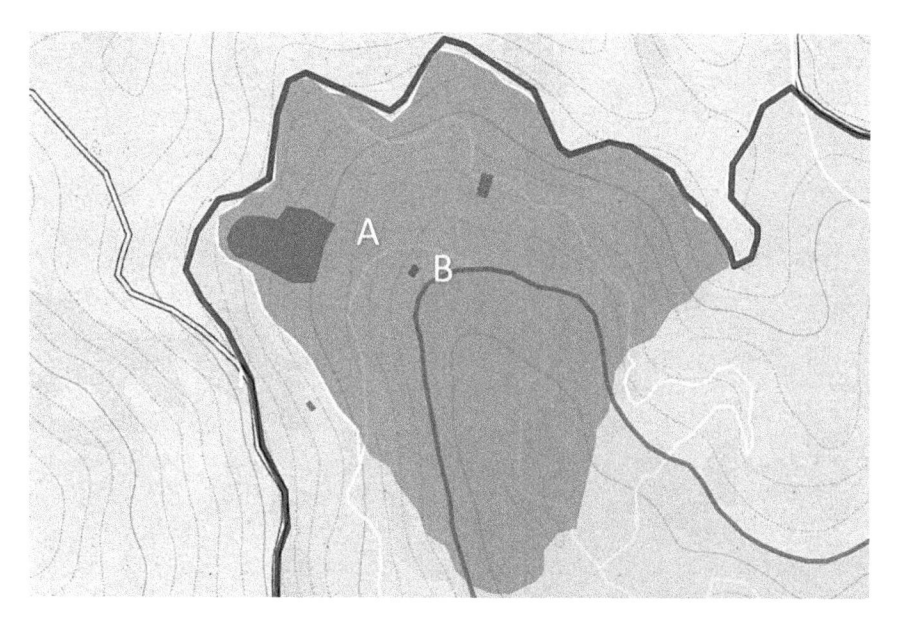

Figure 6.2 Map of L-khel (dark grey area) in the northwest quadrant of Kohima village: 'A' – fieldwork residence; 'B' – traditional location of village gate between old settlement boundary (bold dark grey line) and village path (thin light grey line)

Source: Author's drawing

out spaces to non-clan members inside the village boundary cease and desist or pay hefty fines. I follow this example with a brief theoretical discussion arguing for the inextricable nature of spaces in relation to events, and further the capacities for manoeuvre in relation to spatial configurations of power and constraint as manifested in dreams. I then turn to the ethnographic example exploring the main themes in greater depth, followed by the chapter summary.

The LYO ultimatum

L-khel, in the northwest quadrant of Kohima village, straddles the old settlement which is the highest level (the domain of humans) and encompasses lower areas that were once forested (the domain of spirits). The outer line of the expanded settlement area (post 1950s) is the new boundary, and traditional gates were erected to symbolically demarcate the new line. The old village boundary is largely imaginary, though at times a stone wall marks the line. My fieldwork residence (marked with 'A' in Figure 3) stands about 5 metres from the old boundary line (which is invisible).

Membership in the Lhisemia Youth Organisation (LYO) is comprised of lineage group members, and thus mostly men with some unmarried clan women. The organisation itself does not have any official capacity within the clan councils per se, but regularly participates in organising clan meetings, sports events, village cleaning drives and other clan activities. Its capacity to enforce its various khel-wide edicts is proportional to its capacity to intimidate with violence. It nevertheless acts on its own accord. The use of threats is common, and the LYO while for instance calling clan children over van-mounted loudspeakers to attend sports events might typically announce: 'the LYO will be taking attendance, and if you do not show up, we will remember. When you are in a difficult situation do not expect us to come to your aid'. Clan families are generally relaxed about LYO activities, mainly because they have little to worry about, and either hold membership or have close relatives that do. Many of the edicts and warnings that the LYO circulates relate to rubbish in the streets, stray dogs, the hiring of Muslims for construction work or any other kind of work within the village boundary (which is strictly enforced, with physical assaults on the workers being not uncommon) and other 'disruptions', violators being punished with hefty fines of between 5,000 and 15,000 rupees.

It was at the the tail end of monsoon in August 2014 that I was shown a copy of the notice, drafted and circulated by the LYO, stating that 'all non-Lhisemia inhabitants must leave the village'.[1] There was no doubt that this affected me. In fact, even kinship relations outside of the lineage group – i.e. *Lhisemia* daughters with non-*Lhisemia* spouses – were not exempt. It was an unsettling moment, and my host family, somewhat apprehensive, consulted a few close neighbours to ask whether this was as serious as it sounded.

The clan women met, as they often did, down by the road by the small betel-nut shop to discuss the matter. It was mid-morning, and Ruopfünuo* was particularly upset. Her raised voice gave the impression that she was entirely indignant about what the notice implied for her family and for many others living in the clan vicinity. The daughter of a prominent village elder, her spouse was Chakhesang, and she ran a large grocery store in the basement of a house she and her husband had purchased adjacent to my host family's clan compound some 30 years ago. Ruopfünuo employed non-*Lhisemia khel* Naga women from low-income families and had been a prominent leader in the women's groups in the Baptist church. I found out later that the discussions the women were having revolved around the sudden departure of two families – one Rengma, the other Chakhesang – employed in the government middle school just inside the old boundary and residing adjacent to the school. Both families had been threatened, and thus decided to leave.

Later in the evening, Ruopfünuo visited my residence and asked to speak with me personally. 'Michael, don't worry about this letter, and I am so sorry about the confusion. These are our youths and they are so misguided'.[2] We sat down for tea, and she continued 'they think we do not understand the customary laws, and they are wrong'. Here, she was referring to the women in the room. She went on to explain that a wall once marked the boundary, separating the village above from the land outside where spirits of deceased relatives were believed to reside.

> The customary law is clear about *kemo-Lhisemia* (lit. 'no house-Lhisemia') inside the village boundary. But this compound is outside, we are all outside. Those poor families, I feel so ashamed. These youths are thugs, and make everyone think that we don't know the customary laws, and sent the letter to everyone trying to take advantage.[3]

After tea, we walked down to the road, and up towards the middle school. Ruopfünuo stopped and indicated a place on the ground with her arm. 'The gate used to be here, that is all. If people don't know, they just become victims. The line is here, and after this used to be all forest. I built our house when your compound was still forest'.[4]

Though knowledge and enforcement of the old customary laws fell to clan councils, the women knew them well and understood when lineage group members overstepped. Indeed, knowledge of invisible demarcations had the capacity to overwrite a dictat by descent-group members – the lord 'writ large' of clan land. That these structures are invested with final jural force despite being invisible – with not so much as a stone or hedge to indicate their presence – did not inspire confidence that the matter was settled. The LYO threat – I was told later – was intended for families employing or renting space to non-Naga residents and labourers. But it was a bluff. Several families did indeed leave the village, and the LYO was correct in assuming that some would be ignorant of the old laws. But, though the barriers – once constructed like citadel walls – are no longer visible, they actively 'enplace' and 'displace'. Indeed, they are unseen but not absent, and offer some protection to non-lineage kin dwellers (and their labourers and tenants) though only if these reside outside but in close 'proximity' to the bounded settlement.

This was an important moment in my ethnographic research. I (and my field-work) had been saved by the knowledge or memory of an invisible gate in a neighbour's consciousness. It stands roughly five metres behind my bedroom window and was certainly present for the remainder of our stay. But more than that, the experience concretised a set of notions that had only cursorily appeared in my field notes, namely that this ancient 'ancestral space' endures because it is continuously remembered and reconstructed. Though the current arrangement of concrete buildings and narrow paved and unpaved roads appears chaotic, it is a space governed by an imagined symbolic spatial order – a 'ghostly' skeletal structure of a village. But this older spatial arrangement is a formation always emerging, a continuously imagined formation, and foundational to the spatio-temporal perpetuity of the village's corporate descent groups.

Political narratives are, of course, closely linked to territory, and the phrase 'time immemorial', which is often used in Naga political texts, seeks to under-score the historical legitimacy of the Nagas vis-à-vis the histories of their neigh-bours. The spatial relationships that underpin the contemporary political discourse of Naga nationhood are sourced in a hybridisation between Judaeo-Christian ideas associated with divine promise and its linkages to clearly demarcated land and traditional Angami ideas rooted in the construction of protective perimeters. These boundaries serve to demarcate congruous clan territory within villages, but the more critical village perimeters are those erected around the village periphery, symbolically uniting often antagonistic clans in the face of common threats – the hostility of human enemies, or indeed vengeful spirits. Here the numerous heavily fortified clan gates once functioned as border crossings managed politically at the clan level but spiritually at the village level under the supervision of the elders and the *Kemovo*. The *Kemovo*, the traditional descendent of the original village founder, united the political and spiritual concerns of the village as a whole. He functioned both as the human repository of the combined genealogical knowledge of the clans, and as a result was the only village-wide ritual practitioner.

Spatial configurations and power

When Keith Basso suggested that 'placeless events are an impossibility; every-thing that happens must happen somewhere' (1988, p. 86), he articulated an idea that is particularly salient when applied to events registered in our dreams and in dream narratives. As we have seen in the above story of the LYO ultimatum, space and spatial configurations that create distance and separation are fundamental to descent group clan power, and this kind of discourse continually structures com-munity life. But one way to explore the ways in which embodied relationships to space are negotiated and find expression in day-to-day interaction and relation-ships is by looking at how these coordinates are indexed and negotiated in the spaces that appear in dreams narratives.

Perhaps the first to highlight these features within dreams, Michel Foucault, in his introduction to Binswanger's *Dream and Existence*, suggests that

> In the darkest night, the glow of the dream is more luminous than the light of day, and the intuition borne with it the most elevated form of knowledge. [The dream] can throw into bright light the secret and hidden power at work in the most manifest forms of presence.
>
> (1993, p. 59)

Critiquing Freud, and psychoanalysis generally, Foucault states unapologetically that 'psychoanalysis has never succeeded in making images speak' (ibid., p. 38). In other words, it is a mistake to privilege dream symbols and images at the expense of important spatial relationships and constructions. Foucault emphasises that spatial configurations in dreams speak very specifically about the way human beings encounter constraints and find space in which to exercise agency. Indeed, he suggests that 'the forms of spatiality disclose in the dream the very "meaning and direction" of human existence' (ibid., p. 60). Here, one's capacity to navigate depends on one's authoritative facility to command a dream's specific spatial formations and other selves inhabiting those politically demarcated spaces.

Echoing Foucault, Kempf and Hermann (2003) have suggested that dream experiences and dream narratives are indissolubly linked to the political process of spatial construction. They show how descriptions of landscape in dreams narratives among the Ngaing of Papua New Guinea are revealing in terms of their relation to important spatio-political concerns, and specifically in regards to their relationship to colonialism and Christian missionaries. They suggest, for example, that

> The interplay between hegemonic pervasions and indigenous reconstitutions of body and space has fostered not only local self-awareness of an existence at once peripheral and subordinated; it has also called forth local counter-versions of the dominant discourses. These spaces can only be understood in the context of historical contacts and multiple interactions. Dreamscapes are subject to continuous change and are woven into the constitution of counter-spaces or 'heterotopias' that focus attention on the instability, discontinuity, and ambiguity of spatial orders.
>
> (Kempf and Hermann 2003, p. 80)

Dream narratives, in other words, may offer a glimpse into the unique ways in which space and spatial relationships are conceptually developed in different cultures and how these relate to histories of violence. Keeping these ideas in mind, when reflecting on the Naga revival meetings of the 1950s and 1970s in chapter 4, we can observe the ways in which the sometimes unpredictable, sometimes vengeful spiritual landscape outside village settlements seemed to provide a grammar of anxiety for a new set of unpredictable, often vengeful threats, this time at the hands Indian military and paramilitary forces. This 'grammar' of inside and outside remains a constant, though real and perceived threats may change. In the recurring dreams of two of my informants in Kohima – a mother and her daughter originally from Khonoma village – the mother stated that she regularly had nightmares in which she was chased and ambushed. Those pursuing her in her dream were always the same: soldiers of the Indian Army. She stated that she always feels a deep sense of fear when stopping at highway checkpoints, or passing the Assam Rifles base in the centre of Kohima town. Her daughter, on the other hand, while often having a very similar dream of being chased or ambushed, stated very plainly that her pursuers are in fact always the Naga underground – 'I don't fear the Indian Army, but I do fear the underground groups', she said. 'They are unpredictable, they're wild'. Here, we recall Foucault's notion of the historically situated place event and its coordinates of coercion. While the experience of fleeing or evacuating homes due to the outbreak of violence is first-hand experience for many of my informants, and while these experiences remain largely unspoken of, they are forms of violence that continue to to live internalised by a great many Naga families and communities and surface in episodes that continue to haunt dream narratives.

Having briefly touched on the relationship between historical contingency and spatial formations in dreams, I turn briefly to the notion of 'place-names' as developed by Keith Basso based on his work among Apache communities in Arizona. Here we can observe the ways in which narratives are integrally linked to location, and that visualising events in the process of narration requires specific spatial cues that can create the intended localisation of an event in both the teller and the audience. Basso suggests that

> insofar as places and place names provide the Apache with symbolic reference points for the moral imagination and its practical bearings on the actualities of their lives – the landscape in which the people dwell can be said to dwell in them. For the constructions the Apache impose upon their landscape have been fashioned from the same cultural materials as constructions they impose upon themselves as members of society. Both give expression to the same set of values, standards, and ideals; both are manifestations of the same distinctive charger for being-in-the-world. Inhabitants of their landscape, [they] are thus inhabited by it as well, and, in the timeless depth of that abiding reciprocity, the people and their landscape are virtually as one.
>
> (1998, p. 102)

Here, the relationship between the community and the landscape is ultimately one of reciprocity, and as its formations become indelibly imprinted in their consciousness, the landscape becomes 'sentient' – its meanings become incorporated into a community's deepest forms of experience. An example of this is the relationship between each Kohima village household and their respective paddy fields located several kilometres from the village. Large stones, streams, sometimes trees and unusual features such as sudden protrusions in the earth that one visits over a lifetime on the long treks to and from the field, and in the fields themselves, conjure up passed down legends linking the landscape with ancestral kin and are left undisturbed as sacred places. Streams and water holes in particular can be endowed with spiritual forces and often require careful negotiation when crossing or constructing crossings. But by showing discretion and respect for sacred objects and areas, one also maintains a positive relationship with the land's spirit owners, and this translates positively in times of cultivation and harvest. That sentient landscapes and their sentient beings – forests, mountains, rivers and their spirits – feature so prominently in traditional folk-narratives in the region is indicative of their symbolic currency. Indeed, returning to Foucault, in this animate landscape

> everything says 'I', even the things and the animals, even the empty space, even objects distant and strange which populate the phantasmagoria. The dream is an existence carving itself out in barren space . . . To dream is not another way of experiencing another world, it is for the dreaming subject the radical way of experiencing its own world. This way of experiencing is so radical, because existence does not pronounce itself world.
>
> (Foucault and Binswanger 1993, p. 59)

This notion of experiencing one's 'own world' in the dream is an important idea that will elucidate the following section in which I introduce an episode of considerable anxiety for Senyü (introduced in chapter 3). His dream narrative brings together many of the above discussed themes, but also recalls the very close relationship between dreams and healing in highland Asia. Senyü's dream experiences were of particular interest to me because, though I had accounts of 'soul travel' from several other informants, including an old healer in a *Pochury* village east of Kohima who spoke about his leopard spirit, Senyü was willing to go through his memory of his dream sequences and to explain what he thought each step was about and what it means for him. A significant theme in his dreams, he attests, is the ways the separation of his mother and his father registers as both familial and spatial estrangement in his dreams, a theme he recognises has been recurring for a great part of his life. Raised by his mother and grandmother in a semi-rural township in Dimapur, he was raised in a protective circle that was both separate from his 'entitled' placement within his patrilineal descent group in Kohima and geographically apart – a 70-kilometre distance linked by a legendarily difficult, and militarised road. In other words, his dream accounts entangle a domestic narrative with a political one, namely physical affliction with forms of political violence, on the one hand, and healing with release and a 'distancing' from the centre of affliction on the other. We thus see the entanglement of the domestic terrain with historically contingent terrains of power. In other words, landscapes collapse into 'dreamscapes', and I demonstrate the reversibility of this 'collapse' as illustrated in one particular dream sequence.

Moreover, we may trace linkages between these dreams in which landscape is a central aspect of the dream experience, with shamanic practices that are also closely related to landscape and feature prominently in the ethnographies of the highland cultures running northwards through Arunachal Pradesh and Tibet, and northwestwards towards Nepal (see for example Desjarlais 1989, 1991; Blackburn 2008; Aisher 2007). This is the case specifically in relation to notions of soul-entrapment and the aid the healer requires from helping spirits in tracking the lost soul while negotiating passage with and through unfamiliar, and possibly unfriendly, spirits. This will be discussed briefly, followed by further examination of the ways in which the notion of the 'familiar' and 'unfamiliar' in dreams heightens awareness in waketime reality of aspects of social process that otherwise are hidden or taken for granted. In this way, dreams can serve to unsettle the quotidian, and thereby heighten perception of what is perhaps not visible but not absent either.

Senyü's dream and the sacred forest

Senyü reaches out with his left hand and pulls his teacup closer – gazing somewhat blankly at its contents. There is a moment of silence in between sentences. We are sitting in the upper room of his small business complex in Kohima Town, and an employee stands by quietly waiting for a break in our conversation. He finds his chance and approaches Senyü with a brief under-the-breath consultation. Up until this moment, Senyü has been describing a trip he took a couple years ago right out of college, in the midst of which he became deliriously ill. In his capacity as an architect, and also a Catholic, he had been invited by the Kohima Diocese to visit neighbouring Arunachal Pradesh to survey a section of a large forest that had been undisturbed by local villages in the vicinity. Locals had warned the team that it was a sacred forest guarded by a master spirit. But the group from the Kohima Diocese disregarded the warnings and proceeded to conduct a survey of the area for the purpose of developing a Catholic youth camp. In the group there was a government surveyor who had brought a Global Positioning System and spent the afternoon drawing out the perimeter. Senyü spent his time discussing a set of structures that could be easily built using local materials. He had dreamed of a kind of architecture that mixed local vernacular building techniques and materials with the practicalities and safety of modern construction.

Towards evening Senyü began to feel lightheaded and skipped dinner to lie down. As the night approached, his temperature rose, and he began to shiver with fever. The Diocese father, and leader of the group, was in the next room, but he did not want to disturb him. It had been a long day, and everyone was tired. He did not sleep at all, and by the morning Senyü had become so delirious that the team became alarmed and cut their trip short to return to Kohima. It was in that first evening when he got a fever that Senyü began to experience unusual dreams:[5]

> I was in a village and I was trapped – I couldn't go anywhere. There was a lot of land . . . and I was thinking 'I need to go home; I need to go home'. And then this dream started developing into . . . I started seeing people wearing black lungis [a traditional garment worn around the waist in most of South and Southeast Asia]. I was trying to read where I was.

I saw something written in Tamil and I was saying 'is this Sri Lanka, or South India?' I need to go back but I need to know the name of this place, where I am. So in my dream I was just searching where to go. Slowly the dream started becoming more and more beautiful. I was gliding across some very – it must be Australia, that peak, you know – the red rock or something like that. And there would be some very misty forests and from inside they would be calling my name.

The following night, now back in Kohima, he had a very similar dream. The night after that, he again had the dream and always found it ended in the same place: a landscape and walking along the edge of a riverbank. As time passed in the dream, the landscape seemed to change colour, sometimes becoming more ethereal. But as these changes happened before his eyes, he felt – that is, his dream-self felt – a growing fear. A week passed, and he continued to have fevers, though in the day he felt better. But in his dreams, the reoccurring dream continued to become more terrifying. He would wake up in cold sweats and crawl to the bathroom to throw water on his head, hoping to shake the confusing experiences he was having.

Senyü had been visiting the same landscapes repeatedly now over a week. The one of two doctors he remembers consulting had prescribed some medicine to help him sleep, but they were not able to diagnose the problem. And, eight or nine days after getting back, with no sign of improvement, he began to feel that something had gone terribly wrong in Arunachal. He approached his Catholic parish for help and had a thought that perhaps it had something to do with his dream. As he approached his church to seek help with interpreting the dream, he soon realised there was a problem:

> They [priests] get posted to a new diocese after a few years and it's not possible to develop a long term friendship with them. As a new priest comes in, you would not be sharing your dreams with them. In our Angami society, we always look out for elders regardless of denomination with interpretation of dreams.

He therefore started to ask around for someone who might interpret his dream from Kohima village. A cousin recommended that he consult Jivisenuo, an elderly woman living in Kohima village who worked part-time as a prayer counsellor at the Baptist Revival Church.

> She didn't interpret my dream but she said I was probably being disturbed, and that I needed to come and spend a few days at the prayer centre. So without telling people, I went there – I mean, what will people think 'because of your dream you went on a retreat?' So I went there for three days. It was very boring – I was just praying . . . Then, on the second night in my dream I saw a window and some steps, and I started to climb down.

He had never before had a dream like this, where, despite his own efforts, he had to seek help in figuring out what it was about and what to do about it. But Senyü felt Jivisenuo was right that it was a kind of disturbance, that it was very strange because it did not feel like his own dream, but that he was experiencing the dream of somebody else. After three nights at the centre he decided to return to his work at the small office in the urban development building opposite the war cemetery in town. Though he was feeling only marginally better, he had been away for almost two weeks and was feeling guilty about being absent because of strange dreams that somehow affected his health. He figured he would soon snap out of whatever it was that was afflicting him. On his first night home after having spent the full three days at the prayer centre his dream was now different.

> That night in my dream my mother appeared. She had hired an auto rickshaw, and the driver . . . we had a lot of check-points with a lot of underground insurgent groups manning the gates . . . but this driver was someone who was used to driving out of that place. So he would not stop and he would just go confidently in the centre. And these people would just open the gate, kicking the barrier. So he didn't stop and he didn't slow down, he just kept going and he took me to a place that was very calm – an old tarmac road, or maybe an airport runway. I could not see my mother now after I crossed those gates. And the guy said 'now you move fast from here. You can go by bus or you can go by plane, but this place will soon be overrun again . . . but you go fast'.

Senyü slept well that night and stopped having the cold sweats. The next morning his body was still weak, but he felt as though he had regained his strength. Thinking back, he sees that Jivisenuo had been right – it was a kind of spirit disturbance, or 'soul loss', and that the master spirit of the forest in Arunachal Pradesh, as the villagers had warned, had likely been mischievous and entrapped his soul while he was with the team surveying the area. At one point in the interview he stated, 'There might be some ancient rituals that people do, I don't know. When I was visiting Longkum recently my friend was telling me that if I ever go to a sacred place someone has to call me, or I have to call myself. You have to tell your soul that you are going or leaving'.

As touched on in chapter 1 and in chapter 3, when people in the village speak of a child's *ruopfü*, particularly in the case of 'losing' it to entrapment by a more powerful master spirit, 'it' is characterised as ambivalent with regards to belonging, but more importantly it is characterised as more primordially linked to the spirit world. The child's *ruopfü* must be very carefully and patiently enticed to return to the child's physical body – a process that can take the better part of a day and a large group of clan members. The child's body is unable to 'hold' his or her *ruopfü* without occasional intervention through prayers or by caring to avoid certain forest or river areas. When the child's *ruopfü* is believed to have been lost, possibly taken by a forest spirit such as *Telepfü* (chapter 1), the child is typically lethargic but awake, and often runs a high fever (also one of Senyü's physical symptoms). Once the child's *ruopfü* has been successfully called back and is restored, the body recovers almost immediately, and the child 'awakens' fully. The separation of one's *ruopfü* from the body is also described by adults in sleep as out-of-body experiences, as was discussed in chapter 3. Similar to the young college student from Wokha and an old Reguri healer who could travel through his village in spirit form, his body simultaneously resting in his room, the father in my host family once described his curious sleep experiences in which he consciously leaves his physical body and hovers above the room watching himself snore away as his wife and children sleep next to him.

Also shared in chapter 3, Senyü is sometimes consulted by others who have had strange or disturbing dreams. It is a knowledge he has developed in recent years. Having been just out of college when he visited Arunachal and the forest, he was still new to the idea that the loss of one's *ruopfü* could change one's dreams, and it had not occurred to him that he was in danger. But he said that as he grew more interested in his dreams, he began to remember more details and had realised that he started meeting the *ruopfü* of his deceased mother again, and even his deceased grandmother in his dreams. In fact, his mother often comes and helps him figure out how to solve a problem or get out of a hard place within his dreams. But these kinds of experiences are more recent, and he cannot remember having dreams like this as a teenager or as a child. When his mother appeared with the rickshaw, Senyü understood, 'she was helping me to get out'.

Senyü 'sees', in his dream, what his *ruopfü* sees, and thus his dreamscape while ill did not reflect the landscape within which his body was situated. As he traverses the dreamscape, aided by the two *ruopfüs* – one of whom is his deceased mother – he embarks on a journey of escape. The route taken, however, resembles more and more the precarious militarised landscape already familiar to him in the Naga areas. Along the road connecting Kohima to Dimapur, for example, one might cross up to ten different military, police and underground checkpoints. As Senyü's childhood home stands adjacent to the Dimapur airport, the mention of the wide tarmac road or runway was suggestive – that indeed to find safety his *ruopfü* arrived to a familiar, and possibly safe, place.

In a separate interview, for example, Senyü recalls that as a child living with his mother in Dimapur, she insisted that anytime he travelled to Kohima to visit family he must never stay the night but always return home. Her fear was that, were he not to return the same day, he would be in danger and she would be powerless to help him. In Senyü's dream there is an unmistakable correspondence between his memories of childhood and the experiences he has later in life. In a way, they appear co-temporal within the dream and illustrate the many ways in which dreams index a fuller lived reality, but infusing the now with the corporeality encompassing all of one's lived experience.

Moreover, the entire process of recovery is guided by the spirit of his deceased relative, and this again is consistent with the general understanding among the Angami that deceased relatives live nearby, either in the village or not too far from the village, and meet as well as communicate with the spirits of their living kin in sleep. These kinship ties thus remain in place even after death, and the importance of returning to the childhood home to achieve restoration (if indeed we are to deduce this from the narrative and what we know about Senyü's childhood) illustrates the ways in which familial places remain indelibly imprinted in dream narratives as continuously generative of belonging.

Finally, Senyü's dream experience also points to ways in which the person – in dreams and in navigating the sensorial spaces of waketime reality – navigate the uncertainties of ongoing political conflict. In the following section I explore such terrains in the context of shamanic healing practices in the wider region in which visualising and navigating spatial relationships, cross-ways and landmarks are necessary in restoring a person to health (cf. Stuart Blackburn 2008; Philip Ramirez 2005; Alexander Aisher 2007, 2012; Projit Bihari Mukharji 2015; Stefano Beggiora 2003b, 2004.

Shamanic healing and the political cosmology

Anthropologists in recent decades have recognised the importance of analysing the relationship between shamanic healing practices and socio-political contexts (Crandon 2003; Greenway 2003; Miles and Leatherman 2003; and Ramirez 2011). Among Andean societies in South America, for example, scholars have noted a close relationship between healing practices and cosmology (Silverblatt 1983), while others such as Cloudsley (1999) have highlighted the importance of healing practices in relation to contemporary social processes and the ways historical uncertainties shape the cosmological landscape – the terrain through which such practices draw their resources.

In the case of Senyü, the spirits of the landscape and the barriers that inhibit the smooth reunification of the soul with the body of the person are clothed in familiar representations – in this case military guards that intimidate and disrupt safe passage. The tutelary spirits – in this case the mother and the rickshaw driver – are attune to the fractured political landscape and are successfully able to navigate its barriers towards the final release of Senyü's soul. That there is a spiritual struggle unmediated by a human is a significant feature in the dream's retelling and points to a universe populated by non-human actants that engage in conflict outside human experience. The dreamscape in Senyü's dream is a familiar one, but one that also is backgrounded by repetitiveness and routine. It is only in the dream that a road he has traversed probably hundreds of times, as it connects his mother's home in Dimapur with his father's clan in Kohima, becomes grotesquely accentuated. Indeed, this all-too-familiar highway, in the dream, is intensely strange, and even dreaded, as he calculates his prospects of remaining trapped in it. The imagery in Senyü's dream experience suggests intersections between old and new forms of knowledge and experience. The images and forces impelling him in one direction or the other are not metaphors but representative of forces at play in everyday experience. Senyü's spirit is trapped, and at the prayer centre the notion that it is a spiritual matter seems to suggest he was unaware up to that point of what was happening to him. But this realisation seemed to open up new possibilities, his dreams becoming spaces in which his affliction might come to a resolution. In the earlier account, Senyü is trapped and does not realise it until an interpreter, in this case Jivisenuo, informs him of the problem. And then, once he realises that his illness is connected to the forest that he and the Kohima Diocese were warned about, he can do something about it, things are resolved and he feels better.

The similarities between Senyü's dream experiences and the shamanic practices described by researchers such as Desjarlais (1999) in Nepal are many, indicating significant points of convergence with wider regional beliefs and healing practices. In Desjarlais' accounts, patients consult shamanic healers who engage in their practice by searching landscapes in dream-like states for the lost soul of the patient – often traversing high mountains, valleys and crossing important pathways such as streams – and retrieving the entrapped soul. By drawing the soul out of captivity and ushering it back to the patient, the healer reunites the person with his or her critical life-source, and the person recovers (see also Jeanne Achterberg 1985).

In Senyü's case, the pathway of release towards restoration is embedded in political imagery. That those aiding his release are able to traverse the many blockages that threaten to derail the movement suggests there is room to recreate the pathway to ensure safe passage. Kempf and Hermann suggest that dreamscapes can

> fit into a discursive terrain of indigenous counter-strategies, which reverse hegemonic spatial configurations and use the ensuing foldings to set up alternative versions of space. Dream experiences and narratives shape an imaginative field authorised by ritual power practices, one that constitutes counter-spaces by instigating a strategic extension of the local world. In these discursive counter-strategies lies the real power of dreamscapes.
>
> (2003, pp. 81–82)

In interviews I have had with older informants – Senyü's parent's generation – when speaking of political violence in dreams, they most often attribute such forces to Indian forces, the Indian Army or the Assam Rifles. This suggests there is a great deal of subjective specificity to the dreamscape (as opposed to a more 'general' politico-historical contingency of political violence). The driver of the rickshaw is unknown – faceless, in fact – but that Senyü's escape is not on his own accord but assisted by someone who has specific knowledge needed to overcome the barriers threatening to inhibit safe passage is significant. It indicates that the person's agency – the dreaming 'self' – is not the sole agential figure, and in this case he is virtually powerless and dependent on his spirit guides. The landscape – with its beings – is the prime agent of transformation, and this points to an important interlacing in Angami cosmology and beliefs of bodily affliction with the afflicted terrain and the possibility that bodily wellbeing may be left to other beings that restrict or open up pathways towards restoration.

Concluding remarks

The women in the vicinity of my fieldwork residence, when faced with a threatening notice circulated by the LYO, had sufficient knowledge of old clan laws as to pronounce on the illegitimacy of their claims. Old laws prohibiting non-*khel* decent-group families from residing within the village perimeter had established generations ago the boundary separating human and spirit habitations. By invoking the presence of the spirit domain, my capacity to continue fieldwork was restored. The spatial architecture of the village that remains active as far as clan laws are concerned is entirely immaterial and is continually reconstructed in the memories of lineage group men and apparently non-lineage clan women. But this immaterial architecture of the world, of spaces indexing terrains of power and constraint that must be negotiated, also appear in dreams. And in many respects, their fuller significance may be revealed in dreamscapes, as illustrated in the terrains negotiated by Senyü's *ruopfü* as it escaped, aided by spirits, including the spirit of Senyü's deceased mother, from the entrapment of a master forest spirit in Arunachal Pradesh.

For the Angami, spatial configurations in the landscape are the result of age-old agreements with the spirit domain. Indeed, spaces are a patchwork of spirit and human domains that are the result of generations of negotiation associated with the use of the land for cultivation, animals for hunting and important water sources. Village spaces were safe places, vigorously defended and 'cleansed' through rituals. The clan laws follow these fastidious arrangements, and what remains inside and what remains outside was and is a considerable preoccupation among particular lineage members. Likewise, pathways, mountains and streams are understood to be inhabited by spirits, and in chapter 3 I illustrated how Senyü had been contracted by the state government to 'deal with' the presence of the spirits and to build a structure so as to allow the Indian paramilitaries to move in and appropriate the land. In these instances, the advent of political formations undoubtedly complicates these age-old arrangements, and Senyü's dream in this chapter registers how these overlap but indeed illustrate the imbricated layers of constraint that the Angami and the Nagas navigate daily, whether completely aware of it or not.

The interconnectedness between dreamscapes and landscapes is perhaps best illustrated with an example in the negative. And here I turn to the instance in Senyü's dreaming in which the entire experience is foreign. For over a week he navigated landscapes in his dream that were entirely unfamiliar to him. This was when his soul was elsewhere, and if we take Angami articulations of personhood seriously, it follows that if the always conscious *ruopfü* is not perceiving the immediate world at hand, but indeed an entirely different world, one might surmise that dream narratives generally register the world at hand, and indeed continually apprehends the immediate world at hand. Finally, in Senyü's account of his dream, healing is in many respects juxtaposed to the militarised landscape, and this also raises questions regarding possible linkages, as expressed symbolically in the dream, between the wellbeing of the body and the wellbeing of the land.

In the following chapter, I pick up this theme, namely the restoration of the land and the restoration of a people, though I take it up in the context of a public funeral.

Notes

1 Field notes, LYO ultimatum, Kohima Village, 19 July 2014
2 Field notes Kohima village, 21 August 2013.
3 Ibid.
4 Ibid.
5 Field notes, Kohima town, 20 October 2013

Bibliography

Achterberg, Jeanne, 1985, *Imagery in Healing: Shamanism and Modern Medicine*, Boston: New Science Library, Shambala.

Aisher, Alexander, 2007, "Voices of Uncertainty: Spirits, Humans and Forests in Upland Arunachal Pradesh, India", *South Asia: Journal of South Asian Studies*, 30(3), pp. 479–498.

Aisher, Alexander, 2012, "Coevolving with the Landscape? Migration Narratives and the Environmental History of the Nyishi Tribe in Upland Arunachal Pradesh", in *Origins and Migrations in the Extended Eastern Himalayas*, Toni Huber and Stuart Blackburn, eds., Leiden and Boston: Brill, pp. 63–82.

Basso, Keith H., 1988, "'Speaking With Names': Language and Landscape Among the Western Apache", *Cultural Anthropology*, 3(2), May, pp. 99–130.

Beggiora, S., 2003a, "Buffalo Sacrifice and Megalithic Cults in the Shamanism of Orissa Tribes", *Central Asiatic Journal*, 47(1), pp. 1–15.

Beggiora, S., 2004, "The Subtle Teacher: Typologies of Shamanic Initiation: Trance and Dream among the Lanjia Saoras of Orissa", *Indoasiatica*, 2, pp. 327–344.

Blackburn, S., 2008, "The Stories Stones Tell: Naga Oral Stories and Culture", in *Naga Identities: Changing Local Cultures in the Northeast of India*, M. Oppitz, T. Kaiser, A. von Stockhausen and M. Wettstein, eds., Gent: Snoeck Publishers, pp. 259–270.

Cloudsley, Peter, 1999, "The Art of the Shaman: Healing in the Peruvian Andes", *Journal of Museum Ethnography*, 11, pp. 73–78.

Crandon, Libbet, 2003, "Changing Times and Changing Symptoms: The Effects of Modernization on Mestizo Medicine in Rural Bolivia (the case of two mestizo sisters)", in *Medical Pluralism in the Andes*, Joan D. Koss-Chioino, Thomas Leatherman and Christine Greenway, eds., London and New York: Routledge, pp. 27–41.

Desjarlais, Robert, 1989, "Healing Through Images: The Magical Flight and Healing Geography of Nepali Shamans", *Ethos*, 17(3), pp. 289–307.

Desjarlais, Robert, 1991, "Dreams, Divination, and Yolmo Ways of Knowing", *Dreaming Journal of the Association for the Study of Dreams*, 1(3), September.

Desjarlais, Robert, 1999, "The Makings of Personhood in a Shelter for People Considered Homeless and Mentally Ill", *Ethos*, 27(4), pp. 466–489.

Foucault, Michel and Ludwig Binswanger, 1993, *Dream and Existence*, Keith Hoeller, ed., Forrest Williams and Jacob Needleman, trans., Atlantic Highlands, NJ: Humanities Press.

Greenway, Christine, 2003, "Healing Soul Loss: The Negotiation of Identity in Peru", in *Medical Pluralism in the Andes*, Joan D. Koss-Chioino, Thomas Leatherman and Christine Greenway, eds., London and New York: Routledge, pp. 63–91.

Kempf, Wolfgang and Hermann, Elfriede, 2003, "Dreamscapes: Transcending the Local in Initiation Rites Among the Ngaing of Papua New Guinea", in *Dream Travelers: Sleep Experiences and Culture in the Western Pacific*, Roger Lohmann, ed., New York: Palgrave Macmillan.

Miles, Ann and Leatherman, Thomas, 2003, "Perspectives on Medical Anthropology in the Andes", in *Medical Pluralism in the Andes*, Joan D. Koss-Chioino, Thomas Leatherman and Christine Greenway, eds., New York: Routledge, pp. 3–15.

Mukharji, Projit Bihari, 2015, "Profiling the Profiloscope: Facialization of Race Technologies and the Rise of Biometric Nationalism in Inter-War British India", *History & Technology*, 31(4), pp. 1–21.

Ramirez, Philip, 2005, "Enemy Spirits, Allied Spirits: The Political Cosmology of Arunachal Pradesh Societies", *NEHU Journal, 2005*, 3(1), pp. 1–28.

Silverblatt, Irene, 1983, "The Evolution of Witchcraft and the Meaning of Helaing in Colonial Andean Society", *Culture, Medicine and Psychiatry*, 7, pp. 413–427.

7 The public life of dreams

Sometimes waketime events can appear like dreams. Elements that might be understood to distinguish dreamtime from waketime states – the strange episodic admixture of places, of persons from different epochs, odd discursive juxtapositions and emotive symbolism – appear to characterise some waketime events, particularly in the case of the public funeral of a national hero. In this chapter, the dream-like atmosphere of a funeral reveals the political possibilities generated from 'waking up' in the midst of concentrated 'peak' moments, which in the broader historical context provides a generative space for new vision, albeit rooted deeply in nostalgia for a bygone era.

Figure 7.1 Old warriors stand by Adinno Phizo, President of NNC, during her brother's funeral in Kohima village

Source: Author's photo

Urra uvie! (literally 'Our Land [is] Our Own') is a slogan heard among the Angami and particularly among those close to the Naga National Council. In April 2013 during the funeral of a top NNC leader held in Kohima village, *urra uvie!* was heard frequently and acquired a particular potency because it was invoked by the Phizo family, the 'first family' of Naga nationalism. For the first time in nearly 50 years, the living relatives of late Zhapu Phizo, including Phizo's daughter and NNC president Adinno Phizo, gathered together on Naga soil, and not insignificantly, in the old Baptist missionary compound in Kohima where Zhapu Phizo attended boarding school as a boy. This was one among a myriad of motifs and symbols that appeared as concentrated moments during the funeral events, and I touch on two others: firstly, the appearance of a rainbow as the funeral procession arrived in Kohima prior to the funeral, and secondly, the procession following the funeral service as the body of Kevilevor Phizo was driven to his ancestral village of Khonoma.

The previous chapter explored the relationship between dreams and the sacred ecology or 'sentient landscape', and the ways in which violence – whether clansmen policing village peripheries or Indian paramilitaries manning highway checkpoints – demarcates terrains of power in the landscape that may be registered in dreamtime experience. Drawing on these ideas about the 'sentient landscape', in this chapter I argue that this broader conceptualisation of 'land' can be explored in the context of the funeral as a 'public event', an event which, in its own structure, already enacts or performs *urra uvie* in a context of significant political flux. Important for my argument is the spatio-temporal setting of the event, though it is a waketime experience it takes on the spatio-temporal structure and form of a dream, with all its enigmatic potency and concentrated symbolism, and capable of the kind of 'spill-over' discussed in the context of ecstatic religious expression in chapter 5. Put simply, the main characteristic of group 'dreaming' in the context of a public event is that, while maintaining a tenor of normalcy punctuated with emotive 'peaks', it overall exceeds the normal and the typical and consists of odd spatio-temporal arrangements that, in the event of the 'dream', do not necessarily appear out of the ordinary but begin to form part of a narrative flow which the 'dreamer' as spectator has little chance of affecting. But as in a dream, there are concentrated moments that, in hindsight, seem excessive. We may follow Maria Elisabeth Louw, as she describes this, namely

> dream's sense impressions – images, moods, feelings, sounds and smells – are experienced as extraordinarily real, that is, as real in a more urgent sense than the sense impressions of everyday life: the smells keep hanging in the air even after one's awakening; the fear keeps sitting in one's body; the images seem like something one has seen before, even if they are images of the future.
>
> (2010, p. 280)

If we are to take this description seriously, then we might posit that waketime experiences can exhibit the same characteristics as dreamtime ones, and their amplified 'extraordinarily real' impressions can be likened to 'dreamtime events'.

In order to make this case, I show firstly that such experiences are, in fact, shared, namely that a specific community of people agree that they had the same feelings and experiences. Secondly, I show that there are enough similarities between these waketime events and dream experiences to justify this claim. This can be done ethnographically by documenting the way a particular event or omen is registered by a community of people, identified as an auspicious or ominous sign, and finally that there is a 'group' interpretation, namely a coherence is sought in relation to the sign. Next, having established my claim that these experiences are like dream experiences and thus display the blur of experiences and 'self' discussed in earlier chapters, I will relate the idea of the waketime dream event to political imagination and its potentialities for collective agency. I will then relate the discussion back to the other chapters and particularly in relation to what I have argued about personhood, reversibility and landscapes. I first turn to the day prior to the funeral service in Kohima.

On the eve of the waketime dream

Kevinuo* and her sister Neikehenuo*, both in their mid-30s and originally from *T-khel*, although Kevinuo is married to a man in *L-khel*, are close friends of my host family and were visiting them and discussing the funeral arrangements. They described how the whole village was involved – in cleaning the streets, collecting plastic chairs and even building a large platform for the funeral service. The various Kohima village churches would be taking turns in an all-night vigil of the body once it arrived at the old Baptist Mission compound in the evening. The daily newspapers *Nagaland Post* and *Morung Express* had suggested that Adinno Phizo, Kevilevor's older sister and president of the NNC, would be accompanying the body. 'After 50 years in London . . . she will be totally out of touch with Nagaland . . . a lot has happened in five decades', remarked Neikehenuo.

Khonoma village, where the Phizo family had its roots, was either too small for the large crowd they expected or it proved too risky a place to host representatives from the rival Naga factions. The arrangements allowing for Adinno's return were likely done high up in Delhi and had placed conditions on the event, namely that it be an open area that could be adequately surveilled by Indian paramilitaries. There was a thick early morning fog hanging over the village, and we were sharing a cup of hot tea when Kevinuo received a call from her husband. 'He is such a push-over', she said as she put down the phone. Spending most of his week working for a government contractor in Kiphire district, Kevinuo's husband is home only for a few days, spending precious time with their 1-year-old daughter. 'They're calling him to go to Dimapur airport to help bring Kevilevor's body. He has a truck, but a lot of people in the village have trucks', Kevinuo grumbled. 'So much hype over this Phizo who nobody even knows'.

Kevinuo's response was not unexpected. Born in the early 1980s she and her age group were only familiar with the factional fighting and occasional shoot-outs in the middle of town between the now multiple Naga underground groups. Kevinuo,

a mother and school teacher at the Baptist school, and Neikehenuo, an architect –
both holding master's degrees from universities in Delhi and Hyderabad – were
not in the least nostalgic about the NNC or Naga nationalism. As far as they were
concerned, it had no purpose, and only fuelled rivalries between Nagas. A total of
30 rounds of talks had taken place since the August 1997 ceasefire between the
NSCN-IM and the Indian government and yet twice as many Nagas had died in
factional clashes since the ceasefire than in the 17 years they fought the Indian
forces before the ceasefire.[1]

The disillusionment with the political process in Nagaland was particularly pal-
pable in those few months prior to the funeral. In November 2012 when I arrived
for fieldwork, there was a sense of expectancy in the air as the word around the
village, and discussed in the newspapers, was that a 'final settlement' to the Naga
political problem was imminent. Dramatic headlines in the papers appeared daily,
such as 'Hoped solution, expected election & general confusion',[2] or 'Ready to
dissolve [government] if solution comes: NPF' [Naga People's Front was the ruling party in the state government],[3] and '[Government of India] told to make offer
of settlement',[4] all fuelling a general sense that the long-awaited time had come.
Earlier in the year, on the 19th of July, 2012, the 60-member Joint Legislative
Forum (JLF) made up of ruling and opposition party members of the Nagaland
Legislative Assembly publically pledged to resign and vacate their offices once
the settlement was confirmed, adding a sense of finality.

December was no different, and it seemed as though the regular high-level
meetings being held in the midst of the holiday season – in Kohima, Chumuke-
dima, Dimapur and Delhi – were about the details of transition. Christmas and
New Year would be, everyone felt, historic days that the world would forever
remember. Would the final agreement – the final settlement of Asia's longest running conflict – be symbolically inked on the day of Christ's birth?

Yet, Christmas arrived, and there was no announcement. The first morning
of the New Year was even more unusual. The village awoke with the sense of
having been tricked or duped. The hangover lasted a full day, and on the 2nd
of January, the Election Commission of India announced that state elections
would take place in March, dealing a deafening blow to the entire exercise.[5]
Within days, the circus-like wheels of state election politics began circulating neighbourhoods, as though oblivious to the deeply disillusioned populous,
reflected particularly in the anger expressed in social networking sites such
as The Naga Blog. The JLF had not resigned but were instead campaigning,
flush with cash, on behalf of their respective party candidates. Loud-speakers
attached to minivans circulated the village blaring party songs and slogans,
ignoring the visibly irritated elders, and well-paid campaigners honked and
cheered through the village. The front pages of the papers that once covered the
various high-level meetings associated with the settlement were now littered
with the images of the same politicians being detained by election monitors and
photographed with seized bags filled with cash, boxes of liquor and firearms
intended to buy votes.

The state government had entirely lost its legitimacy, and the elections had been so openly corrupt that no one had any illusions of representational legitimacy. And it was in the midst of this deep flux in the political landscape that news of Kevilevor's death of a massive heart attack was announced.

The oneiric public funeral

The morning was grey, clouded over and raining. I decided to visit Atsa's house for early morning tea and to inspect a window that had broken a short while back (discussed in chapter 4). It looked temporarily patched by Atsa's step-son – a carpenter who visits them on occasion – but I felt it needed a proper repair so she would not dwell on the omen she saw in it. Atsa asked me if I had seen the rainbow yesterday. She said it had appeared as the funeral procession was coming up into Kohima in the afternoon. Outside her broken window, Atsa had a good view of the War Cemetery and the winding road descending towards Zubza and would have had a full view of the rainbow as it appeared around 4pm in the midst of a light afternoon fog.

I had not seen the rainbow, but it seemed that everyone I met that day had. The significance of the rainbow is directly associated with Zhapu Phizo himself, as he saw a rainbow over Kohima when he returned from imprisonment in Burma in June of 1946. It then became a symbol of Naga national aspirations and is the central symbol on the Naga flag. Zhapu Phizo died in London in April 1990, where he had lived in exile for three decades, and when his body was brought to Kohima, a large rainbow again appeared over Kohima. Images of that rainbow have been in circulation ever since then – in family photo albums, cut-outs of old newsprints and in various publications, including the official publications of the Naga National Council, the organisation that Phizo headed from 1950 until his death in London in 1990. His funeral is an event that many of my informants experienced and remember well.

Though this current rainbow had appeared on a relatively clear day, the funeral was conducted in the midst of intermittent showers which had started as I reached the Mission compound. Ten minutes from Atsa's house, the road near the open ground of the compound was already filling up with vehicles, indicating a large contingent of dignitaries, but most striking was the heavy presence of Indian security personnel in all directions. This was immediately alarming because the dailies had clearly stated that there would be no Army interference. It was also inside the village gate and only a few blocks from the Transit Peace Camp where the Naga National Army was based. As I looked at people's faces in the gathering crowd, I could see in their expressions an uneasiness with the heavy military presence. Representatives from all of the Naga underground groups, with the notable exception of the NSCN-IM would be sending representatives. I looked for a place to sit and was soon approached by a man I had only met once before, a well-known and respected elder who served in the Department of Forestry for many decades before his retirement. An outspoken critic of the current Nagaland state government, he was an NNC supporter (though not an uncritical one judging from his writings in the dailies) and seemed equally irked by the security presence. 'The planning committee will not be happy with the Indian forces standing there in such large numbers', he said. 'Some of the delegates are very angry, this really is a Naga affair. If they allowed Kevilevor's coffin to reach Kohima all the way from London, and for Adinno to come as well, then they should be respectful, and leave the grieving family alone to conduct the funeral they intend, without provocation'. I nodded, took a few pictures and asked if he was going to Khonoma for the burial. 'No, but if you need help getting there in a private vehicle I can help you'. He introduced me to another man, a Mr Keza (introduced in chapter 2, his wife and daughter had the same dream), who offered to help. (I discovered later that Mr Keza would drive Adinno and her brothers to Khonoma in his own vehicle as they refused to step foot in the government vehicles provided for them).

By the time the service was to start, the military presence surrounding the event seemed to have thinned out to a few dozens. On the stage sat a large group of family, extended family and clergy, and standing in front of the stage was a fearsome looking line of Khiamniungan Naga men from Eastern Nagaland in full ceremonial dress, wielding spears and large shields decorated elaborately with black and white paint. That there was a significant contingent of representatives from the Eastern Naga groups is not insignificant. Factional fighting had divided the Naga areas, and many communities, including many Eastern Naga groups, had remained loyal to the old NNC.

The service began at noon and included prayers, a few musical numbers and nearly two hours of remembrances, most notably a short speech by Adinno herself:

> We are returning to our homeland; after 50 years for me, and my dear brother Kevilevor is coming home to rest after 46 years . . . His love, dedication, and unstinting loyalty to the Nagas will always be remembered . . . I take this opportunity to salute him and all those Naga patriots who have gone home serving the Naga nation in various capacities and forms. My thoughts and prayers are always with them, and their near and dear ones.

She was then followed by several musical pieces, and a special selection chosen specifically by the Phizo family before a soloist rose to the stage to begin an operatic rendition of the theme song for the 1960s film 'Exodus', written by Pat Boone. A bulletin insert was then quickly distributed to the funeral attendees, in which a *Tenyidie* translation accompanied the English lyrics of 'This Land is Mine'. At the bottom of the insert the words, 'by request of the Phizo family' were clearly printed. As I looked around, the mourning attendees were visibly moved by the song, wiping tears away, while the soloist himself began to express emotion as each phrase intensified and rose in pitch. The final lines, declaring a willingness to lay down one's life for the land, were particularly chilling, given the presence of Indian paramilitaries. As the microphone was placed on the stool next to the podium, there was a 'thump' in the speakers, followed only by a long and deafening silence, as the next presenter slowly rose to the podium. But in that moment, one could conclude with little reservation that a message of utter defiance had just been relayed and witnessed by as many as 2,000 people and erasing whatever sense, certainly in my own mind, that the funeral was anything but a political homecoming for an erstwhile divided Phizo family. The Angami *urra uvie* slogan necessarily taps into a complex magico-religious vision among the Angami,[6] relating in a first instance with a deeply felt interconnectedness between the Angami people, other beings and the natural world. As illustrated above, it also seeks, in the eyes of the NNC leadership, to symbolically graft the Naga national cause with the divine 'covenant' with Israel.

The song continued to resonate throughout the rest of the funeral, as the once very formal speeches by well-wishers became more visceral expressions, often becoming impassioned. Yet, as a leader who had lived in exile in London for a half century, Adinno made no gestures to keep the speeches short. When representatives from the Naga underground groups spoke, their voices seemed somewhat muffled by the earlier moments, and following several civil society leaders, the service was concluded with family members sharing final words and a short exhortation and prayer by one of the local Baptist ministers.

The public had already started to move before the service had ended as traffic, it was clear, would be jammed. An entourage of vehicles soon formed with two Mahindra Gypsy trucks in the lead carrying four Khiamniungan men each, standing in the back, wielding their shields and spears. Mr Kezha had mentioned that Rev. Linyü – the Baptist pastor handling the proceedings at the burial site – was nervous about the show the Khiamniungan men were putting on, as the hair on their spears was taken from the corpses of Indian soldiers. The long locks of brown and black hair were clearly visible, and the men did not seem to care very much that they were displayed openly, photographed and probably televised – just as they passed within a few feet of the Indian security forces along the side of the narrow village road.

Mr Kezha had arranged for me to ride in the entourage along with members of the Angami Youth Organisation. The drive through Kohima was smooth, the snake of vehicles greeted by curious onlookers in the town. As we turned at the War Cemetery junction I received a text message from Abu. A house near Atsa's house was in full flames. I later found out it had been an explosion of a propane tank, and the wooden structure would be entirely consumed. The owners of the house were in the entourage, and the double-lane, one-way procession seemed unlikely to stop or turn around. As we exited Kohima and proceeded down the hill, we could see smoke billowing from the village across the hills. The smoke would have been visible to everyone in the entourage and undoubtedly contributing to the mix of emotions that began to stir with the remembrances and musical numbers during the funeral service.

All along the way vehicles progressed quickly. Construction on the road was underway – it had been considerably widened, with a drainage ditch being constructed on the left side along the rising slope to channel away heavy monsoon downpours. But large puddles had already formed in the road, and landslides had buried long sections of the newly poured ditch. At a rest area about halfway to the village, the procession was met by a line of Khonoma men in ceremonial dress, each firing a muzzle-loading musket in the air to deafening effect. With strict laws governing the ownership of firearms in the state, the display was one of emotion and defiance, and each shot seemed to jolt the vehicles as they passed. We would hear this gunfire throughout the rest of the journey. The warriors were not smiling but were emotionally charged. The rains that now blurred our vision contributed to enlivening the forest canopy, and the terraced rice fields that stretched into the horizon were fluorescent green and filled with water – the landscape seemed to be participating in the theatre, and the thin mist that hovered only accentuated the oneiric feel to the whole event.

We arrived, and I disembarked right in the centre of the village and just below the old village gate – a gate photographed by Hutton in his 1921 monograph – standing as it always has despite the multiple occasions over two centuries when the village has been burned by British and then Indian forces. As I got out, the smell of gunpowder, the loud cracks of the muskets and the sight of people standing in every veranda, vantage point and porch was overwhelming.

Just below the main junction on the southward slope, a few steps below the street, was the above-ground tomb in the old Phizo house plot. The house that once stood there was burned down in 1964, the day Atsa fled to the south. Nothing had been constructed since, so we stood on the foundation, and a few straddled the outline where the timber walls once stood. The convenors of the interment service stood under a small tent that sheltered them from the light rain. I was motioned to enter, but I stayed at the steps leading down into the space where the ceremony was held. I was the only white foreigner and likely the only non-Naga in Khonoma that day. Though I knew many of the people present, it would have been a mistake for me to be too casual.

Hymns were sung and shortly after a speaker asked everyone to stand in attention ready for the ceremony to begin. Soldiers in the Naga Army stood in full uniform, carefully folded the Naga flag and handed it to Adinno's younger brother. Rev. Kevi then began a short liturgy, followed with a final prayer. The coffin was brought to the tomb where I was standing and slid into place. The ceremony was over, and I was directed down some steps to a wooden hall where I again met Mr Keza. We ate a traditional rice and pork meal, and I was soon fetched by the people from the Angami Youth as they were anxious to leave.

Reconstructing the dream narrative

The emotive power of a given dream is sometimes only realised in hindsight, as concentrated moments within the dream narrative appear like peaks in a valley of normalcy. The disjointed nature of the dream narrative as it unfolds may elicit reflexivity, but is generally insufficient to 'wake' the dreaming subject, and more often than not, as little more than a spectator, the dream carries the subject along in its narrative sensical and nonsensical ebbs and flows. I would suggest that the events surrounding Kevilevor's funeral encompass an uninterrupted narrative beginning with the appearance of a rainbow during the ascent of the funeral procession into Kohima, and we might view the all night vigil of Kevilevor's body taken up by the various village congregations, as transitional, contributing to this uninterrupted flow. The endpoint would then come with the evening of the second day following the interment. In hindsight, the waketime dream, as dream narratives often are, is reconstructed or remembered as a summary of concentrated moments. It is in relation to these concentrated moments that one imagines one's agential capacity to decide or to passively observe and be caught up in the directionality of its various coordinates.

The importance of such concentrated moments or 'happenings', in the context of a 'waketime' dream I am suggesting, is directly proportionate to their collective or shared significance, and this is dependent on collective memories of other familiar events. And, collective memory depends on very specific kinds of symbols that elicit general equivalences among a majority, but more importantly, decisions among a concentrated group within that majority. There were many people who were involved, or who attended the events of the funeral that understood, for example, the importance of the rainbow, understood the Phizo legacy in relation to Naga nationalism, and recognised the sense of 'chosen-ness' felt in common with Israel, as expressed in the song 'This Land is Mine'. That is to say, there was a level of recognition among a majority of these meanings. Many of the younger generation attendees, though perhaps recognising the motifs as significant, had little or no frame of reference with regards to their significance in relation to the conflict. In fact, though the signs themselves are meaningful, they are also inextricably linked to the defining era of the Naga nationalist political struggle, namely the height of the conflict in the 1950s and 1960s. In order to illustrate this in a sense of 'third' layer of signification, Naga scholar Visakhonü Hibo, writes on the shared memories among women that recall the early years of the movement:

> The Naga Movement's inception provided a sense of duty and social service which blended well with the culturally inherent qualities of the Naga people. It was also a manifestation in quest for a separate political identity, fear of domination, aspiration and struggle for complete sovereignty. The Naga cadres recruited into the movement were highly valued, revered and romanticised, augmented by the ideological goal of complete sovereignty. Collectivism as against individualism was the unspoken standard which existed both amongst the civilians and the underground cadres. The tentacles of tribalism within the rank and file of the movement were alien. The unity and the common goal gave a ready acceptance as in the case of A.Z. Phizo or whosoever was qualified and ready for self sacrifice toward the cause.[7]

This kind of characterisation of Naga nationalism, of widespread consensus and support, would not be an experience most Naga young adults and youth shared. One aspect of the early movement that significantly distinguished it from the character of the underground insurgency from the 1980s onwards is that the NNC had no absolute central controlling pattern, but was largely decentred, and a show of resistance, sustained through solidarity networks. In other words, like the 'hearthen economy' and indeed sustained, fed, networked and generally aided by the 'hearthen economy', it was ad hoc and collectivist, and in many respects eluded institutionalisation. No longer an active, popular movement, it has evolved into an archaic institution of reference, indeed less an institution than a symbol, relying on nostalgic reification through symbolic elicitation in the context of events.

It would be a mistake, however, to dismiss the capacity for such symbolic elicitations to re-enact the past in the present in powerful ways. I suggest here that, by conceptualising the events surrounding Kevilevor's funeral as a 'waketime dream', we can see that this is precisely what happened. That the waketime dream event did not endure beyond the evening of the interment, indeed that the re-enactment was temporary in the grand scheme of things, is not to suggest it was not a significant and indeed a powerful 'peak', with capacities to spill over into the present context. Caroline Humphrey, reflecting on the ways in which individual subjects make decisions in relation to significant life events or a 'decision-event', suggests:

> The event then is a creative switch. In that it separates off times, the time of Before and the time After, it can be considered itself as a-temporal; it could be an instant or more likely drawn out over a sequence of happenings; in either case, it breaks apart earlier bodies of knowledge or re-jigs them by forcing them to be seen in a particular light.
>
> (2008, p. 374)

We must remember that the funeral events took place within the context of an essentially 'failed state' following the collapse of settlement talks and the fiasco of state assembly elections. It was in that significant void that the events of the funeral spawn an alternative vision, albeit firmly rooted in a nostalgic past. Indeed, as Hoffman and Lubkemann, suggest, recognising the importance of studying events in contexts of conflict, we might join the call for an 'analytical recasting of the "event" as a moment in which cultural creativity is harnessed to the tasks of effecting and legitimizing the social transformations that crises often demand' (2005, p. 315). And what I am suggesting here is that conceptualising 'events' by employing the unique structure and experience of dreams, and the way we remember them, enables us to see the political possibilities that result from heightened lucidity in the midst of historical contingency. This is very much in line with Walter Benjamin's interest in understanding the ways in which the past and present overlap or indeed bleed into each other, and the dream provides this kind of structure. He writes, for example, that:

> The realization of dream elements, in the course of waking up, is the paradigm of dialectical thinking. Thus, dialectical thinking is the organ of historical awakening. Every epoch, in fact, not only dreams the one to follow but, in dreaming, precipitates its awakening.
>
> (1999, p. 13)

Benjamin contrasts his thesis with the prevailing Marxist theory of historical narrative that places political counter-narratives along a teleological continuum by suggesting that 'politicised history' is more like the dream – indeed it is 'intense, mundane, obscure, revelatory and potentially transformative' (Lusty and Groth 2013, p. 143). Indeed, consonant with 'reversibility' as it has been developed in this book, Benjamin refutes the notion that the dream and waking reality exist in separate realms, choosing instead to operate with the premise of a single realm theory, namely

> 'dream' and 'waking' experience are *both* inextricably grounded, and which progresses not in a gradual, seamless, linear continuum, but instead proceeds unevenly in jolts, leaps and unexpected reversals.
>
> (Calderbank 2003, p. 10, emphasis original)

It must be remembered that most dream research has, if for only practical reasons, sustained this conceptual divide between the person narrating his or her dream, and the 'dream-subject' – the 'self' that offers the first-person perspective within the dream narrative. This is not altogether problematic. As was discussed in chapter 2, cross-cultural dream accounts often describe the 'dream-self' as engaging in a dream plot unaware that it is a dream at all. In circumstances where the dream-self suddenly becomes conscious, it appears as though there are in fact two 'selves' – the one that perceives the whole context of the experience as if all of a sudden aware of everything, and the 'self' that retains his or her role within the dream plot. What proves problematic is that these two 'selves' remain, as it were, caught in two separate dimensions of experience, relating obliquely – at least theoretically – to waking experience (unless we are willing to explore, perhaps, the conscious presence of an 'alter-ego'). In chapter 5, I demonstrated that apprehending a single ontological landscape that does not relegate humans and spirits to separate realms or dimensions is critical in understanding Angami ideas about a world co-habited by humans, spirits and ancestors, and by extension dreams and dreaming experiences. Brian Morris articulates this well in the context of his ethnographic writing of the sacramental kinship between humans and non-human animals and spirits in Malawi. He suggests, for example, that:

> People in Malawi do not articulate a 'two world theory', but conceive of spirits (and the deity) as being a part of this world. They do not make a radical division, as in the metaphysics of Plato (and many world religions), between an empirical world of appearances, and a spiritual realm, or a world of (true) Being (cf. Arendt 1978, pp. 23–5). The powers and hidden force of nature, which are particularly manifested in animals, though ultimately derived from the deity, are within this world.
>
> (2000, pp. 228–229)

In Angami thought, the 'real' is that which can be consciously perceived – whether visible or invisible, and as discussed throughout the book (and in particular chapter 4), most individuals both perceive and draw insights from omens which not only appear in dreams, but also appear to them while they are awake. These may be incomplete messages or patterns that only form a narrative when shared with the interpretive insights of others. Developing a fuller knowledge of what is being communicated (by spirits, ancestors or the divine) requires a community of perception, with the memory resources to bring messages into their 'fuller' meaning. And this requires us possibly to rethink approaches common in cross-cultural dream research that privilege the functional thesis, namely that dreams bring hidden meanings for the individual that may be deciphered, offering invaluable resources in constructions of self and identity. This theory, we can recall, holds that the dream becomes a unique space in which individuals spar with their own personal struggles, confronting and negotiating complex situations in preparation for the 'real' historical experiences they will face when situated in social relations – awake and fully conscious to the world. In this chapter I have argued that the process of 'awakening' from the context of an event-as-dream allows us to see the agential and indeed generative possibilities that can become buried in 'un-eventful' everyday-ness, especially in the midst of the 'normalcy' resulting from political censure.

Signs of homecoming

Perhaps the most significant, and memorable, sign or omen to appear in the midst of the funeral event was the rainbow over Kohima. The procession had started in Dimapur in the airport parking lot, and in the midst of tight security, a large crowd gathered to pay their respects and to see Phizo family members who had not set foot in Nagaland for many decades. The long procession then slowly ascended into the hills. It took over three hours to cover 70 kilometres, but from the Zubza area, about 30 minutes northwest of Kohima, the rainbow could be seen – by the snaking vehicles gradually ascending but also by the residents of Kohima.

One of my informants, Mr Iralu, Zhapu Phizo's nephew and a well-known Naga historian, asked me if I had seen the rainbow when it appeared over Kohima. I told him I had not, but that I had heard that it was quite vivid and seen by people across in Kohima. He agreed, but then suggested that it was actually a double rainbow, though I was not sure whether there was any additional significance to the remark. Reflecting back on our conversation, however, I was struck by his interest not only in the sign, significantly potent as it was for anyone making a connection between the Kevilevor funeral and the Nagaland flag, but that it gained a fresh insight unique to the event and indeed another layer of meaning in Iralu's understanding. Nevertheless, he described in a newspaper column his response and that of others upon seeing the rainbow over Kohima:

> I have heard that many people in Kohima as well as in the funeral convoy cried when they saw the rainbow that appeared over the skies of Kohima just as the funeral cortege of late Kevilevor Phizo entered the outskirts of Kohima town. For me also, I found it very difficult to drive as my own tears had

completely blurred my eyesight . . . The sight of Kohima town in the background and the funeral convoy slowly winding its way towards Kohima with a brilliant Rainbow [sic] welcoming them was a most beautiful and moving scene. As far as I am concerned, no other hand than that of our Heavenly Father's hand 'set his bow' (Gen. 9:13) over the skies of Kohima to remind all Nagas that He still loves us. After all, the Rainbow is the symbol of our Naga national flag. Long live the rainbow coloured national flag of Nagaland. May you soon adorn the Asian skies with your unsurpassable beauty in total freedom and sovereignty.

(Kaka D. Iralu, The Morung Express, 30 April 2013)

As with the deeply impressionable signs appearing in dreams, signs, such as Iralu's double rainbow appearing over Kohima, have the capacity to evoke a deep sense of nostalgia amongst its witnesses, and a sense of timeless wonderment not unlike dream sequences that bear elements of powerful past memories. In Kohima, for as long as the Indo-Naga conflict has endured, there has been a virtual absence of nationalist symbols, memorials and other mnemonic devices associated with the movement in the public spaces. Though villages like Khonoma, Phizo's ancestral village, are an exception, this censorship extends to all district hubs and major towns in the state. Such restrictions do little, however, to defuse the evocative quality of national symbols when they suddenly do make an appearance. That the sign is also an omen that can be traced to the covenant between Yahweh and Noah in the Judeo-Christian tradition just adds an additional layer of significance, as illustrated in the commentary I included by noted Naga historian Kaka Iralu.

When the funeral is recalled in conversation, the omen of the rainbow is generally remembered more vividly than the various funerary activities that took place throughout the day. Like a strong sign appearing in a dream, the omen of the rainbow is understood to be both a revelation and a reminder of a future eventuality that is rarely questioned. One Naga author notes that the rainbow has appeared as many as ten times at the funerals of leaders in the nationalist movement (generally under the NNC), as well as during Naga national holidays (Heimi 2000, p. 25). The broad and ongoing circulation of miraculous signs, messages and omens obtained through dreams, visions and prophecy by individuals associated with the underground movement act to keep this continually unfolding process of divinely imparted messages buoyant in the popular psyche. What these revelations entail in terms of political vision, however, is not always clear. For sure, it is generally understood to include the official acknowledgement by India of the unique history of the Nagas, and by extension their right to self-rule or sovereignty. Some plans have suggested demands should include the total political unification of all Naga ancestral lands. Popular consensus, however, generally centres on the expectation of fulfilment of the divine covenant with the Nagas. Generally speaking, however, the political narrative of Naga nationalism has increasingly followed the logic of messianic fulfilment, which in many respects thrives on the forestalling of any final, culminating political event.

It must be said that the nationalist discourse, co-opted by the more militarily active underground groups (i.e. the NSCN-IM, and to a lesser extent the NSCN-K, NSCN-KK and NSCN-R political groups), has done little to rouse public support for the mechanisms ostensibly acting on their behalf to realise this vision. Their divisions, constant infighting and perhaps above all else their heavy taxation demands have all contributed to an erosion of trust in their capacity genuinely to advance the 'national cause'. The relative weakness – resource-wise – of the NNC, and the confinement of its Naga Army to the various Peace Camps scattered around the region as a result of the signing of the 1975 Shillong Accord have more or less spared the NNC from the increasing public outburst of frustration, primarily over the issue of taxation. That signs such as the Phizo rainbow maintain such emotive resilience in places like Kohima that may be said to be largely removed from the stark realities of most interior Naga communities is testament to the still broad belief that the promises of the nationalist political vision may yet be fulfilled. But who will take the leadership role in this endeavour?

A younger generation that has grown up largely removed from the heat of the war has followed a more pragmatic line, and this has invariably resulted in public expression of frustration directed at the underground. Here, the expectant blind adherence to the demands of the nationalist movement have not gone unquestioned. Among the most vocal is an organisation formed in May 2013 during my fieldwork, the Action Committee Against Unabated Taxation – ACAUT. ACAUT led public protests, calling for greater transparency and condemning the high taxation demands of underground groups. The movement drew wide support among young people through social media, and gauging the response in daily papers and blogs such as The Naga Blog, ACAUT has been viewed favourably by the Naga public at large.

However, ACAUT hit squarely at the heart of a system of obligation and patronage that finds its roots in the enduring pattern of clan patriarchal authority. In response to ACAUT's public events, the NSCN-IM, in a manner similar to the threat-espousing character of the Lhisemia Youth Organisation described in chapter 6, responded by accusing the ACAUT of 'treachery', having a 'hidden agenda'; of 'jeopardising the ongoing political dialogue' and acting 'like fools dancing to the tune of (outside) powers' (Nagaland Post, 30 July 2013). What is important to note here is that ACAUT, true to its name, sought limits to 'unabated' abuses. The attempt was not to wholly discredit or malign, but to temper the overreach of power that had come to characterise the various nationalist factions and was seen to cause harm in Naga communities. In 2014, ACAUT ramped up its efforts by touring the Naga areas and holding town-hall meetings. It increasingly drew public support for its campaign for greater transparency, and in many respects, the broad public appeal and support it achieved had not been seen since the early years of the nationalist movement and possibly as far back as the 1951 Naga plebiscite directed by Zhapu Phizo. One very significant difference setting ACAUT apart from previous efforts is the visible presence and participation of women in its leadership. No other organisation, from mainstream Baptist churches and the state government all the way to the underground factions – with the exception of the NNC – invites or allows women to participate in leadership.

The homecoming of the Phizo family, including Adinno Phizo, was in many respects a new page for the Phizo family and for the NNC. They would no longer be divided between the UK and Nagaland, and the office of the NNC presidency would be effectively hands-on and not in absentia. Having chosen a different path to that of the heavy taxation programmes of the other outfits, limited finances have translated into limited ways or avenues for manoeuvre or influence. The NNC and its various bodies have been actively involved in such activities as celebrating Naga national holidays, holding remembrance ceremonies for Naga martyrs and maintaining a presence, albeit a limited one. These events, as with the Kevilevor funeral, serve to maintain the vast repertoire of signs and meanings that lay dormant for now. However, they have every expectation that dreams of a sovereign Naga people will be realised one day. Indeed, that is the covenant, and the promise, and the signs have continued to appear with these messages.

Concluding remarks

In this chapter I argued that by conceptualising the events of Kevilevor Phizo's funeral as an event not unlike a dream, or indeed as a waketime 'dream-event', we could observe the ways in which its odd spatio-temporal juxtapositions, the gathering of persons from different epochs, of rival Naga underground factions and the Indian paramilitaries, of men dressed as old warriors, and of songs of exile associated with Israel, all within a concentrated space and time, may be studied as a dream. Critical to this observation were the various emotive signs that punctuated the 'normalcy' of the event, as well as narratives that necessarily invested in the nationalist discourse of belonging and alienation with renewed clarity.

Within the sentient landscape that encompasses both dream-time and emergent waking reality, self- and group-knowledge and positionality are contingent upon the ongoing, collective process of interpreting the signs encountered throughout a person's life. In this chapter I have sought to map out the process by which the heightened awareness of 'self' possible in oneiric events becomes historical, revealing the way dreaming experience relates to social process and to the creative capacities and insights that spur political vision.

Notes

1 R. N. Ravi, the main negotiator between the Indian Government and the Naga political groups, stated that 'Over 1,800 Nagas have been killed in some 3,000 fratricidal clashes since the beginning of the "ceasefire" (1997–2013) during the 17 years preceding the "ceasefire" (1980–1996) some 940 Naga lives [were lost] in 1,125 clashes mostly with the security forces", in The Hindu, 23 January 2014.
2 The Morung Express, 25 November 2012.
3 The Morung Express, 19 November 2012.
4 The Morung Express, 11 December 2012.
5 The Morung Express, 3 January 2013.
6 Here I speak only about Angami ideas about nationalism, as it is encapsulated in the *urra uvie* slogan. 'Nagaland for Christ' is, for example, a slogan used by Naga nationalists across Naga groups, and each distinct language and dialect will undoubtedly have

their own slogans, and as such there are likely dozens of 'meanings' to sovereignty, and indeed what Naga 'nationhood' entails.

7 Visakhonü Hibo 2013 'Naga Movement: Alternative perception of Naga women', unpublished paper presented at the 2013 Hutton Lectures symposium, Kohima. Cited with permission from the author.

Bibliography

Arendt, Hannah, 1978, *Life of the Mind* (unfinished), Mary McCarthy, ed., 2 Vols., New York: Harcourt Brace Jovanovich.

Benjamin, Walter, 1999, "Dream Kitsch: Gloss on Surrealism", in *Selected Writings: 1927–1934, Vol. 2, Part 1*, Michael Jennings, ed., Cambridge MA: Belknap Press of Harvard University Press, p. 3.

Calderbank, Michael, 2003, "Surreal Dreamscapes: Walter Benjamin and the Arcades", *Papers of Surrealism*, 1, Winter, pp. 1–13.

Heimi, Thomas W. Shapwon, 2000, *God's Hand Upon the Nagas*, Kohima: Self-Published.

Hibo, Visakhonü, 2013, "Naga Movement: Alternative Perception of Naga Women", presented at 2013 Hutton Lectures Symposium, 4th December, Kohima, India (unpublished).

Hoffman, Daniel and Lubkemann, Stephen C., 2005, "Warscape Ethnography in West Africa and the Anthropology of 'Events'", *Anthropological Quarterly*, 78(2), Spring, pp. 315–327.

Humphrey, Caroline, 2008, "Re-Assembling Individual Subjects: Events and Decisions in Troubled Times", *Anthropology Theory*, 8(4), December, pp. 357–380.

Louw, M.E., 2010, "Dreaming up Futures: Dream Omens and Magic in Bishkek", *History and Anthropology*, 21(3), pp. 277–292.

Lusty, Natalya and Groth, Helen, 2013, *Dreams and Modernity: A Cultural History*, London: Routledge.

Morris, Brian, 2000, *Animals and Ancestors: An Ethnography*, Oxford: Berg Publishers.

8 The reversibility of dreaming

This ethnographic study set out to explore the relationship between dreams and agency among the Angami Nagas in Northeast India and identifies in the Angami concept of *ruopfü* – one's spirit or soul – a continuity of consciousness between waking and dreaming states expressed in Angami personhood, enabling the inhabitation of both spaces simultaneously, thus allowing for their 'reversibility'. Situated within a clan community in Kohima village in Nagaland state, this project follows the ordinary and extraordinary dream experiences of ordinary and gifted men, women and young people, as expressed in both narrated dream sequences and their interpretations, often by close kin, but also elders and occasionally church

Figure 8.1 View from fieldwork residence in Kohima village

Source: Author's photo

prayer counsellors. Most conversations occur in typical settings around kitchen hearths, in which I also participate in dream sharing and become inculcated into the great collective effort to cull insights from dream-mediated knowledge and waketime omens, or what in this book I call the 'interpretive community'. The political situation was not an immediate concern as the focus of the study was generally situated within the broad perimeters of the *L-khel* clan group, and even broader village perimeter, with occasional accompanied excursions to outside villages. Nevertheless, there were times when tensions surfaced between villagers and Indian security forces, or between clan members and non-clan members, reminding us that this project was conducted in the midst of a deeply fraught and marginalised landscape, only thinly concealed beneath the quiet normalcies that accompanied day-to-day domestic routine.

For most of my informants, there has never been a time without war and the accumulated tensions, from personal experiences and those passed down through the 'post-memories' of past generations, often translate into dreamtime anxieties that are both traumatic and recurring. Indeed, as I argue in chapter 6, dream narratives can sometimes deconstruct the ways in which communities culturally conceptualise space in landscapes that have sustained significant upheaval. And the spatial coordinates in the dreams of my informants reflect the constraints of movement, particularly the room they have to negotiate for safe passage. Such narratives remain entrenched in these historically positioned topographies of power, continually aggravated by the empty promises of Naga politicians, and the indifference to Naga concerns in Indian political discourse.

The Christian presence, which is significant in the Naga areas, offers a substantial respite in this regard, and high church attendance may be considered a response to the uncertainties and moral ambiguities encompassing community life. In the absence of civic spaces, church buildings fulfil other needs associated with group gatherings and with reaffirming group identity. But, ultimately, this is a church with multiple fractures, and traditional Baptists have for a long time depended on the liturgies, hymns and church programming established by American Baptist missionaries, modelled on ecclesiologies developed in 19th century New England. The archaic character of the church undoubtedly reflects a crucial phase in the transformation of Naga society, reminding us of the ways the new religion came to transform warring communities into brethren. Charismatic groups, on the other hand, have long challenged the hegemony of the traditional Baptist church and continue to draw on their strong roots in the revivals that swept through Nagaland in the 1950s and 1970s.

Acknowledging these inspirational religious experiences and practices that are part of daily life in many community households (which go unacknowledged or are discouraged by traditional Baptist leaders), charismatic churches have grown significantly over the past decade. As I argue, the proximity of traditional Baptist institutions and clan patriarchy, with similar governance structures, and a reverence for the 'enduring pattern' of genealogical tradition that underwrites much of their activities are undeniable. Unlike the traditionalists, charismatics incorporate women into positions of leadership, are more accepting of non-clan and non-village members and have grown critical of clan and clan group xeno-phobia towards outsiders seeking to establish ties or exchanges with the village community.

Important in this research are the inspirational religious expressions, experiences and practices that are accommodated by the charismatic church. The growth of prayer centres that maintain round-the-clock prayer counselling and services are indicative of a shift towards acknowledgement of a deep-seated cultural responsiveness to spiritual activity and, I suggest, points to a regeneration of inspirational practices that resemble the spontaneous, sometimes chaotic meetings that sparked the charismatic movement in the 1950s. As I note in chapter 4, what is particularly significant is the way pre-Christian ritual narratives associated with the propitiation of malignant spiritual forces are consistent with the language of spiritual warfare incorporating many New Testament texts and being used regularly in charismatic services. Through these liturgies, the purity of the prayerful gathering is set in opposition to the dark hostile world outside. Prayers are seen to clothe adherents with a kind of invisible cloak of spiritual protection, and individuals receiving messages in signs and in their dreams help to direct and give insights in navigating the ever-present malignant fog that, at any given moment, could form a concerted attack.

As was the case with the early revivals, however, there is a great deal of theological incoherence at play in the charismatic movement, and informants suggested that any resemblances between the 'gifts of the spirit' and Angami vernacular divinatory practices rooted in communicating with the spirits of deceased relatives are purely coincidental. Indeed, though church members spoke of prophetic dreams, they were articulated entirely in Christian theological language as messages from *Kemesa Ruopfü* (lit. 'Clean Spirit', or Holy Spirit) or directly from *Kepenuopfü*. Undoubtedly, despite the myriad theological colleges and seminaries dotting the Naga landscape, explorations into the efficacy of vernacular divinatory experience in relation to the experiences of Christian charismatics are limited.[1] As is the case in anthropological studies of dreams and dreaming, central to the task of cosmological disambiguation in the midst of overlap between multiple systems is the task of clarifying local constructions of personhood. And in this book, I engage with Angami personhood, and in particular, Angami understandings of *ruopfü* – the Angami term for 'spirit'.

I suggest that, as the always perceiving 'self' of Angami personhood, the concept of *ruopfü* entails a continuity of consciousness and resembles the pre-conceptual 'body' in the late works by French philosopher Maurice Merleau-Ponty, from whom I borrow and seek to ethnographically substantiate the concept of 'reversibility'. As I show, elevating dreaming experience to a primary status in perception, Merleau-Ponty argued that, whether one sleeps or is awake, one never ceases to be in relation to the world, and thus 'sleep is a modality of perceptual activity' (1970 [1968], p. 47). I also suggest that to ignore the importance of 'reversibility' in the way the Angami Nagas experience and act upon the world is to misunderstand the Angami.

These explorations, both into the communicative practices, as well as into Angami understandings of personhood, were partly spurred by J.H. Hutton's suggestion that there is indeed a 'science' behind what he saw as a complex and vibrant Angami dream culture (Hutton 1921, p. 246). In the Introduction of this book, I include two detailed reflections (one of which is published in his 1921a monograph), which, I suggest, offer the ideal blueprint for such a 'science'. For one, they express the importance of symbols in dreams, which is important because the concentrated moments in dream sequences expressed using signs is a universal experience across cultures. But, perhaps more importantly, it enlists an interpretive community that then sieves dream narratives, always attentive to their transformative potential. Moreover, Hutton's observations acknowledge the broad set of extraordinary dream experiences that are generally only described by gifted dreamers, including people with shamanic abilities. To develop a single theory that fails to encompass the full gamut of experiences would be short-sighted because it would foreclose the possibility of 'bleed' between one set of experiences and another. In other words, in suggesting a continuum (as I have, following Hutton) I am also suggesting that traces from across this continuum can at times invade the dream experiences of typical dreamers. And the element of 'surprise', of suddenly being able to consciously navigate the dreamscape, or to speak with deceased relatives, is a recurrent theme throughout this project.

In chapter 2, I trace the development of the anthropological study of dreams and suggest that Freud's psychoanalytic influence was so considerable that it shaped the entire trajectory of anthropologies of dreams and dreaming for the better part of the 20th century and that this influence continues today. At issue is precisely the problem of constituting the 'real' and the 'dreamed' within the same realm of 'primary' experience, thus also attributing agency to the subjects and selves appearing in dreams. Indeed, the agency of spirits, deities and the animate natural world documented by anthropologists for well over a century are generally 'explained away in rationalist terms' as van der Heide suggests (2015, p. 128), stripping them of their power and significance. C. G. Seligman, too, followed this logic and as a foot-soldier for Freud sought to test the latter's theory of the universality of 'dream types' by isolating them from context. Hutton, on the other hand, though fulfilling Seligman's request with a short table of dream symbols and their Angami meanings, also included a great deal of context. In one of the accounts, he places himself in the plot – in this case, a spatially situated (in the Baimho bungalow), tormenting spirit that appeared to him in a dream. Injecting an element of scientific seriousness, he sets up an experiment to test whether or not he was hallucinating, and indeed cites British officers and subjects by name who attested to having experienced the same terrifying spirit. It would be speculative to suggest that Hutton began to appreciate the broader possibilities that such an experience entailed; however, a quick survey of his article titles, including 'Leopard-men in the Naga Hills' (1920) and 'Lycanthropy' (1931), suggests an interest in enigmatic spiritual phenomena.

From what we know, Seligman was not moved, and indeed had he sought to contextualise the hundreds of lists collected from officers and missionaries in the British colonies and around the world, he likely would have never completed his project. Had he attended to local dream theories, as Hutton sought to do in his detailed descriptions, perhaps Angami ideas would have contributed to shifting the course of dream anthropologies towards the possibility of analyses in which ethnographic data was not subordinate to Freudian theory, but which might have been allowed to enter productive dialogue with it (a strategy in which the self of Western intellectual thought is brought into question through encounters with non-Western understandings, more typical of the mid-late 20th century anthropological endeavour). But, though Freud should receive the brunt of criticism for launching a field that isolates dream experience from its social contexts, I suggest that he also contributed to correcting this error. In chapter 3, I explore Merleau-Ponty's development of the pre-conceptual 'body' thesis, and argue that it is precisely in this concept that the correction begins, because it draws significantly from Freud's theories of the subconscious. Merleau-Ponty initially criticises Freud's theory of the subconscious as 'a second thinking subject whose creations are simply received by the first' (Merleau-Ponty, 1970 [1968], p. 49). For Freud, the 'subconscious' is underneath, and indeed he gives it a secondary or derivative status in perception. In other words, Freud's twofold construction, according to Merleau-Ponty, 'leads to a monopoly of consciousness' (ibid., p. 49). But Freud had always articulated the 'subconscious' as perceptual. By simply shifting Freud's notion of the subconscious forwards so that it is no longer hidden or behind, but positioned beside consciousness, Merleau-Ponty succeeds in transforming Freud's seminal study of dreams into a 'phenomenology' of dreaming.

It is within this discussion that I identify linkages between Angami articulations of *ruopfü* and Merleau-Ponty's concept of *chiasm*. Here, perception of the 'other' is dependent on a reciprocal exchange, or 'looping' effect between the perceiver and the perceived. The link between Merleau-Ponty's late working through of the 'reversibility' of *chiasm*, and his equally late discussions on dreams, is discussed by philosopher James Morley (1999). Morley seeks to complete Merleau-Ponty's unfinished project of collapsing the dreaming 'subject' with '*chiasm*', enabling it to inhabit both dreamtime and waketime experience.

As was discussed in chapter 2, Angami personhood articulates a continuum of consciousness between the dream-self and waketime self. Here, the active subject in waketime and dreamtime experience necessarily needs to be understood in terms of an undivided continuum of experience. As this continuum traverses the boundary between awakeness and sleep, we can see that personhood entails a blurring of this line. As I show, the Angami concept of *ruopfü* corresponds to this theory, and indeed if we are to gain intellectual purchase on *ruopfü* it is only by taking this model at face value that we can do so. What this study contributes to this body of literature, and the concept of a continuum of experience, is the argument that, in Angami understandings of *ruopfü*, the continuum does not flow in only one direction, but is instead a reciprocal flow; which is to say it entails 'reversibility'. 'Reversibility' thus elucidates how the waketime *ruopfü* can influence the dreamtime *ruopfü*, and, importantly, the dreamtime *ruopfü* can then reverse the influence to the waketime *ruopfü*. Resembling Merleau-Ponty's notion of the 'looping' motion in his concept of *chiasm*, dream 'reversibility' describes the process by which *ruopfü* can develop and can be understood, and importantly, become integral for understanding the Angami's understanding of dreams and their influence on everyday action.

These theoretical premises help us to visualise a process that I then develop ethnographically in the remaining four chapters. In this regard, chapter 4 shifts to the intimate spaces of the domestic sphere, and specifically to the cramped rooms of a small house below the clan boundary in Kohima village. Here, Atsa interpreted her own dreams in relation to signs that appeared around her and the pain in her own body as an omen. Together, the signs pointed towards a mostly unspoken truth about her husband's frailty and the likelihood of his approaching death. Dreams in this chapter take on a heaviness, a physicality that contrasts with more ethereal descriptions typical of dream research. The ghost of Atsa's mother was ever-present, and Atsa's seeming ambivalence with regards to dreamtime ancestor or spirit visitation belied her desire to glean insights from her encounters, known and unknown, in her sleep. Similarly, Atsa's hearth, though an intimate and familial place, was characterised by its openness to outsiders, and specifically to non-clan visitors – vegetable vendors from Bihar, meat vendors from Manipur, Nepali milkmen – that frequently visited Atsa's kitchen, staying for tea and a chat. Atsa's openness to strangers, her always growing 'hearthen economy' in waketime and sleeptime, offered room for coextensive kinship relations with persons human and non-human, visible and invisible. When her husband died, unable to rely on clan relations for help, she turned to her motley collective of vendors who were happy to help move her belongings to her new place deep in clan territory. As the men arrive early in the morning to carry her furniture and luggage, they avoid trouble with the clan men, and she quietly defies patriarchal laws of separation.

From the place of the hearth, I shift to the place-making of Christianity within the clan community. Thus, in chapter 5, I focus on the idea of 'interference' in dreams, namely the process of bringing private foretelling dream experiences into the interpretive community to be deliberated and blessed. In the case of ominous dreams, 'interference' aids in defusing disruptive supernatural knowledge. This dynamic of 'sieving' inspirational religious practice is important in maintaining the relationship of tensions between different modalities of interaction between, on one hand, the openness to outsiders exemplified by Atsa, and on the other the clan's insistence on patrilineal purity. Moreover, these tensions are further evident in the relationship between the domestic sphere more generally and the morality of sin predicated from the pulpit of the traditional Baptist church. Charismatic variants, however, have sought a middle ground. As discussed already, recognising the ubiquitous nature of dreams and other forms of divination, the charismatic church opened its doors to clan and non-clan members seeking the 'interference' of intercessory prayer, many coming in response to an urgency about the future felt in their dreams. Yet, the kind of 'interference' required by the clan was the containment of new knowledge.

A significant dynamic of worship in the charismatic church was a positioning of the congregation in opposition to the outside landscape wherein resided sin and hostile forces. In chapter 6, I develop this idea further by shifting outside the village gates, turning from specific places such as domestic hearths, clan meeting platforms and church sanctuaries, to the valleys, forests, mountains and human settlements beyond. As touched on earlier, the importance of space is fundamental to the notion of 'reversibility' because dreamscapes often reflect the fraught terrains of waketime landscapes, especially when these are zones of conflict. In this chapter, a young software developer and architect, Senyü, shared his experience of losing his soul while visiting a sacred forest, and when guided by his ancestors in his dreams towards its recovery, he needed to negotiate the militarised roadblocks along the Kohima-Dimapur highway to regain it. As with Atsa's willingness to remain open, and to negotiate with the unknown, Senyü sought to negotiate the animated terrain, and followed the advice of his deceased mother's spirit in negotiating with the spirits that entrapped his soul.

Nationalism, and indeed the idea of a Naga 'ancestral' land, is inextricably linked to cultural conceptualisations of space and landscape, and the Naga national slogan *urra uvie!* along with the Judaeo-Christian symbol of promise – the rainbow – share in constructing a political space that fuses Naga cosmological space with the ideas of state, of identity and of national belonging, which gather potency in the context of the funeral of a national leader of the Naga National Council, or NNC. In chapter 7, I thus seek to substantiate 'reversibility' in terms of political discourse and shift to the public domain and the role of signs in political narrative. Here I highlight the oneiric quality of the April 2013 funeral of Kevilevor Phizo, son of the late Zhapu Phizo, the father of Naga nationalism. Important for the discussion are the different ways in which the political narrative of Naga nationalism has been articulated by the various underground insurgent groups, especially in relation to divine calling – communicated through dreams, visions and prophecy. Most, however, followed the pattern of clan lineage obligation and patronage, and I demonstrate how Kevilevor's funeral is illustrative of a different path taken, as compared to the path that other underground groups have taken.

Theoretically, I explore how waketime events are remembered or imagined along with elements that, together, are not unlike the jagged spatio-temporal backdrops of dreams. In all cases, there is a certain bodily disposition vis-à-vis an emotionally charged set of encounters; one stands witness and is charged to act or behave in reaction to, or in relation to, the experience. One no longer participates in a flow of routine activity, but suddenly stands tilted towards a particular telos. One must respond in the midst of a flow of instigations. Importantly, the waketime 'dream-event' has many witnesses and encounters with highly concentrated moments are collectively experienced. The group understands its position, as if becoming all-of-a-sudden aware and awakened to new possibilities. In other words, as with the person, the collective of witnesses is affected in a certain way by the surroundings which elicit a heightened awareness, an emotionally charged response, not unlike the inspirational religious practices found in the local charismatic church, a movement with deep roots in the charismatic outpourings that emerged at the height of the war.

Critical for this book has been locating predispositions towards receptivity to new forms of knowledge within clan communities and by extension the accompanying temperance of this knowledge (because of its powerful capacities for radical transformation). This comes in light of the balance and cohesion desired and maintained, though imperfect, by existing patrilineal structures. At the heart of this predisposition is the recognition of the participation of a transcendent community – of ancestors, of spirits and of the divine – in continually informing and shaping the unfolding presence among individuals and their community. These processes are all the more prescient in contexts of great conflict such as is characteristic of the Naga areas in Northeast India. Dreams certainly register these anxieties, but they are also spaces for incubating hopes about how their lives will turn out. As M.E. Louw suggests,

> recognising dream images, feelings, sounds and smells as potential omens, people enter a virtual realm, a subjunctive state, where they can imagine and orient themselves toward various potential future scenarios and test the social and moral resonance of these scenarios.
>
> (2010, p. 277)

I argue that this 'virtual realm' or 'subjunctive state' need not be confined to sleep. Drawing upon the Angami articulations of *ruopfü*, such experiences can be understood as a function of one's all-perceiving soul or life-being, or 'that other thing, which does not sleep' drawing on Schopenhauer's notion of the Will (1958, p. 239). Put differently, such experiences of signs and omens that breach the divide between immaterial and material realms are reversible, because, as was the case with Atsa's knee in chapter 4, they may appear to the attentive person regardless of whether they are awake or asleep. In this regard, there are important insights to be drawn from Tylor's, albeit unfortunately phrased, claim that 'the entire life of primitives was nothing but a long dream' (1870, p. 137), because it reflects the character of reversibility as observed in this ethnography among the Angami. As a guiding principle of Angami personhood, dreaming and the general attentiveness to ancestral knowledge, whether awake or asleep, opens avenues for exploring, understanding and creating possible lives. This challenges the givenness to the future that is patterned by patriarchal authority. And as I show in this concluding chapter, this fraught symbiosis between the radical passivity of the hearthen economy and the enduring pattern of clan authority provide a conceptual basis for further explorations into their significance in terms of important historical events, significant political and religious movements, and contemporary studies, such as on gender, health, childhood development, education and other social studies. Moreover, this book elaborates an important dynamic that does not feature significantly in debates surrounding indigenous resistance vis-a-vis the state, as developed by authors such as James Scott. My hope is that, by exploring Angami notions of personhood in relation to dreaming, this book will open new areas of research in the region. Such research would centre on local constructions of personhood, the relationship between personhood, social processes and landscape and what this can tell us about local capacities to draw inspiration and engage politically.

Note

1 An exception to this is the Journal of Tribal Theology published by the Eastern Theological College, Jorhat, Assam, and works especially by Wati Longchar and Vashum (1998; Longchar and Davis 1999; Longchar 2000).

Bibliography

Hutton, J.H., 1920, "Leopard-Men in the Naga Hills", *The Journal of the Royal Anthropological Institute of Great Britain and Ireland*, 50, pp. 41–51.

Hutton, J.H., 1921, *The Angami Nagas*, London: Palgrave Macmillan.

Hutton, J.H., 1931, "Lycanthropy", *Man in India*, 11, pp. 208–216.

Longchar, Wati and Vashum, Y., 1998, *The Tribal Worldview and Ecology*, Jorhat: Tribal Study Centre.

Longchar, Wati, 2000, *The Tribal Religious Traditions in North East India: An Introduction*, Jorhat: Eastern Theological College.

Longchar, Wati and Davis, L.E., eds., 1999, *Doing Theology With Tribal Resources*. Jorhat: Tribal Study Centre.

Louw, M.E., 2010, "Dreaming up Futures: Dream Omens and Magic in Bishkek", *History and Anthropology*, 21(3), pp. 277–292.

Merleau-Ponty, M., 1970 [1968], *Themes From the Lectures at the College of France: 1952–1960*, J. O'Neill, trans. Evanston, IL: Northwestern University Press.

Morley, James, 1999, "The Sleeping Subject: Merleau-Ponty on Dreaming", *Theory and Psychology*, 9(1), pp. 89–101.

Schopenhauer, Arthur, 1958 [1818], *The World as Will and Representation*, E.F.J. Payne, trans., Indian Hills, CO: The Falcon's Wing.

Tylor, Edward, B., 1870, *Researches Into the Early History of Mankind and the Development of Civilisation*, London: John Murray.

van der Heide, N., 2015, "When Dreams Shape Our Day", in *Leiden Anthropology Blog*, posted 15 April 2015. Online source: www.leidenanthropologyblog.nl/articles/when-dreams-shape-our-day, accessed 15 January 2015.

Index

Abbot, G. 63
Abram, D. 73
absences 98; become object-like 86
Achterberg, J. 132
activeness 62; of 'activity' in dreams 62; in both waketime and dreaming 50
agency 5, 22, 35, 66, 75, 81, 96, 124, 132, 138, 155; ability consciously to navigate 5; to affect or alter 49; among the Angami Nagas 152; or force that impels 61; or power to produce themselves 61; in relation to cultural practices 21; of spirits, deities and the animate 155
agential 132, 147; capacities of ruopfü 59; capacity to decide 144; qualities attributed to bodiliness 61
Agha, A. 48
Aisher, A. 127, 131
akhuni 85, 93
alienation 96, 150
alter-ego 146
alter-politics 22
ancestors 13, 16, 30, 44, 45, 48, 59, 74, 110, 147; communicate in dreams 13; external influences from 5; gain insights from 1; guided by his 158; lineage system unites the 8; participation of a transcendent community of 159; trance to communicate with 110; *upfutsa-nuo ruopfü* 47; world co-habited by humans, spirits and 146
ancestral 47, 158; intervention 46; kin 126; knowledge 3, 44, 87, 102, 159; land 35; laws 13; space 123; spirits 4, 5, 58, 72, 74, 113, 120; village 137, 148
Angami 1, 3, 5, 7, 9–11, 13, 14, 16, 18, 23, 25, 29, 37, 42, 48, 50, 55, 56, 58, 59, 61–63, 72, 75, 80, 81, 90–93, 102–104, 119, 120, 123, 130, 132, 133, 137, 142, 143, 146, 150, 152, 156, 159, 160; clan councils 103; clan families 6; clan men 101; community life 4, 6; concept of ruopfü 80, 156; cosmology and belief system 63; dream culture 7, 12, 20, 23, 50, 155; dreamers 45; dreaming 29; dreams 16, 29; dream symbols 15; Eastern 110; festivals 17; food 93; kinship 43, 96; land 10; life stage events 30; myth of origin 12; old beliefs 89; patrilineal clan life 8; personhood 56, 80, 152, 154, 156, 159; philosophy of knowledge 30; public rituals 113; raids 9; ruopfü and reversibility 23; science of dreaming 29; settlements 90; shaman 13; shawls 41; society 128; thought 146; traditions 56; understandings of personhood 155; vernacular divinatory practices 154; villages 1, 8, 91
Angami Youth Organisation 86, 142
Angelova, I. 109, 117
animal 13, 60, 63, 65–66, 77, 80, 126, 146, 151; animating 12; actions 65; bodies 66; for hunting 133; kind 66; kinship 66; non-human 56, 63, 64–65; spirits 4, 12, 67, 74; and spirits 66, 146; tame 91; wild 13, 64; world 12
animate, bodies 60; by beings 111; landscape 63, 126; natural world 155; oneness 80; terrain 158
animism 59, 60, 66, 76, 77
Anthropocene 22
anthropological, examination 1; accounts 75; approach 23, 34; contributions 33; discussions 81; dream research 23, 50; endeavour 156; monographs 20; research 22, 65; study 30, 154, 155; traditional goal 19; work 17, 21